Mastering Chef

Build, deploy, and manage your IT infrastructure to deliver a successful automated system with Chef in any environment

Mayank Joshi

BIRMINGHAM - MUMBAI

Mastering Chef

First published: June 2015

Production reference: 1240615

Published by Packt Publishing Ltd.

Livery Place

35 Livery Street

Birmingham B3 2PB, UK.

ISBN 978-1-78398-156-4

www.packtpub.com

Credits

Author
Mayank Joshi

Reviewers
Omri Bahumi

Evgeny Goldin

Panagiotis Papadomitsos

Commissioning Editor
Edward Gordon

Acquisition Editor
Meeta Rajani

Content Development Editor
Parita Khedekar

Technical Editors
Manali Gonsalves

Taabish Khan

Copy Editors
Trishya Hajare

Aditya Nair

Project Coordinator
Suzanne Coutinho

Proofreader
Safis Editing

Indexer
Priya Sane

Graphics
Sheetal Aute

Disha Haria

Production Coordinator
Komal Ramchandani

Cover Work
Komal Ramchandani

About the Author

Mayank Joshi works for Indix as a DevOps engineer. He has worn many hats during his 10-year long career. He has been a developer, a systems analyst, a systems administrator, a software consultant, and for the past 6 years, he has been fascinated with the phenomenal growth witnessed in cloud environments and the challenges of automation associated with the hosting of the infrastructure in such environments. Prior to Indix, he worked for start-ups such as SlideShare, R&D organizations such as CDAC, and even had a stint at a highly automated chemical plant of IFFCO.

I would like to thank all my fellow colleagues at Indix for their wonderful support and allowing me to get some spare time amid some very tight work schedules.

I wouldn't have been able to work on cloud platforms and configuration management systems had I not associated with SlideShare. Thanks much, guys!

I would also like to thank my family for bearing with me while I was spending most of the time either working or writing the book.

Last but not least, special thanks to the wonderful team at Packt, especially Parita and Meeta, who really pushed me whenever I was losing focus.

About the Reviewers

Omri Bahumi started his relationship with Linux in 1999 at the age of 12. Since then, he has managed to engage with various areas of Linux-based production systems— from high performance network servers to low-level debugging and advanced networking trickery. He serves in EverythingMe's operations team, where he's in charge of designing, building, and deploying multi-data center cloud infrastructures for developers and users alike. A typical day in his life includes a mixture of having coffee, coding in various languages, managing AWS stacks, taming Docker and Chef, and working with engineers on upcoming features (not necessarily in this order). In his spare time, he likes to hack on Arduino, Raspberry Pi, ESP8266, and all sorts of programmable hardware, making cool electronic projects.

Evgeny Goldin is a Ruby, Groovy, and Scala software developer who turned into an automation and release engineer to introduce order where chaos usually reigns. On an average day, all things related to cloud, automation, and continuous delivery get his immediate attention. Back at home, he's a proud father of a 1-year-old son, dreaming of a day when a proper tech talk would happen between the two! When he has any spare time left, he explores the subjects of aviation safety, functional programming, and web security. He's an open source developer, speaker, and passionate advocate when it comes to tools and techniques that lead to smooth and painless release processes.

Panagiotis Papadomitsos is a senior software engineer in the mobile intelligence division of Splunk, which is responsible for the design, implementation, and maintenance of a self-healing, always on highly distributed application mesh that spans three clouds and receives requests from more than 500 million mobile devices from all over the world. He's been working with distributed systems for the past 10 years in various companies and positions, with responsibilities ranging from designing and implementing complex heterogeneous infrastructures using Chef and the Chef ecosystem to architecting and coding low-latency distributed applications in Erlang and Nginx/Lua, contributing code back to the community whenever possible. He is a performance-tuning enthusiast; you'll often find him measuring and optimizing critical code execution paths from the application level down to the OS kernel level. When away from the computer screen, he enjoys surfing, snowboarding, and playing the guitar.

www.PacktPub.com

Support files, eBooks, discount offers, and more

For support files and downloads related to your book, please visit www.PacktPub.com.

Did you know that Packt offers eBook versions of every book published, with PDF and ePub files available? You can upgrade to the eBook version at www.PacktPub.com and as a print book customer, you are entitled to a discount on the eBook copy. Get in touch with us at service@packtpub.com for more details.

At www.PacktPub.com, you can also read a collection of free technical articles, sign up for a range of free newsletters and receive exclusive discounts and offers on Packt books and eBooks.

https://www2.packtpub.com/books/subscription/packtlib

Do you need instant solutions to your IT questions? PacktLib is Packt's online digital book library. Here, you can search, access, and read Packt's entire library of books.

Why subscribe?

- Fully searchable across every book published by Packt
- Copy and paste, print, and bookmark content
- On demand and accessible via a web browser

Free access for Packt account holders

If you have an account with Packt at www.PacktPub.com, you can use this to access PacktLib today and view 9 entirely free books. Simply use your login credentials for immediate access.

Table of Contents

Preface

The core philosophy behind configuration management systems has its roots in the US Department of Defense, where it was adopted as a technical management discipline. Today, the philosophy has been adopted by many other disciplines, including systems and software engineering. The basic idea behind a configuration management system is to establish and maintain the consistency of a system or product throughout its lifetime. The following are the fundamental activities associated with any configuration management system:

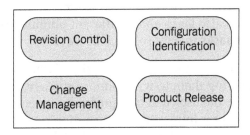

The purpose of configuration management systems is to ensure that the state of the system isn't residing in the minds of people, but inside a revision control system, from which it's easy to figure out the current state of the system along with the changes that have been made to the underlying system over the course of time. It not only allows to record "what" changes were made, but also "why" the changes were made.

With a phenomenal increase in the usage of cloud platforms, new challenges have emerged for system architects, as they now need to design systems that are able to scale up the size of the infrastructure upon the demands laid down by the application's needs, and the manual configuration of systems in such a dynamic environment is just not possible.

Chef is a configuration management system developed by Opscode and is one of the most widely used systems in its category. It allows you to define the infrastructure as a code, and it can be used to build, deploy, and automate your infrastructure. With Chef, the infrastructure becomes as versionable, testable, and repeatable as an application code.

Mastering Chef is an attempt to provide in-depth knowledge of the underlying system. It provides users with insights into different components of the underlying system and also provides users with insight into the APIs that can be used to either extend Chef, or build toolsets around the ecosystem.

What this book covers

Chapter 1, Introduction to the Chef Ecosystem, serves as a reference to new users of Chef. After a brief introduction, we jump into the anatomy of a chef-client run and at the end, we'll see how to go about setting up our workstation for the development of a Chef code that is thoroughly tested before being pushed to the production environment.

Chapter 2, Knife and Its Associated Plugins, introduces the reader to one of the most widely used tools in the Chef ecosystem, called Knife. We will learn to use Knife to bootstrap instances and also learn about different plugins that can be used to accomplish daily routine tasks in a more efficient way.

Chapter 3, Chef and Ruby, brings a user up to speed with the required Ruby knowledge, thereby allowing them to write a more efficient infrastructure code. By the end of this chapter, the user will be equipped with enough knowledge of Ruby to extend the code for infrastructure provisioning, beyond what can be accomplished by merely using the DSL provided by Chef.

Chapter 4, Controlling Access to Resources, introduces the concept of organization, groups, and users, and explains how you can allow fine-grained access to different types of objects residing on the Chef server.

Chapter 5, Starting the Journey to the World of Recipes, introduces the reader to the most fundamental unit of code written by Chef developers— "recipes". We'll learn about the different components of a recipe and get an understanding of the different resources that can be used to manage our infrastructure.

Chapter 6, Cookbooks and LWRPs, introduces users to cookbooks and how you can extend chef-client through the use of lightweight resource/provider. Readers will also learn how to create their own custom LWRPs by the end of this chapter.

Chapter 7, Roles and Environments, explains that, most of the time, a server is not just associated with one particular task and can perform many different operations. For example, you might have a web server that is also performing the role of an application server and a proxy. Roles allow users to attach multiple recipes to a server. Also, in most organizations, infrastructure is classified into different environments depending upon the use. For example, an organization might have a dev, QA, staging, and production environment. The configuration of applications running across these environments will be different to some extent. This chapter will explain what a role is, how we can group multiple recipes in a role, and how to use roles inside a recipe to do things conditionally. We'll also learn how you can manage different environments in your infrastructure using Chef.

Chapter 8, Attributes and Their Uses, explains that every service and a server can be identified with a role and set of properties associated with it. Some properties are system specific, such as the IP address, kernel, hostname, and so on. While they are necessary, an effective infrastructure code always needs more properties that can define the services and the server itself in a more precise manner. In this chapter, we'll see what the different types of attributes are and how to override values of the attributes.

Chapter 9, Ohai and Its Plugin Ecosystem, explains that as part of a chef-client run, many details related to the underlying system, such as architecture, operating system, network details, filesystem, and so on, are required to be collected by Chef. Ohai is a tool that allows for this. In this chapter, we'll learn about Ohai and its plugin-based architecture and associated plugins. We'll also learn how to write our own custom Ohai plugins.

Chapter 10, Data Bags and Templates, explains that in highly dynamic environments such as cloud, a configuration management system is only as good as its support for allowing the specification of the configuration in a form that is dynamic. Templates are just what the doctor ordered for this use case. Data bags, on the other hand, are data stores containing the data stored in a JSON format. In this chapter, we'll learn how to make effective use of databags and templates to define our infrastructure.

Chapter 11, Chef API and Search, explains that the Chef API is perhaps one of the most powerful features of Chef. Chef has a really wonderful API and its search facility is what makes it really fun to use. There are lots of cases where you can make use of Chef's API to build tools that can help in the efficient automation of the tasks. In this chapter, we'll look at Chef's API, using search in a recipe using Chef API, and also using a search through Knife.

Chapter 12, Extending Chef, covers the writing of a custom code suited for our requirements that will help us to extend the functionality of Chef. We'll learn how to write custom Knife plugins and custom Chef handlers.

Chapter 13, (Ab)Using Chef, explores some fun uses of Chef, which will allow an increase in productivity, while managing a large scale infrastructure. We'll see how we can extend tools such as Capistrano by using Chef API. We'll also learn how to manage large distributed clusters using an extension of Chef called Ironfan. We will also look at tools such as the Push Job server, which can be used for the orchestration of chef-client runs across a set of instances.

What you need for this book

All the code in this book is written/tested against Chef 12.x. A basic list of software required to run the code in this book is as follows:

- Operating system: Mac OS X/Linux/Windows
- Ruby: 1.9.3+
- Chef: 12.x
- Git
- Editor: Atom/Sublime/Vi/Emacs/TextMate

Who this book is for

This is a book for anyone who is interested in learning about Chef. You are not required to have any prior experience with the use of Chef or any configuration management system. You aren't expected to have experience with programming in Ruby; however, some experience with the fundamentals of programming will definitely be helpful.

Conventions

In this book, you will find a number of styles of text that distinguish between different kinds of information. Here are some examples of these styles, and an explanation of their meaning.

Code words in text, database table names, folder names, filenames, file extensions, pathnames, dummy URLs, user input, and Twitter handles are shown as follows: "Let's see what the `knife` command has to offer to us."

A block of code is set as follows:

```
knife[:aws_access_key_id] = "AWS_ACCESS_KEY"
knife[:aws_secret_access_key] = "AWS_SECRET_KEY"
```

When we wish to draw your attention to a particular part of a code block, the relevant lines or items are set in bold:

```
node_name               'mayank'
client_key              '~/keys/chef/mayank.pem'
validation_client_name  'chef-validator'
```

Any command-line input or output is written as follows:

```
$ knife search '*:*'
```

New terms and **important words** are shown in bold. Words that you see on the screen, in menus or dialog boxes for example, appear in the text like this: "Once you are done with it, click on the **Create Role** button."

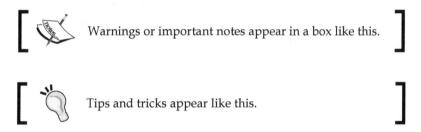

> Warnings or important notes appear in a box like this.

> Tips and tricks appear like this.

Reader feedback

Feedback from our readers is always welcome. Let us know what you think about this book—what you liked or may have disliked. Reader feedback is important for us to develop titles that you really get the most out of.

To send us general feedback, simply send an e-mail to feedback@packtpub.com, and mention the book title via the subject of your message.

If there is a topic that you have expertise in and you are interested in either writing or contributing to a book, see our author guide on www.packtpub.com/authors.

Customer support

Now that you are the proud owner of a Packt book, we have a number of things to help you to get the most from your purchase.

Downloading the example code

You can download the example code files for all Packt books you have purchased from your account at http://www.packtpub.com. If you purchased this book elsewhere, you can visit http://www.packtpub.com/support and register to have the files e-mailed directly to you.

Errata

Although we have taken every care to ensure the accuracy of our content, mistakes do happen. If you find a mistake in one of our books—maybe a mistake in the text or the code—we would be grateful if you would report this to us. By doing so, you can save other readers from frustration and help us improve subsequent versions of this book. If you find any errata, please report them by visiting http://www.packtpub.com/submit-errata, selecting your book, clicking on the **errata submission form** link, and entering the details of your errata. Once your errata are verified, your submission will be accepted and the errata will be uploaded on our website, or added to any list of existing errata, under the Errata section of that title. Any existing errata can be viewed by selecting your title from http://www.packtpub.com/support.

Piracy

Piracy of copyright material on the Internet is an ongoing problem across all media. At Packt, we take the protection of our copyright and licenses very seriously. If you come across any illegal copies of our works, in any form, on the Internet, please provide us with the location address or website name immediately so that we can pursue a remedy.

Please contact us at copyright@packtpub.com with a link to the suspected pirated material.

We appreciate your help in protecting our authors, and our ability to bring you valuable content.

Questions

You can contact us at questions@packtpub.com if you are having a problem with any aspect of the book, and we will do our best to address it.

1
Introduction to the Chef Ecosystem

Chef is a configuration management system written partly in Ruby and Erlang.

Before we begin our exciting journey towards becoming Chef masters, I think it would be prudent on our part to understand the underlying ecosystem.

The Chef ecosystem is primarily comprised of the following components:

- WebUI: This is a Rails application that is used to view information about the Chef server over the Web.

- ErChef: Prior to version 11.x, the Chef server API core (the code responsible for catering to requests by Knife or chef-client) was written in Ruby. However, since 11.x, this code has been rewritten in Erlang.

- Bookshelf: This is used to store cookbooks content such as files, templates, and so on, that have been uploaded to chef-server as part of a cookbook version.

- chef-solr: This is a wrapper around Apache Solr and is used to handle the REST API for indexing and search.

- Rabbit MQ: This is used as a message queue for the Chef server. All items that are to be added to a search index repository are first added to a queue.

- chef-expander: This is a piece of code that pulls messages from the RabbitMQ queue, processes them into a desired format, and finally posts them to Solr for indexing.

- PostgreSQL: This is another major change since version 11.x. Earlier, CouchDB used to be the data storage; however, since version 11.x, PostgreSQL has become the data storage solution used by Chef.

- chef-client: This is a Ruby application that runs on every machine that needs to be provisioned. It handles the task of authenticating with chef-server, registering nodes, synchronizing cookbooks, compiling resource collections, handling exceptions and notifications, and so on.

- Knife: This is a Ruby application that provides an interface between a local chef repository and the Chef server.

The typical architecture of the Chef ecosystem can be understood by looking at the following figure:

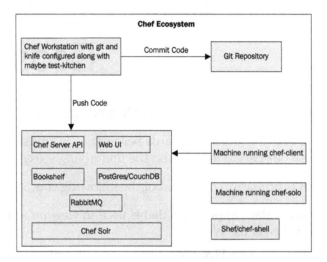

Other than these components, we've **chef-shell (shef)**, Ohai, and chef-solo that form an integral part of the chef ecosystem. We also have chef-zero, which is being adopted by people to quickly test their code or deploy chef code locally. It's a small, fast, and in-memory implementation of the Chef server and it helps developers to write a clean code without all the hooks that were earlier placed into the code to ensure that chef-solo can execute the code.

With the understanding of the Chef ecosystem, we will be covering the following topics in this chapter:

- Different modes of running Chef
- Terminology used in the world of Chef
- The anatomy of a Chef run
- Using the Chef Solo provisioner
- Setting up a work environment

Different modes of running Chef

Chef can be executed under different modes. It's generally set up in a client-server fashion. However, if you were to just bootstrap your machine using Chef code, you don't need to worry about setting up a Chef server. Chef also provides a way of running as a standalone executable. If you are a developer writing a new piece of infrastructure code and want to test it, you can even run it in an IRB-like shell.

The most used mode of running Chef is the client-server model. In this model, we've a Chef server and an agent called chef-client that runs on machine(s) that need to be set up. The Chef client communicates with a chef-server and bootstraps the machine appropriately depending upon certain parameters, which we'll learn about shortly.

In a client-server architecture, the Chef ecosystem is comprised of a chef-server, which in turn is a name given to a set of services running on an instance (chef-server-web-ui, chef-solr, chef-expander, chef-core-api, and so on) and chef-client, which is an agent running on machines.

The chef-solo is the tool to be used if you just want to provision an instance using Chef. With chef-solo, we can do everything except for using the search functionality or accessing remote data bags that the chef-server provides. The chef-solo tool is expected to be deprecated in the near future and chef-zero is the expected way to run the code locally.

Shef is more like a debugging tool that allows you to set breakpoints within a recipe. It runs as an IRB session. It provides support for interactive debugging too.

By default, chef-shell loads in a standalone mode. However, it can also run as a chef-client and be used to verify the functionality of a Chef run. Set up `chef-shell.rb` with the same settings as those in `knife.rb` and run with the `-z` option:

```
$ chef-shell -z
```

We'll cover more about using Shef for debugging purposes later in this book.

The Chef server can either be set up privately, or you can choose a managed hosting service provided by Opscode. Here again, you've a choice of using an open source Chef or Enterprise Chef.

Enterprise Chef adds the following additional features on top of an open source Chef:

- Enhanced management console
- Centralized monitoring and reporting
- Role-based access control
- Push client runs

Terminology used in the world of Chef

Before jumping into a new territory, it's always wise to learn about the terminology used by the people already living in the environment. In this section, we'll try to make sense of what all those terms mean. After you are familiar with the terms, everything will start making more sense:

- **Node**: Any machine or cloud instance that you are configuring using Chef is known as a node. On a Chef server it's an object comprising of attributes and a run list specific to the instance.

- **Chef server**: A Chef server is a machine running chef-core-api, chef-solr, chef-web-ui, chef-expander, and chef-validator along with a backend data store such as PostGre/CouchDB and a messaging system such as RabbitMQ.

- **Workstation**: This is the machine where we'll be writing our Chef code.

- **Repository**: This could be a svn/Git repository where we'll be committing our code. This is useful to maintain revisions of code.

- **Knife**: This is a tool that you can use to manage different aspects of Chef.

- **Cookbook**: This is where you define anything and everything related to your infrastructure code. Cookbooks contain recipes, attributes, files/directories to be set up, templates, and so on.

- **Recipes**: Theses are part of a cookbook and most of the code meat goes into recipes.

- **Attributes**: Every code requires variables, and attributes are like variables holding values, which can be overridden.

- **Roles**: These are a way of arranging cookbooks together. For example, a web server is a role and it can comprise of cookbooks to set up the Nginx web server along with OpenSSL and a few other things.

- **Run-list**: This is an ordered list comprising of roles and/or recipes. The chef-client looks at items in `run_list` and executes them in an order specified in `run_list`.

- **Resources**: The chef-client does multiple tasks such as setting up packages, creating users, setting up cron jobs, executing scripts, and so on. Since Chef is meant to be platform-agnostic, we don't use service providers explicit to the system to do these jobs. For example, we don't say `yum` installs this package, instead we use a resource provider called package, which internally decides which underlying system to choose for the job eventually. This is pretty useful as it helps keep Chef code agnostic to platform changes.

- **LWRP**: **Lightweight resources and providers (LWRP)** are custom resources and providers that provide a way to perform a certain action. For example, you may write your own LWRP to manage Git repositories or install packages using Makefiles and so on.

- **Metadata**: A metadata file describes properties of a cookbook such as version, dependencies, and so on, and it's used to verify that a cookbook is deployed correctly on a node.

- **Templates**: Often, all we want to do is to specify a configuration that changes due to certain parameters, such as environment and so on. Templates allow for the creation of such configurations.

- **chef-client**: This is an agent that will run on instances that we want to bootstrap using Chef.

- **Ohai**: This is a piece of code that allows us to fetch useful information about a system along with other desired information. Ohai is used extensively to generate attributes that help in defining a node during a chef-client run.

- **DSL**: Chef cookbooks are primarily written in Ruby. Chef provides a **Domain Specific Language (DSL)** that helps to write a code easily and quickly.

- **chef-solo**: It's a tool similar to chef-client that will help us to execute a chef code.

- **chef-zero**: It's a lightweight, in-memory implementation of the Chef server, which can be invoked on a node using **chef-client -z**. This is going to be a standard going forward and will be replacing chef-solo in the future.

Now that we know the language, let's jump into the world of Chef and see what happens when a chef-client run happens.

The anatomy of a Chef run

A Chef run here implies either the execution of chef-client or chef-solo, and we'll look at each of them separately.

A Chef run using chef-client

As we learned earlier while understanding terminology, a chef-client is an agent that runs on machines that are meant to be configured using Chef. The chef-client agent is meant to be executed in an environment where we are using Chef in a client-server architecture.

Upon the invocation of a chef-client, the following things happen:

- Ohai is executed and automatic attributes are collected, which are eventually used to build a node object
- Authentication with a chef-server
- Synchronization of cookbooks
- Loading of cookbooks and convergence
- Checking for the status of chef-client run, reporting, and exception handling.

The chef-client, by default, looks for a configuration file named `client.rb`. On Linux/Unix-based machines this file is located at `/etc/chef/client.rb`. On Windows, this file is located at `C:\chef\client.rb`.

The `chef-client` command supports many options. The following option indicates which configuration file to use. By default, `/etc/chef/client.rb` is used for the purpose of a Chef run:

```
-c CONFIG, --config CONFIG
```

> **Downloading the example code**
>
> You can download the example code files for all Packt books you have purchased from your account at `http://www.packtpub.com`. If you purchased this book elsewhere, you can visit `http://www.packtpub.com/support` and register to have the files e-mailed directly to you.

The following option indicates that chef-client will be executed as a daemon and not as a foreground process. This option is only available on Linux/Unix. To run chef-client as a service in a Windows environment, use the `chef-client::service` recipe in the chef-client cookbook:

```
-d, --daemonize
```

The following option specifies the name of the environment:

```
-E ENVIRONMENT, --environment ENVIRONMENT
```

By default, a chef-client run forks a process where the cookbooks are executed. This helps prevent issues such as memory leaks and also helps to run a chef code with a steady amount of memory:

```
-f, --fork
```

The following option specifies the output format: summary (default), `.json`, `.yaml`, `.txt`, and `.pp`:

`-F FORMAT, --format FORMAT`

The following option indicates that the `formatter` output will be used instead of the `logger` output:

`--force-formatter`

The following option indicates that the `logger` output will be used instead of the `formatter` output:

`--force-logger`

The following option specifies a path to a JSON file, which will be used to override attributes and maybe specify `run_list` as well:

`-j PATH, --json-attribute PATH`

The following option specifies the location of a file containing a client key. The default location is `/etc/chef/client.pem`:

`-k KEYFILE, --client KEYFILE`

When a chef-client first registers a new machine with a chef-server, it doesn't have `/etc/chef/client.pem`. It contacts the chef-server with a key called `validation_key` (default location: `/etc/chef/validation.pem`). Upon contacting the chef-server, the chef-server responds with a new client key, which is stored in `/etc/chef/client.pem`. Going forward, every communication with a chef-server is authenticated with `/etc/chef/client.pem`:

`-K KEYFILE, --validation_key KEYFILE`

The following option is the name with which a machine is registered with a chef-server. The default name of the node is FQDN:

`-N NODENAME, --node-name NODENAME`

The following command replaces the current run list with specified items:

`-o RUN_LIST_ITEM, --override-runlist RUN_LIST_ITEM`

The following option provides a number in seconds to add an interval that determines how frequently a chef-client is executed. This option is useful when a chef-client is executed in daemon mode:

`-s SECONDS, -splay SECONDS`

The following command indicates that the chef-client executable will be run in the why-run mode. It's a dry-run mode where a chef-client run does everything, but it doesn't modify the system:

```
-W, --why-run
```

The following command specifies the location in which **process identification number (PID)** is saved. This is useful to manage a chef daemon via a process management system such as Monit:

```
-P PID_FILE, --pid PID_FILE
```

Let's presume we've already written a cookbook to install and configure a popular web server called Nginx.

We will create two files on our target machine:

- client.rb: For our setup, the location will be /etc/chef/client.rb. It is a default configuration that will be used by a chef-client executable:

  ```
  log_level          :info
  log_location       "/var/log/chef.log"
  chef_server_url    "http://chef-server:4000"
  environment        "production"
  ```

  As you can see, we've mentioned in our configuration that log_level is INFO, the log file is stored at /var/log/chef.log, chef-client will connect to a Chef server hosted at a machine accessible by the name chef-server, and finally we have our setup distributed across different environments and this machine is in the production environment.

- roles.json: For our setup, the location will be /etc/chef/roles.json. This is a .json file that defines attributes, and a run_list which will be used to fetch the concerned cookbooks from a chef-server and the bootstrap machine;

  ```
  {
    "run_list":["role[webserver]"],
    "app_user": "www-data",
    "log_dir": "/var/log",
  }
  ```

  As you can see, we've defined a run_list that comprises of a role called webserver. Along with this, we've specified two attributes: app_user and log_dir.

With `client.rb` and `roles.json` in place, now you can run chef-client as follows:

```
#chef-client -j /etc/chef/roles.json
```

The following image describes the steps as they happen during the chef-client run:

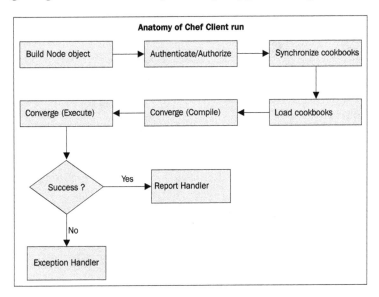

Let's look at each step closely.

Step 1 – Building a node object

As a first step, a chef-client will build the node object. To do this, the system is profiled first by Ohai.

Ohai returns a bunch of information about the system in a `.json` format. The following is an output from the Ohai run on our `chef-eg01` instance:

```
# ohai
{
  "languages": {
    "ruby": {
      "platform": "x86_64-linux",
      "version": "2.1.0",
      "release_date": "2013-12-25",
      . . .
    },
    "python": {
      "version": "2.6.6",
```

```
      "builddate": "Jun 18 2012, 14:18:47"
    },
    "perl": {
      "version": "5.10.1",
      "archname": "x86_64-linux-thread-multi"
    },
    "lua": {
      "version": "5.1.4"
    },
    "java": {
      "version": "1.7.0_09",
      "runtime": {
        "name": "Java(TM) SE Runtime Environment",
        "build": "1.7.0_09-b05"
      },
      "hotspot": {
        "name": "Java HotSpot(TM) 64-Bit Server VM",
        "build": "23.5-b02, mixed mode"
      }
    }
  },
  "kernel": {
    "name": "Linux",
    "release": "2.6.32-220.23.1.el6.x86_64",
    "version": "#1 SMP Mon Jun 18 18:58:52 BST 2012",
    "machine": "x86_64",
   },
    "os": "GNU/Linux"
  },
  "os": "linux",
  "os_version": "2.6.32-220.23.1.el6.x86_64",
  "lsb": {
    "id": "CentOS",
    "description": "CentOS release 6.2 (Final)",
    "release": "6.2",
    "codename": "Final"
  },
  . . .
  "chef_packages": {
    "ohai": {
      "version": "6.14.0",
```

```
        "ohai_root": "/usr/local/rvm/gems/ruby-2.1.0/gems/ohai-6.14.0/
lib/ohai"
      },
      "chef": {
        "version": "11.10.4",
        "chef_root": "/usr/local/rvm/gems/ruby-2.1.0/gems/chef-11.10.4/
lib"
      }
    },
    "hostname": "chef-eg01",
    "fqdn": "chef-eg01.sychonet.com",
    "domain": "sychonet.com",
    "network": {
      "interfaces": {
        "lo": {
          . . .
        },
        "eth0": {
          . . .
        }
      }
    },
    "ipaddress": "10.0.0.42",
    "macaddress": "0A:F8:4C:7A:C3:B2",
    "ohai_time": 1397945435.3669002,
    "dmi": {
      "dmidecode_version": "2.11"
    },
    "keys": {
      "ssh": {
        "host_dsa_public":"XXXXXXX",
        "host_rsa_public":"XXXXXXX
      }
    },
    . . .
}
```

As we can see, Ohai gave us plenty of useful information about our machine,
such as the different language interpreters installed on the system, kernel version,
OS platform and release, network, SSH keys, disks, RAM, and so on. All this
information, that is automatic attributes, along with the node name, is used to build
and register a node object with a chef-server. The default name of the node object is
FQDN, as returned by Ohai. However, we can always override the node name in the
client.rb configuration file.

Step 2 – Authenticate

We won't want our private chef-server to be responding to requests made by anyone. To accomplish this, each request to the Chef server is accompanied with some headers encrypted using the private key (`client.pem`).

As part of this step, a chef-client checks the presence of the `/etc/chef/client.pem` file, which is used for the purpose of authentication.

If no `client.pem` is present, a chef-client looks for a `/etc/chef/validation.pem` file, which is a private key assigned to the chef-validator. Once the chef-validator has authenticated itself to a chef-server, a chef-server creates a public/private key pair. The chef-server keeps a public key with itself, while a private key is sent back to a chef-client. After this step, our node object built in step 1 is registered with the chef-server.

 After the initial chef-client run is over, the chef-validator key is no longer required and can (ideally should) be deleted from the machine.

Step 3 – Synchronization of cookbooks

Now, since we are authenticated, we can go about fetching cookbooks from a chef-server. However, to send cookbooks to the relevant instance, a chef-server has to know which cookbooks to send across.

In this step, a chef-client fetches a node object from the chef-server. A node object defines what is in `run_list` and what attributes are associated with the node. A `run_list` list defines what cookbooks will be downloaded from a chef-server.

The following is what we have in our `run_list`:

```
"run_list":["role[webserver]"]
```

Our `run_list` comprises of one element called `role[webserver]`. A role is a way in which the Chef world organizes cookbooks together under one hood. Here is what our role looks like:

```
webserver.rb
# Role Name:: webserver
# Copyright 2014, Sychonet
# Author: maxc0d3r@sychonet.com

name "webserver"
```

```
description "This role configures nginx webserver"

run_list   "recipe[nginx]","recipe[base]"
override_attributes(
  :app => {
    :base => "/apps",
    :user => "ubuntu",
    :group => "ubuntu",
    :log => "/var/log/nginx",
    :data => "/data"
  }
)
```

Our role has `run_list`, which comprises of two elements: `recipe[passenger-nginx]` and `recipe[base]`. These recipes contain code that will be used to bootstrap a machine using Chef. Along with this, we've a few attributes:

```
node[:app][:base]  = "/apps"
node[:app][:user]  = "Ubuntu"
node[:app][:group] = "Ubuntu"
node[:app][:log]   = "/var/log/nginx"
node[:app][:data]  = "/data"
```

We will be using these attributes in our recipes to set up a machine according to our requirements. These attributes may already be defined in our cookbook and if they are, then they are overridden here.

Here is what a typical `node json` object looks like:

```
{
  "name": "chef-eg01.sychonet.com",
  "json_class": "Chef::Node",
  "chef_type": "node",
  "chef_environment": "production",
  "automatic": { . . . },
  "default": { . . . },
  "normal": { . . . },
  "override": { . . . },
  "run_list": [ . . . ]
}
```

Once the chef-client has obtained the `node json` object from the chef-server, it expands `run_list`. The `run_list` defined in a node object contains roles and recipes, and roles contain `run_list` that again contains further roles and recipes. During the execution of a chef-client, `run_list` gets expanded to the level of recipes.

Now, with a list of recipes to be executed on the machine, a chef-client downloads all the cookbooks mentioned in the expanded `run_list` from the chef server. Some cookbooks might not really be defined in `run_list`, but might be part of a dependency and those cookbooks are also downloaded as part of this event. A chef server maintains different versions of cookbooks and hence, if we want, we can request a specific version of a cookbook by specifying it as part of `run_list`, as follows:

```
{"run_list":["recipe[nginx@1.4.2]"]}
```

This will set up version 1.4.2 of the `nginx` recipe. We can also mention a version in the dependency or environment as follows:

```
depends "nginx", "= 1.4.2"
```

Alternatively, we can use the following code:

```
cookbook "nginx", "= 1.4.2"
```

Downloaded cookbooks are saved in a local filesystem on a machine at the location specified by `file_cache_path`, defined in `client.rb` (defaults to `/var/chef/cache`).

Upon subsequent chef-client runs, the cookbooks that haven't changed since the last run aren't downloaded and only the changed cookbooks are resynced.

Step 4 – Loading of cookbooks and convergence

Now, with all the cookbooks synchronized, a chef-client loads the components in the following order:

- Libraries: Theses are loaded first so that all language extensions and Ruby classes are available.
- Attributes: An attribute file updates node attributes and recipes.
- Definitions: Theses must be loaded before recipes because they create new pseudo-resources.
- Recipes: At this point, recipes are evaluated. Nothing is done with any resource defined in the recipe.

Recipes are loaded in the order they are specified in `run_list`. This is a very important concept to grasp because it can be a deal breaker if not understood properly. Let's look at our `run_list` in `/etc/chef/roles.json`:

```
"run_list":["role[webserver]"]
```

The `webserver` role in turn defines the following `run_list`:

```
run_list   "recipe[nginx]","recipe[base]"
```

This implies that the expanded `run_list` will look something like the following:

```
run_list   "recipe[nginx]","recipe[base]"
```

Now, if there are things mentioned in `recipe[nginx]` that require things that are being set up in `recipe[base]`, then our Chef run will fail. For example, say we are setting up a user `www-data` in `recipe[base]` and we need Nginx to be started as a service with the user `www-data` in `recipe[nginx]`, then it won't work because the `www-data` user won't be created until the base recipe is executed and it'll only be executed once `recipe[nginx]` has been executed.

At this point in time, all the evaluated resources found in recipes are put in resource collection, which is an array of each evaluated resource. Any external Ruby code is also executed at this point in time.

Now, with resource collection ready for use, a Chef run reaches a stage of execution.

Chef iterates through a resource collection in the following order:

- It runs specified actions for each resource
- A provider knows how to perform actions

Step 5 – Reporting and exception handling

Once a chef-client run has ended, the status of the run is checked. If there has been an error, Chef exits with unhandled exception and we can write exception handlers to handle such situations. For example, we might want to notify a system administrator about an issue with the chef-client run.

In the event of success as well, we might want to do certain things and this is handled via report handlers. For example, we might want to push a message to a queue saying that a machine has been bootstrapped successfully.

Using chef-solo

chef-solo is another executable that can be used to bootstrap any machine using cookbooks.

There are times when the need for a chef-server just isn't there, for example, when testing a newly written Chef cookbook on a virtual machine. During these times, we can't make use of a chef-client, as a chef-client requires a chef-server to communicate with.

The chef-solo allows using cookbooks with nodes without requiring a chef-server. It runs locally and requires those cookbooks (along with dependencies) to be present locally on the machine too.

Other than this difference, the chef-solo doesn't provide support for the following features:

- Search
- Authentication or authorization
- Centralized distribution of cookbooks
- Centralized API to interact with different infrastructure components.

The chef-solo can pick up cookbooks from either a local directory or URL where a `tar.gz` archive of the cookbook is present.

The chef-solo command uses the `/etc/chef/solo.rb` configuration file, or we can also specify an alternate path for this configuration file using the `-config` option during the chef-solo execution.

The chef-solo, by default, will look for data bags at `/var/chef/data_bags`. However, this location can be changed by specifying an alternate path in the `data_bag_path` attribute defined in `solo.rb`. The chef-solo picks up roles from the `/var/chef/roles` folder, but this location again can be modified by specifying an alternate path in the `role_path` attribute in `solo.rb`.

Other than the options supported by a chef-client, the chef-solo executable supports the following option:

```
-r RECIPE_URL, --recipe-url RECIPE_URL
```

A URL from where a remote cookbook's `tar.gz` will be downloaded.

For example:

```
#chef-solo -c ~/solo.rb -j ~/node.json -r http://repo.sychonet.com/chef-solo.tar.gz
```

The `tar.gz` file is first archived into `file_cache_path` and finally, extracted to `cookbook_path`.

Now that we understand how the Chef run happens, let's get our hands dirty and go about setting up our developer workstation.

Setting up a work environment

As we saw earlier, the Chef ecosystem comprises of three components: chef-server, chef-client, and a developer workstation.

We'll be developing all our beautiful Chef codes on our workstation. As we are developing a code, it's good practice to keep our code in some version control system such as `git/svn/mercurial` and so on. We'll choose Git for our purpose and I'll presume you've a repository called chef-repo that is being tracked by Git.

The following software should be installed on your machine before you try to set up your workstation:

- Ruby (Preferably, 1.9.x).
- We need Chef and Knife installed on our workstation and it's pretty easy to go about installing Chef along with Knife using the Ruby gems. Just open up a terminal and issue the command:

  `#gem install chef`

- Once Chef is installed, create a `.chef` folder in your home directory and create a `knife.rb` file in it.

Knife is a tool using which we'll use to communicate with a chef-server. Knife can be used for lots of purposes such as managing cookbooks, nodes, API clients, roles, environments, and so on. Knife also comes with plugins that allow it to be used for various other useful purposes. We'll learn more about them in later chapters.

Knife needs the `knife.rb` file present in the `$HOME/.chef` folder. The following is a sample `knife.rb` file:

```
log_level                 :info
log_location              STDOUT
node_name                 'NAME_OF_YOUR_CHOICE'
client_key                '~/.chef/NAME_OF_YOUR_CHOICE.pem'
validation_client_name    'chef-validator'
validation_key            '~/.chef/validation.pem'
chef_server_url           'http://chef-server.sychonet.com:4000'
cache_type                'BasicFile'
cache_options             (:path => '~/.chef/checksums')
cookbook_path             [ '~/code/chef-repo/cookbooks' ]
```

Connect to your chef-server web interface and visit the client section and create a new client with a name of your choice (ensure that no client with the same name exists on the chef-server):

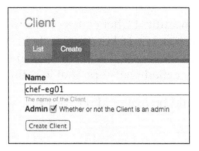

Once you've created the client, a chef-server will respond with a public/private key pair as shown in the following screenshot:

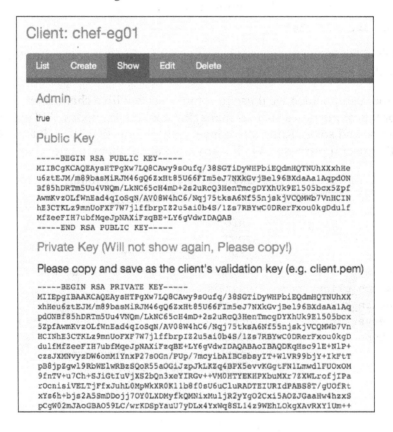

Copy the contents of the private key and store them in `~/.chef/<NAME_OF_YOUR_CHOICE>.pem`

Also, copy the private key for the chef-validator (/etc/chef/validation.pem) from the chef-server to ~/.chef/validation.pem.

Specify NAME_OF_YOUR_CHOICE as the node name.

As you can see, we've specified cookbook_path to be ~/code/chef-repo/cookbooks. I'm presuming that you'll be storing your Chef cookbooks inside this folder.

Create the following directory structure inside ~/code/chef-repo:

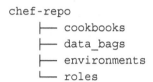

```
chef-repo
        ├── cookbooks
        ├── data_bags
        ├── environments
        └── roles
```

The cookbooks directory will hold our cookbooks, the data_bags directory will contain data bags, the environments directory will contain configuration files for different environments, and the roles directory will contain files associated with different roles.

Once you've created these directories, commit them to your Git repository.

Now, let's try to see if we are able to make use of the Knife executable and query the Chef server:

```
$knife client list
chef-validator
chef-webui
chef-eg01
```

This command will list all the available API clients registered with the chef-server. As you can see, chef-eg01 is a newly created client and it's now registered with the chef-server.

Knife caches the checksum of Ruby and ERB files when performing a cookbook syntax check with knife cookbook test or knife cookbook upload. The cache_type variable defines which type of cache to make use of. The most used type is BasicFile and it's probably best to leave it at that.

The cache_options is a hash for options related to caching. For BasicFile, :path should be the location on the filesystem where Knife has write access.

If you want the Knife cookbook to create a command to prefill values for copyright and e-mail in comments, you can also specify the following options in your `knife.rb` file:

```
cookbook_copyright "Company name"
cookbook_email "Email address"
```

With this setup, now we are ready to start creating new cookbooks, roles, and environments, and manage them along with nodes and clients using Knife from our workstation.

Before we jump into cookbook creation and other exciting stuff, we need to ensure that we follow a test-driven approach to our Chef development. We will make use of test-kitchen to help us write Chef cookbooks that are tested thoroughly before being pushed to a chef-server.

test-kitchen can be installed as a gem:

```
$ gem install test-kitchen
```

Also, download Vagrant from `http://www.vagrantup.com` and install it.

If you want some help, use the `help` option of the `kitchen` command:

```
$ kitchen help
Commands:
  kitchen console                            # Kitchen Console!
  kitchen converge [INSTANCE|REGEXP|all]     # Converge one or more
instances
  kitchen create [INSTANCE|REGEXP|all]       # Create one or more instances
  kitchen destroy [INSTANCE|REGEXP|all]      # Destroy one or more instances
  kitchen diagnose [INSTANCE|REGEXP|all]     # Show computed diagnostic
configuration
  kitchen driver                             # Driver subcommands
  kitchen driver create [NAME]               # Create a new Kitchen Driver
gem project
  kitchen driver discover                    # Discover Test Kitchen drivers
published on RubyGems
  kitchen driver help [COMMAND]              # Describe subcommands or one
specific subcommand
  kitchen help [COMMAND]                     # Describe available commands
or one specific command
  kitchen init                               # Adds some configuration to
your cookbook so Kitchen can rock
```

```
kitchen list [INSTANCE|REGEXP|all]     # Lists one or more instances
kitchen login INSTANCE|REGEXP          # Log in to one instance
kitchen setup [INSTANCE|REGEXP|all]    # Setup one or more instances
kitchen test [INSTANCE|REGEXP|all]     # Test one or more instances
kitchen verify [INSTANCE|REGEXP|all]   # Verify one or more instances
kitchen version                        # Print Kitchen's version
information
```

Now, let's create a new cookbook called `passenger-nginx`:

```
$knife cookbook create passenger-nginx
```

Now, we'll add test-kitchen to our project using the `init` subcommand:

```
$ kitchen init
create .kitchen.yml
create test/integration/default
run gem install kitchen-vagrant from "."
Fetching: kitchen-vagrant-0.14.0.gem (100%)
Successfully installed kitchen-vagrant-0.14.0
Parsing documentation for kitchen-vagrant-0.14.0
Installing ri documentation for kitchen-vagrant-0.14.0
Done installing documentation for kitchen-vagrant after 0 seconds
1 gem installed
```

The `kitchen init` command has created a configuration file called `.kitchen.yml`, along with a `test/integration/default` directory.

It also went on to install a gem called kitchen-vagrant. kitchen needs a virtual machine to test run the chef code, and drivers are responsible for managing virtual machines. By default, kitchen makes use of Vagrant to manage the virtual machine.

Let's see what we have in our configuration file, `kitchen.yml`:

```
$ cat .kitchen.yml
---
driver:
  name: vagrant
provisioner:
  name: chef_solo
platforms:
  - name: ubuntu-12.04
```

```
    - name: centos-6.4
suites:
  - name: default
    run_list:
      - recipe[cb-test1::default]
    attributes:
```

The file is divided into four sections:

- **Driver**: This is where we set up basic stuff such as the SSH username and credentials. Under this section, we've a `name` property with a `vagrant` value. This tells kitchen to make use of the kitchen-vagrant driver.

- **Provisioner**: This tells kitchen to make use of a chef-solo to apply the cookbook to a newly created virtual machine.

- **Platforms**: This lists the operating systems on which we want to run our code.

- **Suites**: Here we describe what we wish to test.

Now, let's see what we have on our hands:

```
$ kitchen list
Instance              Driver    Provisioner   Last Action
default-ubuntu-1204   Vagrant   ChefSolo      <Not Created>
default-centos-64     Vagrant   ChefSolo      <Not Created>
```

As you can see, it's listing two instances: `default-ubuntu-1204` and `default-centos-64`. These names are a combination of the suite name and the platform name.

Now, let's spin up one instance to see what happens:

```
$ kitchen create default-ubuntu-1204
-----> Starting Kitchen (v1.2.1)
-----> Creating <default-ubuntu-1204>...
       Bringing machine 'default' up with 'virtualbox' provider...
       ==> default: Box 'opscode-ubuntu-12.04' could not be found.
Attempting to find and install...
           default: Box Provider: virtualbox
           default: Box Version: >= 0
       ==> default: Adding box 'opscode-ubuntu-12.04' (v0) for provider:
virtualbox
```

```
        default: Downloading: https://opscode-vm-bento.s3.amazonaws.
com/vagrant/virtualbox/opscode_ubuntu-12.04_chef-provisionerless.box
      ==> default: Successfully added box 'opscode-ubuntu-12.04' (v0)
for 'virtualbox'!
      ==> default: Importing base box 'opscode-ubuntu-12.04'...
      ==> default: Matching MAC address for NAT networking...
      ==> default: Setting the name of the VM: default-ubuntu-1204_
default_1398006642518_53572
      ==> default: Clearing any previously set network interfaces...
      ==> default: Preparing network interfaces based on
configuration...
          default: Adapter 1: nat
      ==> default: Forwarding ports...
          default: 22 => 2222 (adapter 1)
      ==> default: Running 'pre-boot' VM customizations...
      ==> default: Booting VM...
==> default: Waiting for machine to boot. This may take a few minutes...
    default: SSH address: 127.0.0.1:2222
          default: SSH username: vagrant
          default: SSH auth method: private key
          default: Warning: Connection timeout. Retrying...
      ==> default: Machine booted and ready!
      ==> default: Checking for guest additions in VM...
      ==> default: Setting hostname...
      Vagrant instance <default-ubuntu-1204> created.
      Finished creating <default-ubuntu-1204> (4m4.17s).
-----> Kitchen is finished. (4m4.71s)
```

So, this leads to the downloading of a virtual machine image for Ubuntu 12.04 and, eventually, the machine boots up. The default username for SSH connection is vagrant.

Let us check the status of our instance again:

```
$ kitchen list
Instance              Driver    Provisioner   Last Action
default-ubuntu-1204   Vagrant   ChefSolo      Created
default-centos-64     Vagrant   ChefSolo      <Not Created>
```

So, our Ubuntu instance is up and running. Now, let's add some meat to our recipe:

```
#
# Cookbook Name:: cb-test1
# Recipe:: default
#
# Copyright 2014, Sychonet
#
# All rights reserved - Do Not Redistribute
#

package "nginx"

log "Cool. So we have nginx installed"
```

So, now we've got our recipe ready, let's let test-kitchen run it in our instance now:

```
$ kitchen converge default-ubuntu-1204
-----> Starting Kitchen (v1.2.1)
-----> Converging <default-ubuntu-1204>...
       Preparing files for transfer
       Preparing current project directory as a cookbook
       Removing non-cookbook files before transfer
-----> Installing Chef Omnibus (true)
       downloading https://www.getchef.com/chef/install.sh
         to file /tmp/install.sh
       trying wget...
Downloading Chef  for ubuntu...
downloading https://www.getchef.com/chef/metadata?v=&prerelease=false&nig
htlies=false&p=ubuntu&pv=12.04&m=x86_64
  to file /tmp/install.sh.1144/metadata.txt
trying wget...
url  https://opscode-omnibus-packages.s3.amazonaws.com/ubuntu/12.04/
x86_64/chef_11.12.2-1_amd64.deb
md5  cedd8a2df60a706e51f58adf8441971b
sha256  af53e7ef602be6228dcbf68298e2613d3f37eb061975992abc6cd2d318e4a0c0
downloaded metadata file looks valid...
downloading https://opscode-omnibus-packages.s3.amazonaws.com/
ubuntu/12.04/x86_64/chef_11.12.2-1_amd64.deb
  to file /tmp/install.sh.1144/chef_11.12.2-1_amd64.deb
trying wget...
```

Comparing checksum with sha256sum...

Installing Chef

installing with dpkg...

Selecting previously unselected package chef.

(Reading database ... 56035 files and directories currently installed.)

Unpacking chef (from .../chef_11.12.2-1_amd64.deb) ...

Setting up chef (11.12.2-1) ...

Thank you for installing Chef!

      Transfering files to <default-ubuntu-1204>

[2014-04-20T15:50:31+00:00] INFO: Forking chef instance to converge...

[2014-04-20T15:50:31+00:00] WARN:

* *
* * *

SSL validation of HTTPS requests is disabled. HTTPS connections are still encrypted, but chef is not able to detect forged replies or man in the middle

attacks.

To fix this issue add an entry like this to your configuration file:


```

  # Verify all HTTPS connections (recommended)
  ssl_verify_mode :verify_peer

  # OR, Verify only connections to chef-server
  verify_api_cert true
```


    To check your SSL configuration, or troubleshoot errors, you can use the
    `knife ssl check` command like so:

```

    knife ssl check -c /tmp/kitchen/solo.rb
```

```
* * * * * * * * * * * * * * * * * * * * * * * * * * * * * * * * * * * * *
* * * * * * *


Starting Chef Client, version 11.12.2

[2014-04-20T15:50:31+00:00] INFO: *** Chef 11.12.2 ***

[2014-04-20T15:50:31+00:00] INFO: Chef-client pid: 1225

[2014-04-20T15:50:39+00:00] INFO: Setting the run_list to ["recipe[cb-
test1::default]"] from CLI options

[2014-04-20T15:50:39+00:00] INFO: Run List is [recipe[cb-test1::default]]

[2014-04-20T15:50:39+00:00] INFO: Run List expands to [cb-test1::default]

[2014-04-20T15:50:39+00:00] INFO: Starting Chef Run for default-
ubuntu-1204

[2014-04-20T15:50:39+00:00] INFO: Running start handlers

[2014-04-20T15:50:39+00:00] INFO: Start handlers complete.

Compiling Cookbooks...

Converging 2 resources

Recipe: cb-test1::default

  * package[nginx] action install[2014-04-20T15:50:39+00:00] INFO:
Processing package[nginx] action install (cb-test1::default line 10)


        - install version 1.1.19-1ubuntu0.6 of package nginx


  * log[Cool. So we have nginx installed] action write[2014-04-
20T15:50:52+00:00] INFO: Processing log[Cool. So we have nginx installed]
action write (cb-test1::default line 12)

[2014-04-20T15:50:52+00:00] INFO: Cool. So we have nginx installed



[2014-04-20T15:50:52+00:00] INFO: Chef Run complete in 12.923797655
seconds


Running handlers:

[2014-04-20T15:50:52+00:00] INFO: Running report handlers

Running handlers complete


[2014-04-20T15:50:52+00:00] INFO: Report handlers complete
```

```
Chef Client finished, 2/2 resources updated in 21.14983058 seconds
        Finished converging <default-ubuntu-1204> (2m10.10s).
-----> Kitchen is finished. (2m10.41s)
```

So, here is what happened under the hood when `kitchen converge` was executed:

- Chef was installed on an Ubuntu instance
- Our `cb-test1` cookbook and a chef-solo configuration were uploaded to an Ubuntu instance.
- The Chef run was initiated using `run_list` and attributes defined in `.kitchen.yml`

If the exit code of the `kitchen` command is `0`, then the command run was successful. If it's not `0`, then any part of the operation associated with the command was not successful.

Let's check the status of our instance once more:

```
$ kitchen list
Instance              Driver    Provisioner   Last Action
default-ubuntu-1204   Vagrant   ChefSolo      Converged
default-centos-64     Vagrant   ChefSolo      <Not Created>
```

So, our instance is converged, but we still don't know if `nginx` was installed successfully or not. One way to check this is to log in to the instance using the following command:

```
$ kitchen login default-ubuntu-1204
```

Once you've logged in to the system, you can now go ahead and check for the presence of the binary named `nginx`:

```
vagrant@default-ubuntu-1204:~$ which nginx
/usr/sbin/nginx
```

So, Nginx is indeed installed.

However, with kitchen, we no longer need to take the pain of logging in to the system and verifying the installation. We can do this by writing a test case.

We'll make use of **bash automated testing system (bats)**, called for this purpose.

Create a directory using the following command:

```
$ mkdir -p test/integration/default/bats
```

Create a new file package `test.bats` under the `bats` directory:

```
#!/usr/bin/env bats

@test "nginx binary is found in PATH"
{
  run which nginx
  [ "$status" -eq 0 ]
}
```

Now, let's run our test using `kitchen verify`:

```
$ kitchen verify default-ubuntu-1204

-----> Starting Kitchen (v1.2.1)

-----> Setting up <default-ubuntu-1204>...
Fetching: thor-0.19.0.gem (100%)
Fetching: busser-0.6.2.gem (100%)
Successfully installed thor-0.19.0
Successfully installed busser-0.6.2
2 gems installed
-----> Setting up Busser
        Creating BUSSER_ROOT in /tmp/busser
        Creating busser binstub
        Plugin bats installed (version 0.2.0)
-----> Running postinstall for bats plugin
Installed Bats to /tmp/busser/vendor/bats/bin/bats
        Finished setting up <default-ubuntu-1204> (1m41.31s).
-----> Verifying <default-ubuntu-1204>...
        Suite path directory /tmp/busser/suites does not exist, skipping.
Uploading /tmp/busser/suites/bats/package-test.bats (mode=0644)
-----> Running bats test suite
✓ nginx binary is found in PATH


1 test, 0 failures
        Finished verifying <default-ubuntu-1204> (0m1.03s).
-----> Kitchen is finished. (0m1.51s)
```

So, we see that our test has successfully passed verification, and we can proudly go ahead and upload our cookbook to the chef-server and trigger a chef-client run on the concerned instance.

Summary

With this, we've come to the end of our journey to understanding the Chef ecosystem and various tools of trade. We now know the language used in the world of Chef and we also know how to go about setting up our machines, which will allow us to develop the code to automate infrastructure using Chef.

In the next chapter, we'll see how we can make use of Knife and the associated plugins to make our life a lot easier while managing infrastructure using Chef.

2
Knife and Its Associated Plugins

We learned about the Chef ecosystem in the last chapter and, as we saw, Knife is one of those tools that we'll be using the most while doing development. In this chapter, we'll look at the internals of Knife and we'll also see different plugins, which will make your life a lot easier while managing your infrastructure using Chef.

Introducing Knife

Knife is a command-line tool that comes bundled with the Chef installation. Depending upon how Chef was installed, you may find the binary at any particular location on your workstation. Since I have installed Chef using rvm and gem packaging, it is found at `~/.rvm/gems/ruby-2.1.0/gems/chef-11.8.2/bin/knife`.

Depending upon your setup, you may find it at some other location. Whatever the location, ensure that it is in your `PATH` variable.

Knife is used for almost every aspect of managing your interactions with chef-server. It helps us manage:

- Cookbooks
- Environments
- Roles
- Data bags
- Nodes
- API clients
- Bootstrapping of instances
- Searching for nodes

Let's see what the `knife` command has to offer to us. Just fire up the terminal and enter the command:

```
$knife
ERROR: You need to pass a sub-command (e.g., knife SUB-COMMAND)
Usage: knife sub-command (options)
    -s, --server-url URL            Chef Server URL
        --chef-zero-port PORT       Port to start chef-zero on
    -k, --key KEY                   API Client Key
        --[no-]color                Use colored output, defaults to
false on Windows, true otherwise
    -c, --config CONFIG             The configuration file to use
        --defaults                  Accept default values for all
questions
    -d, --disable-editing           Do not open EDITOR, just accept the
data as is
    -e, --editor EDITOR             Set the editor to use for
interactive commands
    -E, --environment ENVIRONMENT   Set the Chef environment
    -F, --format FORMAT             Which format to use for output
    -z, --local-mode                Point knife commands at local
repository instead of server
    -u, --user USER                 API Client Username
        --print-after              Show the data after a destructive
operation
    -V, --verbose                   More verbose output. Use twice for
max verbosity
    -v, --version                   Show chef version
    -y, --yes                       Say yes to all prompts for
confirmation
    -h, --help                      Show this message


Available subcommands: (for details, knife SUB-COMMAND --help)


** BOOTSTRAP COMMANDS **

. . .


** CLIENT COMMANDS **

. . .


. . .
```

Whoa! That was some output. So that's the power of Knife, and it tells you that you need to make use of subcommands such as `cookbook`, `node`, `client`, `role`, `databag`, and so on. We will look at each of these in detail later.

Before we start using Knife, we need to configure it. During this configuration, we'll specify where Knife can contact our chef-server, where cookbooks are residing on our machine, and so on.

The configuration file for Knife is called `knife.rb` and is typically found in the `~/.chef` folder. This is a Ruby file, as is visible from its extension; you guessed right, it can contain actual Ruby code along with some configuration settings that are required for the working of Knife.

The following are the configuration settings that we'll specify in our `knife.rb` file:

Setting	Description
`chef_server_url`	This defines where to find our chef-server. It's usually the FQDN of chef-server along with the API port.
`node_name`	This is typically the name of your workstation.
`client_key`	As you saw, we created a client for use in the workstation on chef-server. This is the path to the private key we downloaded.
`cookbook_path`	This is the path on your filesystem where cookbooks are residing.
`cookbook_copyright`	Every time we create a new cookbook, role, or environment using Knife, we'll get files with basic stuff such as copyright and so on. This will prefill the value of copyright for you.
`cookbook_email`	Every time we create a new cookbook, role, or environment using Knife, we'll get files with basic stuff such as e-mail and so on. This will prefill the value of e-mail for you.
`validation_client_name`	Usually, it is safe to leave this as `chef-validator`.
`validation_key`	This is the path to the private key for `chef-validator`.
`knife['editor']`	Some Knife subcommands such as `knife role edit` require this configuration to be defined. This contains the path for your favorite editor.

Here is a sample ~/.chef/knife.rb file:

```
log_level               :info
log_location            STDOUT
node_name               'maxc0d3r'
client_key              '~/keys/chef/maxc0d3r.pem'
validation_client_name  'chef-validator'
validation_key          '~/keys/chef/validation.pem'
chef_server_url         'http://chef-server.sychonet.com:4000'
cache_type              'BasicFile'
cache_options           ( :path => '~/.chef/checksums' )
cookbook_path           [ '~/code/chef-repo/cookbooks' ]
```

Just to verify that Knife has been set up properly, run the following command:

```
$knife client list

chef-validator

chef-webui

maxc0d3r
```

So, we queried chef-server about all the API clients and it duly responded back with the list of 3 clients. As you can see, the API client that I'll be using to communicate with chef-server is also available there.

With Knife configured, let's see what we can do with it.

Managing cookbooks

Knife is the tool that we'll be using to do all sorts of operations on cookbooks residing on our development workstation or on a remote chef server. Operations for a cookbook can be the following:

- Creating a new cookbook
- Uploading a cookbook to chef-server
- Deleting a cookbook from chef-server
- Downloading a cookbook from chef-server
- Deleting multiple cookbooks from chef-server
- Listing all cookbooks on chef-server

Creating a new cookbook

In order to create a new cookbook, issue the following command:

```
$knife cookbook create new-cookbook
** Creating cookbook new-cookbook
** Creating README for cookbook: new-cookbook
** Creating CHANGELOG for cookbook: new-cookbook
** Creating metadata for cookbook: new-cookbook
```

This command will create the following directory structure along with some default files in the path you've specified in the cookbook_path variable in the knife.rb file:

```
$ tree new-cookbook/
new-cookbook/
├── CHANGELOG.md
├── README.md
├── attributes
├── definitions
├── files
│   └── default
├── libraries
├── metadata.rb
├── providers
├── recipes
│   └── default.rb
├── resources
└── templates
    └── default
```

We'll look at this structure in detail later while finding out more about cookbooks. For now, it's sufficient for us to know that the new cookbook called new-cookbook has been created.

Uploading a cookbook to chef-server

Now we went on to modify this cookbook as per our requirements; once done, we want to upload this cookbook to chef-server. The following command will help us get this job done:

```
$ knife cookbook upload new-cookbook
Uploading new-cookbook    [0.1.0]
Uploaded 1 cookbook.
```

Cool, so our cookbook was uploaded, but what's this 0.1.0? Well, as we'll see in *Chapter 6, Cookbooks and LWRPs*, chef-server allows us to maintain different versions of a cookbook. The version is defined in the file called metadata.rb and, if you look at new-cookbook/metadata.rb, you will see that the version defined for the cookbook is 0.1.0. You can maintain different versions of the same cookbook on chef-server and use any particular version you want while bootstrapping the instances.

Getting the list of all the cookbooks on chef-server

There are times when we'd like to get a list of all the cookbooks residing on a remote chef-server, and this is all the more important when you are working in teams. The following command will get you a list of all cookbooks on chef-server:

```
$ knife cookbook list
new-cookbook             0.1.0
```

Let's modify the version of our cookbook and upload it once more. To do this, edit the new-cookbook/metadata.rb file and change the version to 0.1.1:

```
$sed -i .bak 's/0.1.0/0.1.1/g' new-cookbook/metadata.rb
```

> You can ignore the .bak extension, but on some platforms it's kind of necessary (such as Mac OS X).

Let's upload the cookbook once more:

```
$ knife cookbook upload new-cookbook
Uploading new-cookbook    [0.1.1]
Uploaded 1 cookbook.
```

Now let's see what cookbooks are on chef-server:

```
$ knife cookbook list
new-cookbook             0.1.1
```

So we see that our newly uploaded cookbook is there. However, where has my previous version gone? Well, it's not gone anywhere, it's just that by default Knife is reporting back the latest version of the cookbook. If you want to see all the versions of cookbooks, use the same command with the -a argument:

```
$ knife cookbook list -a
new-cookbook                    0.1.1   0.1.0
```

Deleting cookbooks

There are times when you'd like to delete a cookbook or some version of your cookbook, as you know that it's not going to be in use now. The following command helps us accomplish this task:

```
$ knife cookbook delete new-cookbook
Which version(s) do you want to delete?
1. new-cookbook 0.1.1
2. new-cookbook 0.1.0
3. All versions

2
Deleted cookbook[new-cookbook] [0.1.0]
```

If we don't specify any version, Knife will list all available versions of cookbooks and ask us to choose one of them for deletion. If you know which version to delete, you can just specify the version:

```
$ knife cookbook delete new-cookbook 0.1.0
Deleted cookbook[new-cookbook] [0.1.0]
```

If you wish to delete all versions of a cookbook, use the command with the -a argument as follows:

```
$ knife cookbook delete new-cookbook -a
Do you really want to delete all versions of new-cookbook? (Y/N) y
Deleted cookbook[new-cookbook] [0.1.1]
Deleted cookbook[new-cookbook] [0.1.0]
```

To avoid confirmation, append -y to the last command or add knife[:yes] to your knife.rb file.

The delete command doesn't purge the entire cookbook or concerned version from chef-server, and keeps one copy of files. If you wish to completely delete the concerned cookbook or a version of it, append the delete command with -purge.

Downloading a cookbook

Let's say you and your friend are working on a cookbook together by collaborating using Git. It so happens that your friend uploaded a new version of the cookbook onto chef-server; however, he/she forgot to push the changes to Git. Now, he is on leave for a week and you want to carry on with the development on this cookbook, but you also want to know what all changes your friend made. This is one area where downloading a cookbook really helps. However, ensure that you aren't using downloaded cookbooks to override content within your SCM repository, or else it can cause issues when trying to merge changes later on, and will eventually corrupt your SCM repository.

You can download a cookbook using the following command:

```
$ knife cookbook download new-cookbook -d /tmp
Which version do you want to download?
1. new-cookbook 0.1.0
2. new-cookbook 0.1.1

1
Downloading new-cookbook cookbook version 0.1.0
Downloading resources
Downloading providers
Downloading recipes
Downloading definitions
Downloading libraries
Downloading attributes
Downloading files
Downloading templates
Downloading root_files
Cookbook downloaded to /tmp/new-cookbook-0.1.0
```

So again, if you've multiple versions of cookbooks, Knife will ask which version of cookbook to download. I've used the -d option to specify which directory to download the cookbook to. If it's not specified, the cookbook is downloaded to the current working directory. If you know which version of cookbook needs to be downloaded, you can specify that as follows:

```
$ knife cookbook download new-cookbook 0.1.1 -d /tmp
```

```
Downloading new-cookbook cookbook version 0.1.1
Downloading resources
Downloading providers
Downloading recipes
Downloading definitions
Downloading libraries
Downloading attributes
Downloading files
Downloading templates
Downloading root_files
Cookbook downloaded to /tmp/new-cookbook-0.1.1
```

Deleting multiple cookbooks

Knife also provides a bulk `delete` subcommand that allows you to delete cookbooks whose names match a regex pattern.

For example, the following command will delete all versions of all cookbooks starting with `new`:

```
$ knife cookbook bulk delete "^new"
All versions of the following cookbooks will be deleted:

new-cookbook

Do you really want to delete these cookbooks? (Y/N) y

Deleted cookbook   new-cookbook                [0.1.1]
Deleted cookbook   new-cookbook                [0.1.0]
```

Managing environments

Usually in any project, the infrastructure is split across different environments such as dev, staging, production, and so on. Chef allows us to maintain different configurations and settings across different environments through the concept of environments.

Creating an environment

To manage environments, create a directory named `environments` in the root of your Chef repository. Your directory structure will look something like the following:

```
.
├── README.md
├── cookbooks
├── data_bags
├── environments
└── roles
```

All the environment-related configs will be kept inside the `environments` directory. Let's presume that we've an environment called production and another one called staging. We like to live on the cutting edge in the staging environment and keep the latest version of our web server package there, whereas, in production environment, we are cautious and always keep a tested version of the web server. We'll create two files, namely `staging.rb` and `production.rb`, in the `environments` directory:

```
staging.rb:
name "staging"
description "Staging Environment"
override_attributes :webserver => { :version => "1.9.7" }


production.rb:

name "production"
description "Production Environment"
override_attributes :webserver => { :version => "1.8.0" }
```

Now, all we need to do is ensure that these configurations get pushed to chef-server. To do this, we run the following command:

```
$ knife environment from file staging.rb
Updated Environment staging


$ knife environment from file production.rb
Updated Environment production
```

When using the files in your SCM repository, to manage environments, ensure that you specify the full path of the `.rb` files when using the Knife environment from the file command.

One can also create environments directly by issuing the following command:

```
$ knife environment create <environment_name>
```

This will open up an editor (ensure that either you've an environment variable called EDITOR set up or the path to your favorite editor specified in knife.rb). You can modify the content of the file opened up by the last command and save it.

Deleting an environment

You may delete an environment using the following command:

```
$ knife environment delete <environment_name>
```

For example, the following command will delete the environment named staging from chef-server:

```
$ knife environment delete staging
Do you really want to delete staging? (Y/N) y
Deleted staging
```

If you wish to override the confirmation, either append the command with -y, or specify knife[:yes] in your knife.rb file.

Editing an environment

You can edit an environment by modifying the files inside the environments folder and rerunning the following command:

```
$ knife environment from file <filename>
```

Alternatively, you can directly modify the environment by issuing the following command:

```
$ knife environment edit <environment_name>
```

Listing all environments

You can see the list of all environments configured on chef-server through the following command:

```
$ knife environment list
_default
staging
```

As you can see, the command listed two environments, namely _default and staging. The _default environment comes along as the default with chef-server, and any node that doesn't have an environment associated with it (more on this later) will have the _default environment associated to it.

Displaying information about an environment

You can view information about an environment through the following command:

```
$ knife environment show <environment_name>
```

Consider the following as an example:

```
$ knife environment show staging
chef_type:              environment
cookbook_versions:
default_attributes:
description:            Staging Environment
json_class:             Chef::Environment
name:                   staging
override_attributes:
  webserver:
    version: 1.9.7
```

Managing roles

Roles are used to group together cookbooks under a single roof and apply them on the node that is to be bootstrapped. Roles in Chef comprise of a run_list and a set of attributes. As with environments, you can manage roles through Knife.

Creating a new role

You can create a new role using the following command:

```
$ knife role create <role_name>
```

This will open your editor with a template, and all you need is to fill that template to your liking and save.

Alternatively, you can create a role separately in a file inside the roles directory and, once you are satisfied with the content of that file, just issue the following command:

```
$ knife role from file <filename>
```

I prefer the second option as it allows me to maintain revisions of code inside a version control system.

Let's create the role named `webserver`. To do this, we'll create the file called `webserver.rb` inside the `roles` folder:

```
#Role to manage webservers

name "webserver"
description "Webserver Role"

run_list  "recipe[webserver]","recipe[logstash]"
```

As you can see, I've specified two recipes in the `run_list`, namely `webserver` and `logstash`. We'll use the `webserver` recipe to install and configure a web server, while the `logstash` recipe is used to push logs from a web server to a central log server running Graylog.

We'll now push this newly created role onto our chef-server:

```
$ knife role from file webserver.rb
Updated Role webserver!
```

Deleting a role

You can delete a role by issuing the following command:

```
$ knife role delete <rolename>
```

Consider the following as an example:

```
$ knife role delete webserver
Do you really want to delete webserver? (Y/N) y
Deleted role[webserver]
```

Editing a role

You may edit an existing role by using the following command:

```
$ knife role edit <rolename>
```

Alternatively, you can edit the corresponding role file in your local Chef repository, and then use the following command:

```
$ knife role from file <role_file>
```

Listing all available roles

You can get a list of all available roles using the following command:

```
$ knife role list
webserver
```

Displaying information about a role

You can use the following command to see what the role is supposedly doing:

```
$ knife role show <rolename>
```

For example

```
$ knife role show webserver
chef_type:            role
default_attributes:
description:          Role to manage webserver
env_run_lists:
json_class:           Chef::Role
name:                 webserver
override_attributes:
run_list:
  recipe[webserver]
  recipe[logstash]
```

Managing nodes

Nodes are the machines that we'll be configuring using Chef. Chef stores information about nodes in node objects, which can be viewed in the JSON format. We can manage details like creating a node, editing a node, listing all available nodes, modifying `run_list` applicable to nodes, overriding some attributes corresponding to a node, deleting a node, and so on, using Knife.

Creating a node

One can create a new node using the following command:

```
$ knife node create <node_name>
```

Alternatively, you can use the following command:

```
$ knife node from file <filename.rb>
```

Nodes need to be created explicitly by you as a chef-client run automatically takes care of creating a new node object for you. However, let's see this command in action:

```
$ knife node create webserver01
```

This command will open up your favorite text editor with the following template:

```
{
  "name": "webserver01",
  "chef_environment": "_default",
  "json_class": "Chef::Node",
  "automatic": {
  },
  "normal": {
  },
  "chef_type": "node",
  "default": {
  },
  "override": {
  },
  "run_list": [

  ]
}
```

Modify the values for chef_environment by replacing _default with staging, and add recipe[webserver], recipe[logstash], or role[webserver] to the run_list:

```
{
  "name": "webserver01",
  "chef_environment": "staging",
  "json_class": "Chef::Node",
  "automatic": {
  },
  "normal": {
  },
  "chef_type": "node",
  "default": {
  },
  "override": {
  },
  "run_list": [
    "recipe[webserver]",
    "recipe[logstash]"
  ]
}
```

Save the file and voilà, you get a response from Knife saying that your new node was created:

```
Created node[webserver01]
```

You could've easily created that JSON file yourself and used the following command:

```
$knife node from file <filename>
```

This would've had the same effect.

Listing all available nodes

Okay, so we've our newly created node on chef-server. Let's see if it's actually there. You can get a list of all available nodes on chef-server using the following command:

```
$knife node list
webserver01
```

Displaying information about a node

If you want to see what all configurations are associated with a particular node, you can do this by using the following command:

```
$knife node show webserver01
Node Name:    webserver01
Environment: staging
FQDN:
IP:
Run List:     recipe[webserver], recipe[logstash]
Roles:
Recipes:
Platform:
Tags:
```

You might be wondering why few fields are empty in the preceding output. If you remember, in *Chapter 1, Introduction to the Chef Ecosystem*, while understanding the anatomy of a chef-client run, we saw that, as the first step in a chef-client run, Ohai is executed that profiles the underlying system and tries to fetch system-related information. This information is finally used to build the node object. When building the node object directly using Knife, the system-related information is not yet collected, and hence the corresponding fields are blank.

Editing a node

You can edit a node object using the following command:

```
$knife node edit <node_name>
```

Alternatively, edit the file containing JSON data for the concerned node and issue the following command:

```
$knife node from file <filename>
```

Adding stuff to the run_list associated with a node

Let's say you've created a brand new cookbook that will add some monitoring stuff to your web server, and you want to add that recipe to a particular node. Now, you can go on and edit a node and modify the run_list, but since it's just a run_list that needs to be modified, you can use the following command:

```
$ knife node run_list add <node_name> [ENTRY]
```

For example, let's presume our monitoring cookbook is called monitoring. Let's add it to our newly created node—webserver01:

```
$ knife node run_list add webserver01 recipe[monitoring]
webserver01:
  run_list:
    recipe[webserver]
    recipe[logstash]
    recipe[monitoring]
```

Cool! So now, our node object has three recipes associated with it.

Deleting stuff from the run_list associated with a node

You can use the following command to delete stuff from a node's run_list:

```
$ knife node run_list remove <node_name> [ENTRY]
```

For example, let's delete recipe[logstash] from the run_list associated with node webserver01:

```
$knife node run_list remove webserver01 recipe[logstash]
webserver01:
  run_list:
```

```
recipe[webserver]
recipe[monitoring]
```

You can also specify multiple entries while deleting elements from the `run_list` as follows:

```
$ knife node run_list remove webserver01 'recipe[logstash]','recipe[monit
oring]'
webserver01:
  run_list: recipe[webserver]
```

Deleting a node object

This is especially necessary for instances running on cloud platforms such as AWS, Rackspace, Azure, and so on. Cloud platform providers have made it very easy for people to provision infrastructure on demand. However, as easy as it is to scale up the infrastructure, it's as hard to maintain it—especially when you've instances going up and down like crazy due to provisions for elasticity. If we are managing instances in cloud, it's very essential to find some way to clean up node objects from chef-server that aren't up-and-running anymore. You can delete a node object using the following command:

```
$knife node delete <node_name>
```

For example, let's presume our node `webserver01` no longer exists in the physical world. Let's get rid of this node object then:

```
$ knife node delete webserver01 -y
Deleted node[webserver01]
```

> With AWS, you can make use of SNS and SQS to build a system where, if an instance goes down, a SNS notification is issued that writes a message to SQS. This message contains the name of the instance (which is a tag). You can then write a daemon that runs on one machine and polls SQS for any message; if there is any message, it pops it out, reads the name of the instance, and issues a command to delete the node from chef-server.

Managing an API client

As with node objects, every instance that communicates with chef-server registers itself as an API client. This client is authenticated with chef-server through a public/private key pair, and every communication with the chef-server REST API is authenticated through this. In general, the node name and client name are usually the same; however, they can be different too. You can create, delete, edit, reregister, and list clients using Knife.

Creating a new client

You can create a new client using the following command:

```
$ knife client create maxc0d3r
```

This will open up your favorite text editor with the following JSON template:

```
{
  "name": "maxc0d3r",
  "public_key": null,
  "validator": false,
  "admin": false,
  "json_class": "Chef::ApiClient",
  "chef_type": "client"
}
```

> If you want to make your client admin, change the value of false to true. As you'll see in later chapters, the admin privilege is something that can be very useful in certain cases. Usually, whenever a new instance registers itself with chef-server, it's registered as a non-admin client. However, a non-admin client doesn't have certain privileges, such as modifying data bag elements, and so on. If you are running the Chef setup in a private network, I would suggest modifying the Chef code so that every client is registered automatically as an admin.

Save this file and exit your editor, and the command will return your private key:

```
$ knife client create maxc0d3r
Created client[maxc0d3r]
```

```
-----BEGIN RSA PRIVATE KEY-----
XXXXXXXXXXXXXXXXXXXXXXXXXXXXXXXX
-----END RSA PRIVATE KEY-------
```

Save this private key in a safe place, and now you can communicate with chef-server as `maxc0d3r` using the private key we just downloaded.

Listing all available API clients

You can find a list of all available clients using the following command:

```
$ knife client list
chef-validator
chef-webui
maxc0d3r
```

The `chef-validator` and `chef-webui` clients come by default along with " chef-server.

Displaying information about a client

You can use the following command to get the required information about an API client from chef-server:

```
$ knife client show maxc0d3r
admin:       true
chef_type:   client
json_class:  Chef::ApiClient
name:        maxc0d3r
public_key:  -----BEGIN RSA PUBLIC KEY-----
XXXXXXXXXXXXXXXXXXXX
-----END RSA PUBLIC KEY-----
validator:   false
```

Deleting an existing client

You can delete an existing client using the following command:

```
$ knife client delete maxc0d3r -y
Deleted client[maxc0d3r]
```

Reregistering a client

It might so happen that on one really bad day, you lost your private key that you'd received while registering the client with chef-server. Well, not everything is lost here. You can reregister your client with chef-server by issuing the following command:

```
$ knife client reregister maxc0d3r
-----BEGIN RSA PRIVATE KEY-----
XXXXXXXXXXXXXXXXXXXXXXXXXXXXXXXX
-----END RSA PRIVATE KEY-------
```

Reregistration of a client will invalidate the previous public/private key pair, and chef-server will return you a new private key that you can use now to communicate with chef-server using the existing client.

The search command

Perhaps one of the most useful use of Chef, while managing large-scale infrastructures, is through the search facility. The Chef server maintains an index using Solr, and this index can be queried for a wide range of stuff such as data bags, environments, nodes, and roles. One can specify exact, wild card, or fuzzy search patterns to search through this index.

You can use the search command as follows:

```
$knife search INDEX QUERY
```

Here, INDEX in the command can either be the client, environment, role, node, or data bag name. QUERY is the query string that will be executed. The default INDEX value is node; if it's not specified, it's implied as a node by default.

Consider the following as an example:

```
$ knife search '*:*'
Node Name:   webserver01
Environment: staging
FQDN:
IP:
Run List:    recipe[webserver], recipe[logstash]
Roles:
Recipes:
Platform:
Tags:
```

If the search query pattern doesn't contain a colon (`:`), the default query is: `tags:*#{@query}*`, `roles:*#{@query}*`, `fqdn:*#{@query}*`, or `addresses:*#{@query}*`.

Let's see some examples of a Knife search in action:

- To find all nodes having the environment as `production` and the platform as `Ubuntu`, the command will be as follows:

  ```
  $ knife search node 'chef_environment:production AND
  platform:ubuntu'
  ```

- To find all nodes having the environment as `production` and the platform as `Ubuntu`, and to show the users configured on these machines, the command will be as follows:

  ```
  $knife search node 'chef_environment:production AND
  platform:ubuntu' -a users
  ```

  The `-a` option is used to restrict the output to attributes that have been specified. This is especially useful if we want to write a script around the output from a Knife search.

- To find all nodes having the environment as `production` and the role as `webserver`, the command will be as follows:

  ```
  $ knife search node 'chef_environment:production AND
  role:webserver'
  ```

- To find all nodes having the environment as `production` and recipes as `logstash`, the command will be as follows:

  ```
  $ knife search node 'chef_environment:production AND
  recipes:logstash'
  ```

Bootstrapping a node

Knife can also be put to effective use to bootstrap a machine. Let's presume you've got a brand-new machine that you want to set up as a web server. For the sake of this example, I'll presume that it's a Ubuntu 12.04 machine. The service provider has given you the hardware and has installed the operating system for you. However, now, in order to configure it with Chef, you need to install the chef-client on the machine. One way to go about doing this is to manually go to the machine and install Chef using the gems or omnibus installer.

However, there is a more easy way. You can use your good old friend Knife to set up chef-client on a newly created instance.

Use the following command to bootstrap your instance:

```
$ knife bootstrap webserver01 -x user01 -i user01.key --sudo
```

This command will use `user01.key` as the SSH key, and try to use SSH to connect to the remote machine (`webserver01`) as user (`user01`). Once it's able to establish SSH connection, this command will then set up Chef using the omnibus installer using sudo. Finally, the command will register the node with the chef-server and trigger a chef-client run.

We'll see more ways to accomplish this job in later chapters.

Some useful Knife plugins

Knife is a wonderful tool on its own. However, there are plenty of plugins available that help extend the functionality of Knife. We'll be writing some such plugins in later chapters. Let's take a sneak peak at a few really useful plugins that will help ease your job of administering a large-scale infrastructure.

The knife-ssh plugin

Say you had around 10 web servers in your infrastructure, with the environment as `production` and the role as `webserver`. Now, one day you realize that you want to clean up a directory, say `/var/log/nginx`, as you've forgotten to clean up logs that have been accumulating over a period of time due to a misconfigured log rotation script.

No worries, the knife-ssh plugin is just meant to handle this situation. Here is how we can use it:

```
$ knife ssh -i <path to ssh key> 'chef_environment:production AND
role:webserver' -x user 'sudo -i rm -f /var/log/nginx/*.gz'
```

This command is presuming that a user named `user` has sudo privileges on all the machines that have `chef_environment` as `production` and `webserver` as `role`.

The knife-ec2 plugin

AWS is one of the most popular public cloud service provider, and one of its offerings is called EC2. This service allows you to create machines that can then be used for a different purpose.

This plugin provides the ability to create, bootstrap, and manage EC2 instances. You'll need to install this plugin before being able to use it. To install this plugin, issue the following command:

```
$gem install knife-ec2
```

Once the plugin is installed, you'll need to add these two additional configuration values to your `knife.rb` file:

```
knife[:aws_access_key_id] = "AWS_ACCESS_KEY"
knife[:aws_secret_access_key] = "AWS_SECRET_KEY"
```

If you aren't in the US-EAST-1 region, you'll also need to specify one other configuration parameter:

```
knife[:region]
```

You could've also provided these values as arguments to the `knife ec2` command, but keeping them in `knife.rb` is perhaps the easiest way.

Once you've the plugin set up correctly, you can list all your EC2 instances using the following command:

```
$ knife ec2 server list
```

You can create a new instance using the following subcommand:

```
$ knife ec2 server create
```

You'll need to supply some information such as the AMI ID, SSH key pair name, and so on, for this purpose. You can find more details about the options that this command accepts using the following command:

```
$ knife ec2 server create -help
```

The knife-azure plugin

This is a plugin very similar to the knife-ec2 plugin, and provides capabilities to manage instances on the Microsoft Azure cloud platform.

The knife-google plugin

This is a plugin on the lines of the knife-ec2 plugin, and provides capabilities to manage instances on Google Compute Engine.

The knife-push plugin

If you are using Enterprise Chef, you might want to try using the push job facility. It's an add-on that allows jobs to be executed on a machine independent of chef-client. A job is a command that has to be executed and the machine on which it needs to be executed is defined by a search query.

Push jobs have three main components: jobs (managed by the push jobs server), a client (which is installed on each machine), and one (or more) workstations.

These components communicate with each other as follows:

- A heartbeat message between the push job server (usually chef-server) and each node.
- The knife-push plugin that provides four commands: `job list`, `job start`, `job status`, and `node status`.
- Various job messages are sent from the workstation to job server.
- A single job message is sent from the push job server to one or more nodes for execution.

You can find more details about push jobs at `http://docs.opscode.com/push_jobs.html`.

Other than these plugins, there are many other plugins available for use. You can find some of them at `https://github.com/chef?query=knife`.

Summary

In this chapter, we learned about one of the most widely used components of Chef's ecosystem, called Knife. We looked at the different subcommands of Knife, configuring Knife, and finally some plugins that can be used to extend Knife's functionality.

In the next chapter, we will see why we need to learn Ruby and write efficient infrastructure code using Ruby.

3
Chef and Ruby

When we say that we will be specifying our infrastructure as a code using Chef, what we mean is that we'll be writing code using **domain-specific language (DSL)** provided by Chef. This code will be executed by chef-client on the concerned machine, and the machine will be bootstrapped as per the guidelines we specify in our code. The DSL provided by Chef is very much like Rake tasks, and Ruby developers will find themselves at home when writing Chef code.

Chef DSL is actually a Ruby DSL, and one can use the full power of Ruby as a programming language when trying to write Chef code. The term "Chef code" is used loosely here, to specify recipes, roles, environments, templates, resources, attributes, libraries, and so on.

Chef provides a DSL that you can use to write your recipes and roles, describe environments, write custom resource providers and libraries, and so on.

The code that you'll write will be stored as Ruby files in the Chef repository. When these files are uploaded to the Chef server, they are converted to JSON. Each time the contents of Chef repository are changed and uploaded to the Chef server, the Ruby files are recompiled to JSON and uploaded. This needs to be emphasized: *recipes and libraries aren't converted to JSON.*

So, do I need to be a Ruby developer now to make use of Chef? This is the question that first bumps into anyone's mind, who is jumping into the world of Chef. The answer to this question isn't as easy as a yes/no. Yeah, you need a certain level of competency with Ruby if you want to really make use of Chef, however, you don't need to be a hardcore Ruby developer to make the best use of Chef. Knowledge of Ruby will be helpful, in any case, as it makes for an excellent choice to write automation scripts.

In this chapter, we'll look at those components of Ruby that you will need to know in order to make the best use of Chef.

Ruby

Ruby is a simple, dynamic programming language created by Yukihiro Matsumoto (also known as Matz). The language is a blend of features provided in different languages such as Perl, Smalltalk, Lisp, and so on. Ruby was developed with an aim to provide a new language that balanced functional programming with imperative programming.

As mentioned earlier, you don't have to be a hardcore Ruby developer. Following are the things that we'll cover in this chapter, which will allow you to make the best use of Chef:

- Variables and types
- Basic operations
- Conditional statements and loops
- Blocks
- Arrays and hashes

Yeah, we just need to learn about these five components of the language and we are all set to conquer the world of Chef.

However, before we go ahead with our journey into the fascinating world of Ruby, let's take a quick look at IRB. This is one of those tools that can really help you while playing with small Ruby code snippets.

IRB

IRB is an acronym for "interactive Ruby". It's a tool that provided alongside Ruby interpreter, which allows for the interactive execution of Ruby expressions. These expressions are delivered to IRB using standard input.

Let's quickly see IRB in action:

```
~ irb
2.1-head :001 >
```

When we enter the `irb` command, it throws a shell at us. The format of the shell prompt is as follows:

```
$RUBY_VERSION :$LINE_NUMBER >
```

You can customize this prompt to your liking. However, for now, just remember that whatever expression you enter at the prompt is interpreted as a Ruby expression and is evaluated right away.

Consider the following as an example:

```
☒  ~  irb
2.1-head :001 > 2+3
 => 5
```

As you can see, we entered an arithmetic expression to compute the sum of two numbers, 2 and 3, and in return IRB returned us the output of computation.

To exit out of IRB, just issue the `quit` or `exit` command at the prompt.

To learn more about IRB and how to customize it to your liking, read the IRB documentation at `http://ruby-doc.org/stdlib-2.1.5/libdoc/irb/rdoc/IRB.html`. Replace `2.1.5` with the Ruby version installed on your machine.

Variables and types

If you are new to programming, then just for a quick reference: a variable is nothing, but a memory location where we can save some data. This memory location can be easily referenced by a name and that name is called the **variable name**. Many languages such as C, Java, and so on, force you to declare variables before you use them, and they also expect you to specify the type associated with the variable. For example. if you want to store a number in the memory in a C program, you'd say the following:

```
int x = 10;
```

This will create a 2 byte memory space and that memory space will contain a binary associated with 10. The memory location where 10 is stored can be referenced through a variable name called x.

Ruby, on the other hand, is pretty lenient and it doesn't expect you to specify data type associated with a variable. Ruby, hence, belongs to a family of programming languages that are called dynamically typed languages. Unlike strongly typed languages, dynamic languages do not declare a variable to be of certain type; instead, the interpreter determines the data type at the time some value is assigned to the variable:

```
x = 10
puts x
x = "Hello"
puts x
```

The preceding piece of code, when executed, will give the following output:

```
10
Hello
```

Variable names in Ruby can be created using alphanumeric characters and underscores. A variable cannot begin with a number. Variable names cannot begin with a capital letter, as the Ruby interpreter will consider it to be a constant.

Variable names can also start with special characters called **sigils**. A sigil is a symbol that is attached to an identifier (this is just the name of the variable, method, or class). We'll see more about methods and classes later in this chapter. Sigils in Ruby are used to determine the scope of variables (scope is the range in your code where the variable can be referenced). We've the following sigils available in Ruby:

- $
- @

Any variable without a sigil is a local variable. This variable's scope is limited to a block, method, or class in which it's defined.

Global variables begin with the $ sign. They are visible everywhere across your program. Though they seem like a good feature, the use of global variables should be avoided in general.

Any variable starting with the @ character is an instance variable. Instance variables are valid inside an object.

Finally, any variable with the @@ character as prefix is called a class variable. This variable is valid for all instances of a class.

There are a few methods provided by Ruby that will help you find `local_variables`, `global_variables`, `instance_variables`, and `class_variables` in a given context of the code. Let's see them in action:

```ruby
#!/usr/bin/env ruby
w = 10
$x = 20
@y = 30
@@z = 40
p local_variables
p global_variables.include? :$x
p self.instance_variables
p Object.class_variables
```

The p method like puts can be used to display output. However, there is a subtle difference between the two. The puts method calls the to_s method on the object and returns a readable version of the object. The p method, on the other hand, calls the inspect method instead of to_s. The p method is better suited for debugging.

The local_variables method gives us an array of all the local variables defined in a specific context. The global_variables method produces a list of all global variables. Since there are a lot of default global variables created by Ruby and we didn't want to list them all, we chose the include method of the Array class, which tells us whether something belongs to the concerned array or not. The self pseudo variable points to receiver of the instance_variables method. The receiver in our case is the main method. Finally, we have an array of class variables associated with Object. The main is an instance of the Object class.

Let's run the code and see what happens:

```
$./sigils.rb
[:w]
true
[:@y]
[:@@z]
```

Often we need to declare some variables at the operating systems' environment level, and we might need to make use of them. The ENV constant gives access to environment variables. This is a Ruby hash. Each environment variable is a key to the ENV hash. The ARGV constant, on the other hand, holds command-line argument values. They are passed by a programmer when a script is launched. The ARGV array is an array that stores arguments as strings. The $* is an alias for ARGV.

Ruby also has some predefined variables such as $0, $*, and $$. The $0 variable stores the current script name. The $* variable stores command-line arguments. The $$ variable stores the PID of the script.

Symbols

Symbols look like variables, however, with a colon (:) prefixed. For example, :symbol_1. Symbols need not be predeclared and assigned a value. Ruby guarantees that the symbol has a particular value, no matter where it appears in a Ruby program.

Symbols are very useful because a given symbol name refers to the same object throughout a Ruby program. Two strings with the same content are two different objects; however, for a given name, there can only be one single symbol object. Let's examine the following example to illustrate this fact:

```
⬚  ~  irb
2.1-head :001 > puts "string".object_id
70168328185680
 => nil
2.1-head :002 > puts "string".object_id
70168328173400
 => nil
2.1-head :003 > puts :symbol.object_id
394888
 => nil
2.1-head :004 > puts :symbol.object_id
394888
nil
```

As you can see, we started by creating a string object with the `string` value and sought its object ID using the `object_id` method. Next, we tried the same thing once more. In both the cases, we received different object IDs. However, when we applied the same concept to a symbol object called `:symbol`, we received the same object ID both the times.

Ruby uses a symbol table to hold the list of symbols. Symbols, like variables, are names—names of instances, variables, methods, and classes. So, let's say we had a method called `method1`; this would automatically create a symbol called `:method1` in the symbol table. This symbol table is maintained at all the times while the program is under execution. To find what is present in this symbol table, you can execute the `Symbol.all_symbols` method.

Symbols are more effective than strings as they get initialized just once. Let's see an example.

Let's call the following code snippet as Code1:

```
day = "Sunday"
if day == "Sunday"
  puts "Holiday!"
else
  puts "Work day"
end
```

Let's call the following code snippet as Code2:

```
day = :Sunday
if day == :Sunday
  puts "Holiday!"
else
  puts "Work day"
end
```

In Code1, we've a Sunday string. It's used once to be assigned to a variable called day and, the next time, we use this string for comparison. In this case, two instances of string objects are created in memory. However, in Code2, we've a symbol called :Sunday and it's declared just once. All later references to the symbol refer to the same old object.

With this knowledge of symbols, a question arises as to when to use symbols and when to make use of strings. There is no easy answer to this, but as a general practice:

- If the content of the object is important, a string is a more apt choice
- If the identity of the object is important, a symbol is a more suitable choice

Basic operations

Like all other programming languages, Ruby comes packed with a whole bunch of operators.

Arithmetic operators

Assume a = 2 and b = 4.

Operator	Description	Example
+	**Addition**: Adds values on either side of the operator	a + b will give 6
-	**Subtraction**: Subtracts the right-hand side operand from the left-hand side operand	a – b will give -2
*	**Multiplication**: Multiplies values on either side of the operator	a * b will give 8
/	**Division**: Divides the left-hand side operand by the right-hand side operand	b / a will give 2
%	**Modulus**: Divides the left-hand side operand by the right-hand side operand and returns the remainder	b % a will give 0
**	**Exponent**: Performs exponential (power) calculations on operators	a ** b will give 2 to the power of 4, which is 16

Comparison operators

Operator	Description	Example
==	Checks whether the values of the two operands are equal or not; if yes, then the condition becomes true.	(a == b) is not true.
!=	Checks whether the values of the two operands are equal or not; if the values are not equal, then the condition becomes true.	(a != b) is true.
>	Checks whether the value of the left-hand side operand is greater than that of the right-hand side operand; if yes, then the condition becomes true.	(a > b) is not true.
<	Checks whether the value of the left-hand side operand is less than the value of the right-hand side operand; if yes, then the condition becomes true.	(a < b) is true.
>=	Checks whether the value of the left-hand side operand is greater than or equal to the value of the right-hand side operand; if yes, then the condition becomes true.	(a >= b) is not true.
<=	Checks whether the value of the left-hand side operand is less than or equal to the value of the right-hand side operand; if yes, then the condition becomes true.	(a <= b) is true.
<=>	This is the combined comparison operator. Returns 0 if the first operand equals second, 1 if the first operand is greater than the second, and -1 if the first operand is less than the second.	(a <=> b) returns -1.
===	This is used to test the equality within a when clause of a case statement.	(1...10) === 5 returns true.
.eql?	This returns true if the receiver and argument have both the same type and equal values.	1 == 1.0 returns true, but 1.eql?(1.0) is false.
Equal?	This returns true if the receiver and arguments have the same object ID.	If aObj is duplicate of bObj, then aObj == bObj is true, a.equal?bObj is false, but a.equal?aObj is true.

Assignment operators

Operator	Description	Example
=	This is the assignment operator. Assigns values from the right-hand side operand to the operand on the left-hand side.	c = a + b will give c the value 6
+=	Adds the operand on right-hand side to the operand on left-hand side, and assigns the result to the left-hand side operand.	c += a is equivalent to c = c + a
-=	Subtracts operand on the right-hand side from the operand on the left-hand side, and assigns the result to the left-hand side operand.	c -= a is equivalent to c = c - a
*=	Multiplies the operand on the right-hand side with the left-hand side operand, and assigns the result to the left-hand side operand.	c *= a is equivalent to c = c * a
/=	Divides the operand on the left-hand side by the operand on the right-hand side, and assigns the result to the left-hand side operand.	c /= a is equivalent to c = c / a
%=	Takes modulus using two operands, and assigns the result to the left-hand side operand.	c %= a is equivalent to c = c % a
**=	Performs exponential calculation on operators, and assigns the value to the left-hand side operand.	c **= a is equivalent to c = c ** a

Bitwise operators

Operator	Description	Example
&	Binary AND	(a & b) = 0
|	Binary OR	(a | b) = 6
^	Binary XOR	(a ^ b) = 6
~	Binary 1s complement	~a = -3
<<	Binary left shift	a << 2 = 8
>>	Binary right shift	a >> 2 = 0

Logical operators

Operator	Description	Example
and	If both the operands are true, condition becomes true	(a and b) is true
&&	If both the operands are true, condition becomes true	(a && b) is true
or	If any of the operands are true, condition becomes true	(a or b) is true
||	If any of the operands are true, condition becomes true	(a || b) is true
!	If a condition is true, logical not will make it false	!(a && b) is false
not	If a condition is true, logical not will make it false	not(a &&b) is false

The Ruby ternary operator

Operator	Description	Example
?:	Conditional expression	If the condition is true, then value x: otherwise value y

Ruby range operators

Operator	Description	Example
..	Creates a range from the start to end point inclusive	1..10 creates a range from 1 to 10
...	Creates a range from the start to end point exclusive	1...10 creates a range from 1 to 9

The Ruby defined? operator

The defined? operator is an operator that checks whether the passed expression is defined or not. If the expression is not defined, it returns nil or else a description of the expression as a string:

* The defined? variable: If the variable is defined, it returns true
* The defined? method: If the method is defined, it returns true

- The `defined?` super: If the method exists that can be called with superuser, it returns true
- The `defined?` yield: If the code block has been passed, it returns true

Conditional statements and loops

Conditional statements and loops allow developers to branch off from the serial flow of execution of code and also iterate through the code. Ruby provides multiple ways to do this job. Let's look at a few of them.

The if statement

The `if` statement is pretty much a basic branching statement that's provided by many programming languages. It's pretty much how we use the "if" statement in natural language—if it's true, do this; if it's not, do something else.

```
x=2
if x == 2
  puts "True"
else
  puts "False"
end
```

If we need to check for multiple conditions, we get an `elsif` statement, that we can embed between the `if` and `else` statements:

```
height = 164
if height > 170
  puts "Tall"
elsif height > 160
  puts "Normal"
else
  puts "Dwarf"
end
```

The fun part of doing this in Ruby is that you can assign values returned by the `if`, `elsif`, and `else` blocks. For example, you might want to save the `Tall`, `Normal`, or `Dwarf` message inside some variable for later use. You can do this quickly in Ruby as follows:

```
size = if height > 170
  "Tall"
```

```
elsif height > 160
  "Normal"
else
  "Dwarf"
end
```

Depending on the value of `height`, whichever block is executed, it'll eventually become the value of `size`.

The unless statement

Often, you would want to make a choice, where if a condition is not true, do this or else do that. In most of the programming languages, and Ruby too, you can accomplish this using the negation operator (`!`) before the condition along with the `if` statement. However, Ruby provides a more convenient and natural way to handle this through the `unless` statement. You can just say this: unless condition, do this or else do that.

An example for this is as follows:

```
day_today = "Sunday"
unless day_today == "Sunday"+

  puts "Working day!"
else
  puts "Holiday time!"
end
```

The case/when statement

Many a times, we'll have multiple conditions to deal with and, if that's the case, then though `if then else` can be used, it will become messy eventually. The `case/when` statement is a much better option in this case:

```
day_today = "Sunday"
case
  when day_today == "Sunday"
      puts "Holiday!"
  when day_today == "Monday"
      puts "Start of week !"
  when day_today == "Wednesday"
```

```
      puts "Mid week crisis !"
  end
```

Alternatively, an even better and concise way to express this would be as follows:

```
day_today = "Sunday"
case day_today
  when "Sunday"
      puts "Holiday!"
  when "Monday"
      puts "Start of week!"
  when "Wednesday"
      puts "Mid week crisis!"
end
```

The while loop

A while loop can continue to execute statements until the condition stated is false. In other words, a while loop can continue to execute statements "while the condition is true".

```
count = 1
while count < 10
    puts count
    count += 1
end
```

This will print the numbers 1 to 9.

The until loop

As unless is the opposite of if, until is the opposite of while. It will continue to iterate over the block of code until the given condition is true:

```
count = 10
until count == 0
  puts count
  count -= 1
end
```

The for loop

The `for` loop in Ruby is more like a `foreach` loop in languages such as Perl or PHP. It's mostly used for iterating over an array or a hash:

```
x = [1,2,3,4,5]
for item in x
  puts x
end
```

This will print all elements of the x array, one at a time.

Methods

Ruby methods are what we refer to as functions in some other programming languages. Many a times, we would want all the statements, operators, and so on that we saw earlier, to be bundled together and used as a single unit. Methods are means to accomplish this feat.

In Ruby, a method name should begin with a lowercase letter. Methods should be defined before they are called upon, otherwise an exception is raised by Ruby.

The syntax to define a method is as follows:

```
def method_name [([arg [= default]]...[, *arg [, &expr ]])]
end
```

Let's look at a few different examples to make this syntax more clear.

Example 1—a simple method:

```
def method
  # Method definition goes here
end
```

Example 2—a method with two arguments:

```
def method (arg1, arg2)
  #  Method definition goes here
end
```

Example 3 — a method with two arguments having some default values. This will pass default values to the arguments if the method is called without passing the required parameters:

```
def method (arg1=val1, arg2=val2)    #  Method definition goes here
end
```

Example 4 — variable number of parameters:

```
def method (*args)
   # Method definition goes here
end
```

In this case, `args` is an array that contains all the parameters that are passed to the method when it's called.

Each method in Ruby returns a value by default. This return value will be the value of the last statement of the method definition, or whatever is returned explicitly by the `return` statement.

Take a look at the following examples.

Example 1 — default return value:

```
def method
   x=1
   y=2
end
```

This method, when called, will return the last declared variable `y`.

Example 2 — explicit return value using the `return` statement:

```
def method
   return 1
end
```

This will return 1.

The method can be called by issuing its name. For example:

- `method` #: This will call a simple method called `method`
- `method("a","b")` #: This will call a method with two arguments
- `method "a","b"` #: This will again call a method with two arguments

You may even assign a value of this method to a variable.

Blocks

Blocks are one of the most powerful features of the Ruby programming language and perhaps one of the most misunderstood ones. Blocks are pieces of code between braces ({ }), or pieces of code enclosed between do-end. These are a way to group statements and they can only appear adjacent to method calls. The code written inside a block is not executed when it's encountered, instead it's called when the method makes a call to yield.

Blocks can have their own arguments as well. There are many methods in Ruby that iterate over a range of values, and most of them can take a code block as an argument. These methods call yield multiple times to allow for the iteration to complete.

Let's explore this using some examples.

Example 1 — a simple code block:

```
Line1    #/usr/bin/env ruby
Line2    def call_block
Line3       i=0
Line4       puts "Start of method"
Line5       while i < 10
Line6         print i + ":\t"
Line7         yield
Line8         i += 1
Line9       end
Line10      puts "End of method"
Line11   end
Line12   call_block { puts "Inside code block" }
```

When executed, we'll get the following output from the preceding code:

```
Start of method
0:   Inside code block
1:   Inside code block
2:   Inside code block
3:   Inside code block
4:   Inside code block
5:   Inside code block
6:   Inside code block
7:   Inside code block
```

```
8:    Inside code block
9:    Inside code block
End of method
```

So, the interpreter looked at the code and figured out that we made a call to the call_block method in Line12. The interpreter then jumps to Line2 where the method is defined. Starting on Line5, we enter a while loop; finally, on Line7 we make a call to the block associated with the call_block method.

Example 2 — a code block with arguments:

```ruby
#/usr/bin/env ruby
def call_block
  i=0
  puts "Start of method"
  while i < 10
    yield i
    i += 1
  end
  puts "End of method"
end
call_block { |i| puts "Call #{i} - Inside code block" }
```

Here, we create a block that accepts an argument. The value passed to the block as an argument is stored inside a local variable named i. This time, inside the call_block method, we call the block through yield along with the argument. The following is the output of running this piece of code:

```
Start of method
Call 0 - Inside code block
Call 1 - Inside code block
Call 2 - Inside code block
Call 3 - Inside code block
Call 4 - Inside code block
Call 5 - Inside code block
Call 6 - Inside code block
Call 7 - Inside code block
Call 8 - Inside code block
Call 9 - Inside code block
End of method
```

Example 3 — a code block using `do-end`

Both the previous examples made use of braces to declare a code block. Let's see how we can create a code block using the `do-end` directives:

```ruby
#/usr/bin/env ruby
def call_block
  i=0
  puts "Start of method"
  while i < 3
    yield i
    i += 1
  end
  puts "End of method"
end
call_block do |i|
 puts "Call #{i} - Inside code block"
end
```

Again, as in the example 2, this code will generate the same output as the previous example:

```
Start of method
Call 0 - Inside code block
Call 1 - Inside code block
Call 2 - Inside code block
End of method
```

Example 4 — let's see how we handle variable scoping with blocks:

```ruby
#/usr/bin/env ruby
x=15
3.times do |x|
  puts "x in the block is #{x}"
end
puts "x out of the block is #{x}"
```

When executed, we'll get this output:

```
x in block is 0
x in block is 1
```

```
x in block is 2
x out of block is 15
```

So the x variable in the block was indeed a local variable.

Now let's see another case:

```
#!/usr/bin/env ruby
x=15
3.times do |y|
  x = y
  puts "x in block is #{x}"
end
puts "x out of block is #{x}"
```

When executed, we'll get this output:

```
x in block is 0
x in block is 1
x in block is 2
x out of block is 2
```

In this case, since x is not a block parameter (variables inside || are called block parameters), both occurrences of x inside and outside the block are one and the same.

There has been a change in how we can handle scoping of block parameters since Ruby 1.9. Since 1.9, blocks have their own scope for block parameters only. For example:

```
#/usr/bin/env ruby
x=15
3.times do |y; x|
  x = y
  puts "x in block is #{x}"
end
puts "x out of block is #{x}"
```

When executed, we'll get this output:

```
x in block is 0
x in block is 1
x in block is 2
x out of block is 15
```

Here, the x variable is a variable local to the block. If you want to specify variables local to the block, just add them as a comma separated list after adding a semicolon to the block parameter list.

For example, if a block has two block parameters, namely x and y, and you want to have two block local variables, a and b, you can specify them as: | x,y ; a,b |.

Arrays

Arrays and hashes are perhaps the two data structures that will be used the most by developers who are writing the Chef code. Be it fetching attributes or values from data bags, you'll be finding these two data structures almost everywhere.

Arrays are an ordered collection of objects that can be accessed through an integer index. Each element of an array can be referenced through an index. The first element of the array is referenced through index number 0 and so on. Ruby also provides support for negative integers as indexes. -1 refers to the last element of the array, -2 is the second last element, and so on.

Unlike other languages, arrays in Ruby aren't tied to one single data type, and they aren't fixed in size either. Ruby arrays grow automatically while elements are added to it. Ruby arrays can also hold other array objects, thereby allowing us to set up multidimensional arrays.

Creating an array

There are multiple ways to create arrays.

Way 1 — using the new method of the Array class:

```
countries  = Array.new
```

Let's create this array with an initial size of 10:

```
countries = Array.new(10)
```

We can find the size and length of the array using the size and length methods:

```
#/usr/bin/env ruby
countries = Array.new(10)
puts countries.size
puts countries.length
```

When executed, this will produce the following result:

```
10
10
```

Let's assign some values to our array:

```
countries = Array.new(3, "India")
```

This will create a `countries` array with values `["India","India","India"]`.

Way 2—using the `[]` method of the `Array` class:

```
countries = Array["India","China","USA"]
```

Way 3—directly initializing an array using `[]`:

```
countries = ["India","China","USA"]
```

Way 4—specifying the range as an argument to create an array:

```
digits = Array(0..9)
```

This is equivalent to saying this:

```
digits = Array.new(0,1,2,3,4,5,6,7,8,9)
```

Or it is equivalent to saying this:

```
digits = Array.new(10) {|x| x}
```

Also, it is equivalent to saying this:

```
digits = [0,1,2,3,4,5,6,7,8,9]
```

With our array created, we can now do lot of things with it. Let's see a few operations that we'll be using most often with objects of the `Array` class.

Accessing elements of an array

Elements of an array can be retrieved using the `#[]` method. It can take either a single integer (absolute index), a range, or start element and length as arguments:

```
digits = [1,2,3,4,5,6,7,8,9]
digits[0] #=> 1
digits[2] #=> 3
```

```
digits[-1] #=> 9
digits [-2] #=> 8
digits [2,3] #=> [3,4,5]
digits[2..3] #=> [3,4]
digits[2..-4] #=> [3,4,5,6]
```

Another way to access an element of an array is to make use of the `at` method:

```
digits.at(2) => 3
```

If you try to access a value beyond the array boundaries, Ruby by default returns nil. However, there might be circumstances where you might want to throw away an error, or return some default value, if someone tries to access values beyond the boundaries of an array. You can make use of the `fetch` method for this purpose:

```
digits.fetch(100) #=> IndexError: index 100 outside of array
   bounds: -9...9
digits.fetch(100,"Out of bounds!") #=> Out of bounds!
```

There are two special methods, namely `first` and `last`. These methods allow you to access the first and last element of an array:

```
digits.first #=> 1
digits.last #=> 9
```

To get the first n elements of an array, make use of the `take` statement:

```
digits.take(4) #=> [1,2,3,4]
```

There is another method called `drop`, which ignores the first n elements and returns the remaining elements:

```
digits.drop(5) #=> [6,7,8,9]
```

To check whether an array has any element at all or not, use the `empty?` method:

```
digits.empty? #=> returns true if array named digits is empty or
   else it'll return false
```

To check whether a particular element is included in the array, use the `include?` method:

```
digits.include?(8) #=> returns true if array named digits contains
   8 or else it'll return false
```

Adding elements to an array

Elements can be added to an existing array using the `push` method or `<<`.

```
digits = [0,1,2,3,4]
digits.push(5) #=> [0,1,2,3,5]
digits << 6 #=> [0,1,2,3,4,5,6]
```

To add an element to the beginning of an array, use the `unshift` method:

```
digits.unshift(9) #=> [9,0,1,2,3,4,5,6]
```

To add an element at a fixed location, use the `insert` method:

```
digits.insert(3,'three') #=>  [9,0,1,'three',2,3,4,5,6]
```

We can also add multiple values, as follows:

```
digits.insert(3,'three','four') #=>
  [9,0,1,'three','four',2,3,4,5,6]
```

Removing elements from an array

Elements can be removed from an array using the `pop` method:

```
digits = [0,1,2,3]
digits.pop
digits #=> [0,1,2]
```

You can use the `shift` method to remove an element from the start of an array:

```
digits.shift #=> 0
digits #=> [1,2]
```

To delete an element in a particular position, you can make use of the `delete_at` method:

```
digits = [0,1,2,3]
digits.delete_at(1) #=> 1
digits #=> [0,2,3]
```

To delete a particular element, use the `delete` method:

```
digits = [0,1,2,2,3]
digits.delete(2) #=> 2
digits #=> [0,1,3]
```

If you want to remove duplicate values from an array, you can make use of the `uniq` method. It has two variants, `uniq` and `uniq!`. The former will return a copy of the array without duplicates, while the second one will remove the duplicate elements within the array itself:

```
digits = [0,1,2,2,3]
digits.uniq #=> [0,1,2,3]
digits #=> [0,1,2,2,3]
digits.uniq! #=> [0,1,2,3]
digits #=> [0,1,2,3]
```

Iterating over an array

There are multiple ways in which one can iterate over an array. You can make use of the loop constructs that we discussed earlier:

```ruby
#!/usr/bin/env ruby
counter=0
x=[1,2,3,4]
while counter < x.length
  puts x[counter]
  counter += 1
end
```

However, like many other classes, the `Array` class includes the `Enumerable` module, which provides a method called `each`. This method defines how and which elements should be iterated. In case of arrays, you can supply a block to this method, and all the elements of the array will be yielded:

```ruby
x = [1,2,3,4]
x.each {|i| puts i}
```

Running this piece of code gives the following output:

```
1
2
3
4
```

There is a `reverse_each` method as well, that as its name suggests, allows for traversal of the array in the reverse order:

```ruby
x = [1,2,3,4]
x.reverse_each { |i| puts i }
```

Running this piece of code gives the following output:

```
4
3
2
1
```

There are times when we would like to create a new array based on the original array, but with some modifications that are consistent across all elements of the array. We can make use of the map method for this purpose:

```
x = [1,2,3,4]
y = x.map { |e| e**2} #=> y=[1,4,9,16]
```

As you can see, each element of the x array was picked up, squared, and pushed into a new array, which can be referenced using variable named y.

Selecting elements of an array

One can select elements specifying certain criteria defined in an associated block. There is a destructive way and a nondestructive way to accomplish this.

The nondestructive way

An example of the nondestructive way is as follows:

```
x = [1,2,3,4,5]
x.select { |i| i > 2 } #=> [3,4,5]
x.reject { |i| i < 3 } #=> [3,4,5]
x.drop_while { |i| i < 3 } #=> [3,4,5]
x #=> [1,2,3,4,5]
```

The destructive way

An example of the destructive way is as follows:

```
x.select! { |i| i > 2 } #=> [3,4,5]
x.reject! { |i| i < 3 } #=> [3,4,5]
```

As you can see, in the nondestructive way, the methods returned an array after performing the operations; however, our original array that is x remained unaffected. However, in the destructive way, the original array itself was modified. We'll see a bit more about this in our next section.

Bang methods

As you might have noticed, we used two different variants of the same method in our previous example where we explained destructive and nondestructive ways of selecting elements from an array. The bang sign after a method doesn't necessarily mean that the method would be destructive, nor does it imply that methods without a bang sign are always nondestructive. It's just a means of specifying the fact that the methods with the ! sign affixed to the method name are more dangerous as compared to methods without it.

The bang methods are generally used to do modifications in place. Now, what this means is that, say I've an x = [1,2,3,4,5] array and I want to remove all elements from this array that are greater than 2. If I chose x.select, then the x array would remain the same; however, a new array object containing [3,4,5] would be returned. However, if I were to choose x.select!, then the x array itself would be modified:

```
2.1-head :001 > x=[1,2,3,4,5]
 => [1, 2, 3, 4, 5]
2.1-head :002 > x.select { |i| i > 2 }
 => [3, 4, 5]
2.1-head :003 > x
 => [1, 2, 3, 4, 5]
2.1-head :004 > x.select! { |i| i > 2 }
 => [3, 4, 5]
2.1-head :005 > x
 => [3, 4, 5]
```

It's generally advisable to choose non-bang variants of a method, as most of the times, we want to ensure that the objects on which we are working are immutable. Hence, we would like to perform operations on a copy of the object, rather than on the object itself.

Hashes

Hashes are also known as associative arrays, and they are dictionary-like objects, comprising keys and their associated values. Hashes are very similar to arrays; however, while arrays allow only integers to be used as an index, hashes, on the other hand, can use any object as a key.

Creating hashes

Hashes can be created easily using their implicit form as follows:

```
scores = { "A" => 85, "B" => 70, "C" => 60, "D" => 50, "E" => 35 }
```

Here, A, B, C, D, and E are keys having associated values 85, 70, 60, 50, and 35, respectively.

Hashes also allow for a form wherein keys are always symbols:

```
scores = { :A => 85, :B => 70, :C => 60, :D => 50, :E => 35 }
```

We may access each key's value using the corresponding symbol as follows:

```
scores[:A] #=> 85
```

We can also create a new hash using the new method of the Hash class:

```
scores = Hash.new
scores["A"] = 85
```

If no default value is set while creating a hash, then, when we try to access the key, it'll return nil. One can always set a default value for a hash by passing it as an argument to the new method:

```
scores = Hash.new(0)
scores["A"] #=> 0
```

Let's now see a few commonly used methods for the Hash class and their corresponding objects:

- hash.clear: This method removes all existing key-value pairs from a hash:

  ```
  x = { :A => "a", :B => "b" }
  x.clear #=> {}
  ```

- hash.delete(key): This deletes all key-value pairs from the hash that matches the key passed into the arguments:

  ```
  x = { :A => 'a', :B => 'b', :C => 'c' }
  x.delete(:A) #=> 'a'
  x #=> {:B => 'b', :C => 'c'}
  ```

- hash.empty?: If the hash is empty, it'll return true or else false.

- `hash.has_value? (value)`: This checks whether the given hash has the corresponding value that was passed as an argument to the method. If it has, then it'll return `true` or else `false`:

```
x = {:A => 'a', :B => 'b'}
x.has_value?('a') #=> true
x.has_value?('c') #=> false
```

- `has.has_key? (key)`: This checks whether the given hash has the corresponding key that was passed as an argument to the method. If it has, then it'll return `true` or else it'll return `false`:

```
x= {:A => 'a', :B => 'b'}
x.has_key?(:A) #=> true
x.has_key?(:C) #=> false
```

- `hash.keys`: This method will return an array containing all the keys associated with the hash:

```
x = {:A => 'a', :B => 'b'}
x.keys #=> [:A,:B]
```

- `hash.values`: This method will return an array containing all the values associated with the given hash:

```
x = {:A => 'a', :B => 'b'}
x.values #=> ['a','b']
```

- `hash.size`: This method will return the length of the given hash:

```
x = {:A => 'a', :B => 'b'}
x.size #=> 2
```

- `hash.to_s`: This method will first convert the hash to an array and, finally, convert this array to a string:

```
x = {:A => 'a', :B => 'b'}
x.to_s #=> "{:A=>\"a\", :B=>\"b\"}"
```

- `hash.invert`: This method will create a new hash with keys and values from the original hash that is swapped:

```
x = {:A => 'a', :B => 'b'}
x.invert #=> {'a' => :A, 'b' => :B}
```

Iterating over a hash

Like array, hashes also include the `Enumeration` module. Hence, we can make use of methods such as `each`, `each_key`, and `each_value`.

An example of the use of the `each` method is as follows:

```
x = {:A => 'a', :B => 'b'}
x.each { |key, value| puts "#{key} #{value}" }
```

If we run the preceding piece of code, we'll get this output:

```
A a
B b
```

An example of the use of the `each_key` method is as follows:

```
x.each_key { |key| puts "#{key} #{x[key]}" }
```

If we run the preceding piece of code, we'll get this output:

```
A a
B b
```

An example of the use of the `each_value` method is as follows:

```
x.each_value { |value| puts "#{value}" }
```

If we run the preceding piece of code, we'll get this output:

```
a
b
```

Classes and objects

Object-oriented programming is a paradigm that has become the foundation of many modern programming languages, and it's at the core of Ruby. In short, the object-oriented programming sees the world as data, modeled in code by "objects". When working with data, this model of programming is most apt, as it allows us to model our program as we would see the real world.

The object-oriented programming paradigm, or OOPs as it's popularly called, is based upon a few principles, let's look at them one at a time:

- **Encapsulation**: This is a concept that ensures a certain functionality is hidden from the rest of the code. Its primary use is to ensure that the underlying data is protected, and can only be manipulated in a way the object desires. Ruby accomplishes this by creating objects. The objects expose certain interfaces (also known as methods), using which the interaction can happen with those objects.

- **Polymorphism**: This is the ability to represent the same thing in multiple forms. In the context of Ruby, this means that we'll have a single interface to entities of different types. One way to achieve polymorphism is through inheritance. This allows one class to inherit functionality of another class. The class from which the functionality is inherited is referred to as superclass, while the class that is inheriting the functionality is called a subclass.

For example, let's say we've a class called Shape that has a method called draw. We'll use this Shape class as a superclass for two subclasses, namely Circle and Square:

```ruby
class Shape
  def draw
    raise NotImplementedError, 'You must implement the draw method'
  end
end


class Circle < Shape
  def draw
    puts "We'll draw a circle here."
  end
end
class Square < Shape
  def draw
    puts "We'll draw a square here."
  end
end
```

Now, let's use these subclasses in our script and see what happens:

```ruby
shape = Circle.new
circle.draw
```

```
shape = Square.new
square.draw
```

When this script is executed, we'll get the following output:

```
We'll draw a circle here.
We'll draw a square here.
```

Another way to achieve polymorphism in Ruby is via modules. Modules like classes contain code that is common in behavior. However, we cannot create an object from a module. A module must be mixed in a class using the `include` keyword. This is referred to as **mixin**. After the mixing of the module, all the behaviors specified in the module are available to the class and its objects. We'll look at modules a little later after being introduced to the concepts of classes and objects.

What's an object and a class?

You might hear this phrase multiple times, "In Ruby, everything is an object!" Though we've not yet touched the concepts of objects so far, it's true that everything in Ruby is an object. Objects are created out of classes. One can consider classes to be the concepts, while objects are real-life incarnations of those concepts. For example, living beings are a concept whereas you, me, our pets, plants, and so on, are all real living beings. Different objects might have different information stored about them; however, all of them might belong to the same class.

Attributes and behaviors associated with an object are defined in a class. Classes define what an object would finally appear like and what all it will be able to accomplish. To define a class, we use the `class` keyword, and use CamelCase naming convention to name the class. The class definition finishes with the `end` keyword. The filename associated with a class is specified in the snake_case format. So we might have a file called `living_beings.rb` that holds the `LivingBeings` class:

```
#living_beings.rb
class LivingBeings
    # Definition of class goes here
end
```

We can now create an object from this class by using the `new` method as follows:

```
humans = LivingBeings.new
```

The process of creating a new object from a class is called instantiation, and hence an object is also sometimes referred to as an instance of a class.

Modules

As we discussed earlier, modules are a way to achieve polymorphism. They also allow for multiple inheritance. A module is a collection of behaviors that is usable in a class via mixins.

Let's look at an example to see modules, classes, and mixins in action:

```
module A
   def methodA1
   end
   def methodA2
   end
end
module B
   def methodB1
   end
   def methodB2
   end
end
class X
   include A
   include B
   def methodX
   end
end
x = X.new
x.methodA1
x.methodA2
x.methodB1
x.methodB2
x.methodX
```

As you can see, we've two modules, namely A and B, and each of them has two methods. Next, we've a class called X, and we've included both the A and B modules in the X class. This class also has its own method called methodX. Finally, when we create an object of this class, the object has access to all the five methods. Thus, we can see that the X class is inheriting from both the modules, and hence is showing multiple inheritance.

Summary

This brings us to the end of our journey in to the world of Ruby. We have looked at variables, operators, statements, and methods, and eventually had a sneak peek into the world of OOPs. We have learned about classes, objects, and modules. We'll make use of most of the stuff we learned here throughout this book. We'll be extending our knowledge of Ruby as and when we move on to structures involving JSON objects and so on.

In the next chapter, we'll cover concepts such as organizations, groups, and users, and how you can allow for fine-grained access to different types of objects on the Chef server.

4
Controlling Access to Resources

So you decided that you were going to set up a Chef server and configure your infrastructure in a smart way. Good for you! However, once you've moved past this stage, the next stage that will come and haunt most organizations is: How do we ensure that everyone is able to contribute towards using Chef, while ensuring that no big mess up happens when everyone is busy modifying the Chef code? Above all, how to ensure that anybody who is not supposed to access resources on the Chef server is denied access?

Chef provides a very fine-grained, role-based access to resources through Enterprise Chef.

Any system that has to provide for such a mechanism has to have two components included in it:

- Authentication
- Authorization

All communication with the Chef server is through the Chef Server API. The API provided by Chef is a REST API, and the access to the API is restricted using authentication mechanisms. Public key encryption is used in both Enterprise and Open Source Chef for authentication purpose. Whenever a node/client is created to communicate with the Chef server, a public/private key pair is created. The public key is stored on the Chef server, while the private key is kept with the client. Every request that is made to the Chef server API contains a few special HTTP headers that are signed using the private key. The public key stored on the Chef server is used to verify the headers and contents. Once a request has been authenticated, the next thing that the Chef server needs to decide is whether the request should return the data to the client who has requested access to it.

In the Open Source Chef server, there are only two types of roles that a client can have: either a client can be admin or non-admin. However, in Enterprise Chef, we can manage access to resources through the role-based access control model.

The bootstrap process

Before we jump into understanding the authentication and authorization mechanisms available in the Chef ecosystem, let's look at the bootstrap process used for the purpose of bootstrapping a new machine using Chef. There are two ways to bootstrap a new node:

- Using the `knife bootstrap` subcommand
- Using a custom orchestrator, which can bootstrap a new machine

In both the cases, unless you are using the chef-client version 12.1 (or higher) and the validator-less bootstrap, you'll require the validator's private key for the first chef-client run on the node. If you are using the Open Source Chef server, this key can be found in `/etc/chef-server/chef-validator.pem`, whereas, for the Enterprise Chef server, this key will be issued to you during the initial setup.

If you are going to use the `knife bootstrap` subcommand, this key should be copied over to the machine from where the `knife bootstrap` subcommand will be invoked. Also, update your `knife.rb` file on the workstation with the path of `validation_key` along with `validation_client_name`.

If you are going to use a custom orchestrator to provision your machines, you might want to copy this key to a location from where it's accessible on a remote machine. For example, if you are working in an Amazon AWS environment, perhaps you will want to keep this key in a S3 bucket and use user data to fetch this key from S3 during the bootstrap process. This method is also useful when trying to do unattended installs.

During the bootstrap process, if a chef-client is not present, it's installed. Next, the necessary keys are generated using the name of the node, which can either be the name provided explicitly, FQDN, machine name, or hostname. Finally, the node is registered with the Chef server. For this purpose, the validator private key is put to use. Once the client is set up, a corresponding private key is created on the node (`/etc/chef/client.pem`). All subsequent communications with the Chef server happen through this key.

As we can see, the `validation.pem` file is the primary source of authentication when trying to bootstrap a machine. Hence, this key should be secured, and unauthorized access to this key should be avoided. Also, any keys issued to the users with admin privileges should be safeguarded as these accounts can be used to perform destructive operations on the Chef server.

Authentication

Communication with the Chef server can be initiated by different mechanisms such as chef-client, Knife, and using API in code. Let's see how authentication works under different circumstances.

chef-client

Every time a chef-client needs to communicate with the Chef server to fetch some data required for bootstrapping a machine, the chef-client needs to authenticate itself with the Chef server. It does so by using a private key located at `/etc/chef/client.pem`. However, as we saw in the bootstrap process, when a chef-client is executed for the very first time, there is no private key on the concerned machine. Hence, a chef-client makes use of the private key assigned to the chef-validator (`/etc/chef/validation.pem`). Once the initial request is authenticated, a chef-client will register with the Chef server using `validation.pem`, and subsequently the Chef server will return back a new private key to use for future communication. Once the initial chef-client run is over, `validation.pem` should be removed from the node. The `/etc/chef/client.pem` file on a node is usable only on the concerned node as it is signed using the node name. This prevents a node from accessing data that isn't meant for it, and also allows the administrators to ensure that only the nodes that are registered with the Chef server are managed by it.

Knife

As a Chef developer/administrator, we are constantly making use of Knife to perform various tasks on the Chef server. RSA public-key pairs are used to authenticate every request that is made using knife.

During the set up of workstation, we run `knife configure` – initially to create `knife.rb` and alongside a `.pem` file that is also generated and that will be used for communicating with the Chef server in future.

One can also generate a new user or client using Chef Web UI. Once a new user or client is generated, you can copy over contents of the private key file into a .pem file, store it in a safe place, and reference it in knife.rb as follows:

```
$ cat ~/.chef/knife.rb
log_level                 :info
log_location              STDOUT
node_name                 'mayank'
client_key                '~/keys/chef/mayank.pem'
validation_client_name    'chef-validator'
validation_key            '~/keys/chef/validation.pem'
chef_server_url           'http://chef-server.sychonet.com:4000'
cache_type                'BasicFile'
cache_options( :path => '~/.chef/checksums' )
cookbook_path [ '~/code/chef-repo/cookbooks' ]
```

Note that the node_name value must be the one that was used to generate the .pem file specified in client_key.

> As you might have noticed, we mentioned that we can create a client or user using Knife, and use it for all subsequent communications with the Chef server. Both the client and user are enough to make use of Chef API; however, the only difference between them is that users can also make use of Web UI to communicate with the Chef server, whereas clients only have access to Chef API.

Custom API calls

On a system where Chef is installed, one can also make use of API calls using different languages. For instance, the following example will make use of Ruby to make a call to the Chef server, in order to list all the nodes belonging to the webserver role:

```
#!/usr/bin/env ruby
require 'chef/rest'
require 'chef/search/query'

Chef::Config.from_file(File.expand_path("~/.chef/knife.rb"))
query = Chef::Search::Query.new
query_string = "role:webserver"
nodes = query.search('node',query_string).first
p nodes.map(&:name)
```

This script when executed, will return names of all the nodes that were bootstrapped with the `webserver` role.

Let's see what happens if we provide wrong credentials. We will modify `knife.rb` to say the following:

```
client_key /keys/chef/foobar.pem
```

This file is not present on our machine. Now, if we try and run our script, we'll get an error as follows:

```
[2014-06-30T00:51:09+05:30] WARN: Failed to read the private key /keys/
chef/foobar.pem: #<Errno::ENOENT: No such file or directory @ rb_sysopen
- /keys/chef/foobar.pem>
/Users/mayank/.rvm/gems/ruby-2.1.0/gems/chef-11.8.2/lib/chef/http/
authenticator.rb:74:in `rescue in load_signing_key': I cannot read /keys/
chef/foobar.pem, which you told me to use to sign requests! (Chef::Except
ions::PrivateKeyMissing)
        from /Users/mayank/.rvm/gems/ruby-2.1.0/gems/chef-11.8.2/lib/chef/
http/authenticator.rb:64:in `load_signing_key'
        from /Users/mayank/.rvm/gems/ruby-2.1.0/gems/chef-11.8.2/lib/chef/
http/authenticator.rb:38:in `initialize'
        from /Users/mayank/.rvm/gems/ruby-2.1.0/gems/chef-11.8.2/lib/chef/
rest.rb:63:in `new'
        from /Users/mayank/.rvm/gems/ruby-2.1.0/gems/chef-11.8.2/lib/chef/
rest.rb:63:in `initialize'
        from /Users/mayank/.rvm/gems/ruby-2.1.0/gems/chef-11.8.2/lib/chef/
search/query.rb:34:in `new'
        from /Users/mayank/.rvm/gems/ruby-2.1.0/gems/chef-11.8.2/lib/chef/
search/query.rb:34:in `initialize'
        from test_api.rb:10:in `new'
        from test_api.rb:10:in `<main>'
```

As you can see, `authenticator.rb` tried to authenticate us with the Chef server, but couldn't do so.

Let's see what happens if we provide the right private key, but a wrong client name. Let's modify our `knife.rb` and state the following:

```
node_name 'foobar'
```

Now, if we'll execute our script, we will get an error like the following:

```
/Users/mayank/.rvm/rubies/ruby-2.1.0/lib/ruby/2.1.0/net/http/response.
rb:119:in `error!': 401 "Unauthorized" (Net::HTTPServerException)
```

```
    from /Users/mayank/.rvm/gems/ruby-2.1.0/gems/chef-11.8.2/lib/chef/
http.rb:140:in `request'
    from /Users/mayank/.rvm/gems/ruby-2.1.0/gems/chef-11.8.2/lib/chef/
rest.rb:104:in `get'
    from /Users/mayank/.rvm/gems/ruby-2.1.0/gems/chef-11.8.2/lib/chef/
search/query.rb:42:in `search'
    from test_api.rb:9:in `<main>'
```

Now that we know that all requests to the Chef server REST API need to be signed, let's see how it is actually done.

As we discussed earlier, the Chef server REST API accepts certain HTTP headers that are signed using our private key. These headers are X-Ops-Authorization-n where *n* can be an integer starting from 1.

Chef makes use of mixlib-authentication for the purpose of signing headers. Apart from other required headers, every request is embedded with X-Ops-Authorization-n headers, and these headers are populated with values using the following piece of code:

```
def sign(private_key, sign_algorithm=algorithm, sign_version=proto_
version)
    # Our multiline hash for authorization will be encoded in multiple
header
  # lines - X-Ops-Authorization-1, ... (starts at 1, not 0!)
  header_hash = {
    "X-Ops-Sign" => "algorithm=#{sign_algorithm};version=#{sign_
version};",
    "X-Ops-Userid" => user_id,
    "X-Ops-Timestamp" => canonical_time,
    "X-Ops-Content-Hash" => hashed_body,
  }

  string_to_sign = canonicalize_request(sign_algorithm, sign_version)
  signature = Base64.encode64(private_key.private_encrypt(string_to_
sign)).chomp
  signature_lines = signature.split(/\n/)
  signature_lines.each_index do |idx|
    key = "X-Ops-Authorization-#{idx + 1}"
    header_hash[key] = signature_lines[idx]
  end
  Mixlib::Authentication::Log.debug "String to sign: '#{string_to_
sign}'\nHeader hash: #{header_hash.inspect}"
  header_hash
end
```

These headers, along with other required headers such as Accept, X-Chef-Version, and so on, are passed along with the request to the Chef server, where they are decoded and verified for integrity. All the headers are Base64 encoded, and hashing is done using SHA1.

The following is the `tcpdump` output, when we tried to execute the `knife node list` command:

```
☒   ~  sudo tcpdump -vvvs 1024 -l -i any -A host chef.sychonet.com


tcpdump: data link type PKTAP
tcpdump: listening on any, link-type PKTAP (Packet Tap), capture size
1024 bytes
19:25:34.303810 IP (tos 0x0, ttl 64, id 28538, offset 0, flags [DF],
proto TCP (6), length 64)
    192.168.200.17.58990 > chef.sychonet.com.http: Flags [S], cksum
0x7630 (correct), seq 1860154782, win 65535, options [mss 1460,nop,wscale
4,nop,nop,TS val 348873058 ecr 0,sackOK,eol], length 0
....E..@oz@.@........
..n.Pn...........v0.............
..ab........
19:25:34.381930 IP (tos 0x0, ttl 63, id 0, offset 0, flags [DF], proto
TCP (6), length 60)
    chef.sychonet.com.http > 192.168.200.17.58990: Flags [S.], cksum
0xf1e2 (correct), seq 261649376, ack 1860154783, win 17898, options [mss
1268,sackOK,TS val 36293234 ecr 348873058,nop,wscale 7], length 0
....E..<..@.?..X..
......P.n..s.n.....E............
.).r..ab....
19:25:34.381959 IP (tos 0x0, ttl 64, id 49771, offset 0, flags [DF],
proto TCP (6), length 52)
    192.168.200.17.58990 > chef.sychonet.com.http: Flags [.], cksum
0x455a (correct), seq 1, ack 1, win 8242, options [nop,nop,TS val
348873135 ecr 36293234], length 0
....E..4.k@.@.8......
..n.Pn.....s... 2EZ.....
..a..).r
19:25:34.382581 IP (tos 0x0, ttl 64, id 56374, offset 0, flags [DF],
proto TCP (6), length 1035)
```

```
    192.168.200.17.58990 > chef.sychonet.com.http: Flags [P.], seq 1:984,
ack 1, win 8242, options [nop,nop,TS val 348873135 ecr 36293234], length
983
....E....6@.@..S......
..n.Pn.....s... 2.......
..a..).rGET /nodes HTTP/1.1
Accept: application/json
Accept-Encoding: gzip;q=1.0,deflate;q=0.6,identity;q=0.3
X-Ops-Sign: algorithm=sha1;version=1.0;
X-Ops-Userid: maxc0d3r
X-Ops-Timestamp: 2015-04-24T13:55:34Z
X-Ops-Content-Hash: 2jmj715rSw0yVb/vlWAYkK/YBwk=
X-Ops-Authorization-1: TkyDvBoWHIg3Fmdq6GYpBZyI9nzmrlr3nvWhsFKiH0qYYN4ocd
XG4BDN+29X
X-Ops-Authorization-2: PY0avZQi9InskpfKV6Qx590uHUY/butQd+kCzDbKcQHObhmDZ3
f9CsQLXN1n
X-Ops-Authorization-3: vrH9A69RYrRswTyGNURg8MlDgr+TWPCnQfdzrTNLjDN8DcuEaJ
HBBPEnwobK
X-Ops-Authorization-4: ecBK9Uw+9rHZ6a06qZ8aMEVTjRzZGhgboMbmbIP2QpZMMyIUzo
J6rLktPjah
X-Ops-Authorization-5: eBTnAHLvE1VOg3eWW/rzLcRQHCf2WuBiO3/
YvyKzmYWvOHzY6p1hxaubiin4
X-Ops-Authorization-6: i9u8OvFVNNNuH8yzBrEICkxeBffT8OcSUF6nyn+w2Q==
Host: chef.sychonet.com:80
X-Remote-Request-Id: c110eb5b-1528-4165-91de-5a879fe1a692
X-Chef-Version: 11.14.2


19:25:34.460756 IP (tos 0x0, ttl 63, id 47454, offset 0, flags [DF],
proto TCP (6), length 52)
    chef.sychoent.com.http > 192.168.200.17.58990: Flags [.], cksum
0x60cb (correct), seq 1, ack 984, win 156, options [nop,nop,TS val
36293312 ecr 348873135], length 0
....E..4.^@.?.C...
......P.n..s.n..v....`......
.)....a.
...
```

As you can see, the following headers were accompanied with the request made by Knife:

- X-Ops-Sign
- X-Ops-Userid
- X-Ops-Timestamp
- X-Ops-Content-Hash
- X-Ops-Authorization-1
- X-Ops-Authorization-2
- X-Ops-Authorization-3
- X-Ops-Authorization-4
- X-Ops-Authorization-5
- X-Ops-Authorization-6
- Host
- X-Remote-Request-Id
- X-Chef-Version

We'll learn more about these headers in our discussion on APIs later in this book. In the meantime, if you are interested in more details about how this is all happening, you can refer to the code for mixlib authentication at `https://github.com/opscode/mixlib-authentication`.

Authorization

As we discussed earlier, users of Chef can only perform actions that they are authorized to perform. There is a difference in the implementation of authorization between the Enterprise and Open Source Chef server.

The Enterprise Chef server makes use of the role-based access control model.

The Open Source Chef server, on other hand, has a fairly simple model, where there are either admin users who have the privilege to read, write, update, and delete resources, or non-admin users who have read-only access to resources on the Chef server.

Let's look at each of these in detail.

The Open Source Chef server

As we discussed earlier, the Open Source Chef server has a very simple model for authorization purpose. We've two sets of users: admin and non-admin. Any user with an admin privilege can read, write, update, or delete any resources on the Chef server, whereas non-admin users have read-only access to the resources on the Chef server.

When a node is registered with the Chef server through an initial chef-client run, it gets registered as a non-admin client. Similarly, if you try to create a new client using Knife, it'll be registered as a non-admin user, unless you explicitly set it as admin.

As a Chef developer/administrator, you'll be adding/updating/deleting resources, such as cookbooks, users, nodes, and so on, on the Chef server. Hence, you should create the client with admin rights.

There are, however, times when you want your nodes to be registered with admin privileges. For example, some time ago I was creating Chef code for an infrastructure on AWS. This setup was being done on an autoscaling group. I wanted all the machines in the autoscaling group to get a proper hostname. To accomplish this, I prepopulated a data bag with a set of hostnames. During the bootstrapping of the machines, I fetched a hostname from the data bag and, once the machine was bootstrapped, I wanted the Chef recipe to remove the hostname that was assigned to the node from the data bag.

Data bags are a resource on the Chef server, and nodes are by default registered with the non-admin privileges on the Chef server. So, we can't just go around deleting stuff from the Chef server using our Chef recipe that is running via the chef-client.

In order to overcome this issue, we will need to modify the code on the Chef server.

Edit the `api_client.rb` file, which can be found inside the `/opt/chef-server/ embedded` folder (search for the file inside this folder).

This file defines a class called `ApiClient`, and its constructor initializes a few variables such as `@name`, `@public_key`, `@private_key`, `@admin`, and `@validator`.

Around line 38, you'll find that `@admin` is set as `false` by default. This is overridden to `true` when we create a client using the `-a` option with Knife. If we want to create all clients with admin privileges, we need to set this as `true`.

Now, whenever a request is made to Chef API for the registration of a new client/ node, it will be created with admin rights.

Before you go about making this change, ensure that you understand the implications because there is a very good reason why it's set up the way it is.

The following requests require admin privileges:

- **Client index**: `knife client list`
- **Client update**: `knife client edit NAME`
- **Client destroy**: `knife client delete NAME`
- **Cookbook update**: `knife cookbook upload COOKBOOK_NAME`
- **Cookbook destroy**: `knife cookbook delete COOKBOOK_NAME`
- **Data bag create**: `knife data bag create DATABAG_NAME`
- **Data bag destroy**: `knife data bag delete DATABAG_NAME`
- **Data bag item create**: `knife data bag create DATABAG_NAME ITEM_NAME`
- **Data bag item update**: `knife data bag edit DATABAG_NAME ITEM_NAME`
- **Data bag item destroy**: `knife data bag delete DATABAG_NAME ITEM_NAME`
- **Environment create**: `knife environment create ENVIRONMENT_NAME`
- **Environment update**: `knife environment edit ENVIRONMENT_NAME`
- **Environment destroy**: `knife environment delete ENVIRONMENT_NAME`
- **Role create**: `knife role create ROLE_NAME`
- **Role update**: `knife role edit ROLE_NAME`
- **Role destroy**: `knife role delete ROLE_NAME`

The following are some requests that require admin privileges if executed from a location where a request was originated:

- **Client show**: `knife client show NAME`
- **Node update**: `knife node edit NAME`
- **Node destroy**: `knife node delete NAME`

The following API requires admin privileges, or is done by the chef-validator during the initial chef-client run:

- **Client create**: `knife client create`

Enterprise Chef

As we discussed earlier, Enterprise Chef makes use of the role-based access control model to grant access to the different resources on the Chef server. Access to objects can be defined by object type, group, user, organization, and so on.

Enterprise Chef uses the concept of organization, group, and user to define this role-based access. Let's look at each of these in brief:

- **Organization**: An organization is the top-most entity for role-based access. Each organization consists of groups such as clients, users, admins, at least one user, and one node. The on-premise Enterprise Chef server provides support for multiple organizations as well. When a setup is being done, the Enterprise Chef server creates one organization by default.

- **Groups**: A group is used to define access to the object types and objects in the Chef server. It also assigns permissions that are used to decide which tasks are available to the members of that group. All the users who are members of a group inherit permissions associated with the group. The Enterprise Chef server provides the following groups by default: admins, clients, and users. Hosted Chef also provides an additional group called `billing_admins`.

- **Users**: A user is any non-admin person who is supposed to manage the data stored on the Chef server. The Enterprise Chef server includes a single user, which is set up initially, and this user is automatically assigned to the admins group.

- **Chef-client**: A client is any agent that makes use of the Chef server API to interact with the Chef server. Every node on which a chef-client is configured is automatically added to the client group.

Whenever a request is made to the Enterprise Chef server for a resource, the Chef server checks whether the requesting entity has permissions over the requested resource or not. If it's permitted, the resource is served. If it's not, the Chef server checks whether the group to which the user belongs has permissions over the requested resource and, if it's permitted, the resource is served back to the user.

Object permissions

The Enterprise Chef server includes the following object permissions:

- **Delete**: This defines whether a user or group can delete the concerned resource.

- **Grant**: This defines whether a user or users belonging to a group can assign permissions over the concerned resource.

- **Read**: This defines which users or groups have access to the details about the concerned resource.
- **Update**: This defines which users or groups have access to edit details associated with the concerned resource.

The Enterprise Chef server also includes the following global permissions:

- **Create**: This defines which users or groups can create the following resources: cookbooks, data bags, environments, roles, nodes, and tags.
- **List**: This defines which users or groups can view the following resources: cookbooks, data bags, environments, roles, nodes, and tags.

Groups

As we saw earlier, Enterprise Chef includes the following default groups:

- **admins**: This group contains all the users who'll have administrative privileges.
- **billing_admins**: This group is specific to Hosted Enterprise Chef. It's used to define a list of users who'll have privileges to manage information related to billing.
- **clients**: This group is primarily meant to contain a list of machines that are registered with the Chef server by a chef-client.
- **users**: This group is generally meant to house all the users who'll make use of tools such as Knife or Chef Web UI.

A single instance of the Enterprise Chef server comes with one organization by default. However, one can set up multiple organizations if needed. Each organization can have a unique set of groups and users. Each organization will manage its own set of nodes on which chef-client is installed.

A user can belong to multiple organizations, provided that role-based access control is configured per organization. Using multiple organizations ensures that the same Chef server is reused to provide support for different groups within an organization. For a large organization, this is a boon as it allows an organization to set up a single Chef server, and have different organizations set up for different groups. Each of these organizations can have different schedules for updates; multiple groups might want to have access to different resources using the same name.

Before we wrap up with authorization, we should note that the endpoints for API requests for the Enterprise Chef server and the Open Source Chef server are not the same.

For the Enterprise Chef server, the endpoint should always include `/organization/organization_name` as part of the name of the endpoint. For the Open Source Chef server, there is no such constraint.

This is also evident in the `knife.rb` file. With the Open Source Chef server, we've `chef_server_url` as `https://chef-server.sychonet.com`, whereas, for the Enterprise Chef server, it will be like `https://api.opscode.com/organizations/maxc0d3r`.

Summary

In this chapter, we went on to understand how authentication happens in the Chef server and how one can make use of custom APIs to connect securely with the Chef server. We also saw different models of authorization used by the Enterprise and Open Source Chef server. I hope by now you know how authentication and authorization happen in the world of Chef and how you can choose the right variant of the Chef server for your use, depending on your requirement s with regard to the granularity of authorization levels needed.

In the next chapter, we'll learn about the most fundamental unit of code written by Chef developers: is a **recipe**. Components of a recipe and its resources (among other things) will be covered next.

5
Starting the Journey to the World of Recipes

We have our Chef server setup done by now. You must be itching to get your hands dirty with writing Chef code and bootstrapping your infrastructure using it. We'll look into the different components that can be managed through Chef using the concept of resources. Once we are familiar with different resources, we'll see how we can utilize them in our recipes. We'll also see some best practices in writing recipes.

Before we start off, we need to understand what the term "recipe" really means.

In the world of Chef, a recipe is the most fundamental unit of code that is executed. It can be considered as the most fundamental configuration element within an organization. A recipe is a piece of code written in Ruby and it defines everything that is required to configure a system or part of it. A system can comprise of different components. For example, you may have a machine that is acting as a database and web server simultaneously. You can either have a single recipe to configure this machine or you can have multiple recipes – one to configure a database, one to configure a web server, and yet another to set up a barebones machine. Eventually, you can apply all these recipes on the concerned machine using a `run_list`. In the course of this chapter, we will cover the best practices to handle these cases and many others.

Recipes are nothing but simple Ruby code that defines how the system is going to get to a particular state. A system comprises multiple components and each of these components is handled by means of a resource.

A resource is a statement of configuration policy. It describes the desired state of an element in our system. Each resource statement in a Chef recipe corresponds to a specific part of infrastructure – a file, cron job, package, service, and so on.

Recipes group together these resource statements and describe the working configuration of the entire system. Cookbooks are eventually used to collect recipes and store them on the Chef server.

As you can see, resources are used to define the different components of a system. However, all these components are handled differently across different platforms. To ensure that resources are handled in the right manner, Chef comes with the concept of providers. There are different providers for different resources and, depending on the platform and `platform_version`, the right provider is selected, which then acts on the concerned resource.

For example, let's assume that we want to install a package called `telnet` and we specify this as follows:

```
package "telnet" do
  action :install
end
```

Now, depending on the platform on which this is executed, the right provider is chosen and the `telnet` package is installed. On Debian-based systems, it will make use of `apt`, while on RHEL/CentOS it'll make use of `yum`.

The platform to be chosen is determined by Ohai. Ohai is a Ruby gem that is installed alongside Chef during standard installation and can be executed as a command – `ohai`. Ohai checks for the platform and `platform_version` on every chef-client run and this information is used to decide the provider. We'll discuss Ohai and its associated plugins at length in later chapters.

In this chapter, we'll learn about the different resources provided by Chef, how providers help execute resources, and eventually how we bundle resources in Chef recipes.

Resources

A resource is nothing but a Ruby block with four components – a type, a name, one or more attributes, and one or more actions. The following is a typical way to declare a resource in a Chef recipe:

```
type "name" do
  attribute "value"
  action :type_of_action
end
```

All actions have a default value. For example, the package resource's default action is :install and hence, if we just want to install a package, we can just say:

```
package "package_name"
```

This will take care of the installation of the latest available version of the package called package_name.

The chef-client handles the processing of recipes in two phases. In the first phase, resource collection is built. In this phase, all the recipes mentioned in run_list are evaluated in the order specified. All the resources described in the recipes are identified and collected into a collection. All the libraries are loaded first to ensure that all Ruby classes and language extensions are available. This is followed by the loading of attributes, then by lightweight resources, and eventually all definitions. Finally, all the resources are loaded in order from the collection. This phase is referred to as the **compilation phase**.

With all the information collected, chef-client configures the system. Each resource is executed in the order identified by the run_list and finally by the order in which it's defined in the recipe. Each recipe is mapped to a provider. The provider takes the necessary steps to complete the action and finally the resource is processed. This phase is referred to as the **convergence or execution phase**.

Every resource in Chef has some actions and some attributes associated with it. There are some actions and attributes that are common to every resource and then there are some that are very specific in nature. Let's look at common actions and attributes first:

Action	Description
:nothing	It defines a resource that does nothing. It is generally used to define a resource that is later notified by another resource.

The following is an example of the :nothing action:

```
service "splunk" do
  action :nothing
  supports :status => true, :start => true, :stop => true, :restart =>
true
end
```

So here we've defined a resource of type `service`, having the name `splunk`. We don't want this resource to do anything for now. Maybe later on we'll use some other resource to do something useful with this resource. For example, maybe we'll use a change in the config file to trigger a restart later on. This concept is referred to as notification/subscription and we'll have a deeper look at this a little later.

Attribute	Description
`ignore_failure`	If the associated resource fails for some reason, it shouldn't let a Chef run fail. This attribute has the value `false` by default.
`provider`	This is used to specify a provider using `Chef::Provider::Long::Name`.
`retries`	This specifies how many times we should catch an exception for this resource and retry. This attribute has the default value `0`.
`retry_delay`	This is used to specify a delay between retries. The default value is `2`.
`supports`	This is a hash of options that help in describing capabilities associated with a resource. This attribute is primarily used by the `user` and `service` resources.

Let's say you have a service that is flaky in nature; however, you want to give it a shot by starting it through Chef. It'll be wise to make use of `ignore_failure` for such services because, in case it's unable to start, the Chef run will fail:

```
service "flaky_service" do
  action :start
  ignore_failure  true
end
```

Now let's say you are setting up the machine for use using the Node.js app. You want to set up an npm package and you aren't aware of redguide/nodejs (`https://github.com/redguide/nodejs`). You went ahead and wrote your very own provider to install the package using npm (we'll learn more about providers later on. For now, just consider them as a mechanism to perform some action). You can easily make use of the `provider` resource to specify which provider Chef should make use of while installing the concerned resource:

```
package "my_npm_package" do
  provider Chef::Provider::Package::NPM
end
```

Coming back to the flaky service, say you wanted to retry the start of the flaky service two to three times before declaring it as a failure. You can do so using the `retries` and `retry_delay` attributes:

```
service "flaky_service" do
  action :start
  retries 3
  retry_delay 5
end
```

Now Chef will retry starting the service three times with a delay of five seconds between each retry. If the service is unable to start, the Chef run will eventually fail.

Guard attributes

There are certain attributes that can be used to evaluate the state of a node during the execution process of a chef-client run. Based on the result of the evaluation, the attribute is used to tell chef-client whether it should continue the execution of that specific resource or not. These attributes are referred to as guard attributes or conditionals. A guard attribute either accepts a string or a block of Ruby code as a value.

If a string is supplied as a value, the string is considered as a command, and if the execution of the concerned command yields 0 as the return value (also known as exit status), the guard is applied or else not.

If a Ruby block is supplied as a value, the block is executed as Ruby code. The block must return either `true` or `false`.

Guard attributes are typically used to ensure that the Chef resource is idempotent. It checks whether the desired state is present or not. If the state is already present, the chef-client run does nothing for the concerned resource.

The following attributes can be used to define a guard:

Attribute	Description
`not_if`	This prevents a resource from being executed if the condition is `true`
`only_if`	This ensures that a resource is executed only if the condition is `true`

The following arguments can be used with the `not_if` and `only_if` guard attributes:

Argument	Description
`:user`	This specifies which user the command will run as
`:group`	This specifies which group the command will run as
`:environment`	This can be used to specify a hash containing environment variables
`:cwd`	This is used to set the current working directory before running a command
`:timeout`	This is used to set the timeout for a command

For example, let's assume that we are installing a package called `package_name` and we want to install it only on systems running RHEL 6.x.

Here is how we can accomplish this using the `not_if` guard attribute:

```
package "package_name" do
  action :install
  not_if { platform_family?('rhel') &&
    node['platform_version'].to_f  <  6.0 }
end
```

Here is how we can accomplish this using the `only_if` guard attribute:

```
package "package_name" do
  action :install
  only_if { platform_family?('rhel') &&
    node['platform_version'].to_f  >= 6.0 }
end
```

Resources that pass strings as argument to guard attributes can also specify an interpreter that can be used to evaluate the string command. This is done using the `guard_interpreter` attribute to specify a script-based resource – `bash`, `csh`, `perl`, `powershell_script`, `batch`, `python`, and `ruby`.

As we saw, we can have an environment attribute associated with a resource. Guard attributes are generally running commands. However, unless `guard_interpreter` is defined, guard attributes won't use environment variables declared using the `environment` attribute. To ensure that the right environment variable is passed to the command that is passed to `guard_attribute`, the environment variable should be explicitly defined for `guard_attribute` or `guard_interpreter`.

For example, say we want to start a Java application but we want to ensure that we don't trigger the start if the application is already running. Being lazy as most of us sysadmins are, we didn't bother creating init scripts to manage the start/stop of the application or check the status. However, our Java application is intelligent enough to report its status if we pass an argument status to our application. Now, being a Java app, we want to ensure that we have the right JAVA_HOME path set before we go about triggering the command to start the app or check the status.

The following is one way to handle this:

```
bash "some_app" do
  environment { "JAVA_HOME" => "/usr/java/default" }
  code "java /apps/some_app/app start"
  not_if "java /apps/some_app/app status"
end
```

However, this isn't the right way to go about handling our situation because the environment variable JAVA_HOME isn't available to the java some_app status command. One way to do it correctly is this:

```
bash "some_app" do
  environment { "JAVA_HOME" => "/usr/java/default"  }
  code "java /apps/some_app/app start"
  not_if "java /apps/some_app/app status", :environment => {
    'JAVA_HOME' => '/usr/java/default' }
end
```

Another way to handle this is using guard_instructor as follows:

```
bash "some_app" do
  guard_interpreter :bash
  environment { "JAVA_HOME" => "/usr/java/default" }
  code "java /apps/some_app/app start"
  not_if "java /apps/some_app/app status"
end
```

Now, maybe we want to execute the command to check the application status as a user called the application and we want to ensure that our current working directory is /apps/some_app while the command is executed. The following example will help us accomplish this:

```
bash "some_app" do
  environment { "JAVA_HOME" => "/usr/java/default" }
  code "java /apps/some_app/app start"
```

```
    not_if "java /apps/some_app/app status", :user => "application",
      :cwd => "/apps/some_app", :environment => { "JAVA_HOME" =>
      "/usr/java/default" }
end
```

Resources can perform some action or trigger an event for another resource using a notification mechanism. The following are the available notifications for all the resources available in Chef:

Notification	Description
notifies	This is used to notify some other resource to take an action if the state of this resource changes
subscribes	If the state of any other resource changes and we want some action to be taken on this resource, then we make use of subscribes

When notified, we may expect action to happen either immediately or we might want all notifications to be queued up and executed at the end of the chef-client run. Chef provides us with the concept of notification timers just for this:

Timer	Description
:immediately	When immediately is specified, the notification results in the immediate execution of an action on the concerned resource
:delayed	This tells Chef to queue up the notification and execute it right at the end of the chef-client run

Let's say we are managing a web server such as Nginx and we want Nginx to reload every time a change is pushed to its configuration file – nginx.conf. We can accomplish this using the notification mechanism very easily:

```
service "nginx" do
  supports :restart => true, :reload => true
  action :enable
end

cookbook_file "/etc/nginx/nginx.conf" do
  source "nginx.conf"
  owner "root"
  group "root"
  mode "0644"
  notifies :reload, "service[nginx]", :immediately
end
```

The is can also be done through the `subscribes` notification as follows:

```
cookbook_file "/etc/nginx/nginx.conf" do
  source "nginx.conf"
  owner "root"
  group "root"
  mode "0644"
end
service "nginx" do
  supoorts :restart => true, :reload => true
  subscribes :reload, "cookbook_file[/etc/nginx/nginx.conf]",
  :immediately
end
```

One thing we need to understand most of all is the fact that notifications on resources are queued. So let's say we have the following piece of code:

```
template '/etc/ntp.conf' do
  notifies :restart, 'service[ntp]'
end
service 'ntp' do
  action :start
end
```

This code will take the following actions:

1. Update the template.

2. Queue the restart of the service.

3. Start the service.

4. Restart the service (due to notification).

Lazy evaluation of attributes

There may be times when we don't know the value of an attribute until the execution/convergence phase of the chef-client run. During such times, lazy evaluation of attribute values can be very helpful. In such cases, we pass on a Ruby block along with the keyword `lazy` to the attribute and the code block is evaluated to figure out the value to be associated with the concerned attribute. For example:

```
cookbook_file "some_file" do
  source "some_file"
  owner lazy { "ruby_block containing some Ruby code" }
end
```

With knowledge about how resources are handled by Chef, let's move on to see what different resources are available for use and how to make best use of them. We'll only look at the most commonly used resources here. You can refer to the documentation at `http://docs.getchef.com/chef/resources.html` for details about specific resources not mentioned here.

The package resource

The `package` resource is one of the most widely used resources. This resource is used to manage packages on a system.

The `package` resource uses the following syntax:

```
package "package_name" do
  attribute "value"
  ....
  action :action
end
```

Here, `package_name` is the name of the package you want to manage and `attribute` refers to some attribute that might be associated with this package; for example, the version of the package. There is an optional `action` value that refers to the action that we want to take against this package. The default action is `:install`, which takes care of the installation of the concerned package.

Consider the following as an example:

```
package "telnet" do
  action :install
end
```

This will install the `telnet` package on the concerned machine.

As we discussed earlier, we can skip specifying the default actions and hence the last piece of code can be written in a much more compact form as follows:

```
package "telnet"
```

Let's say we want to install a specific version of a package. For example, we might be making use of MongoDB in our setup and we had set up a machine a few months back that used version X of MongoDB. However, recently a new version of MongoDB, Y was added to the repositories. Now, whenever the package resource is used, it'll pick up version Y of the package for installation. This can result in lots of issues as there might be compatibility issues between versions X and Y.

To ensure that the same version of the package is installed, you can specify the version of the package while making use of the `package` resource:

```
package "mongo" do
  version "X"
end
```

The `package` resource has the following actions associated with it:

Action	Description
:install	This is the default action and is used to install the package specified.
:upgrade	This is used to ensure that the latest version of the package is installed on the system. If the package is not installed beforehand, then this is equivalent to using :install.
:remove	This is used to uninstall a package.
:purge	This will uninstall the concerned package and will also remove the concerned configuration files.
:reconfig	This action is used to reconfigure a package.

The `package` resource can have the following attributes associated with it:

Attribute	Description
allow_downgrade	This is used by the yum_package resource to downgrade a package to satisfy dependency requirements. The default value is false.
arch	By default, yum will install a version of the package that is in line with the architecture of your system. However, there might be times when you want to install a package with a particular architecture. This attribute can be used to define that architecture.
flush_cache	This is used to flush the yum cache before or after a yum resource is either installed, upgraded, or removed. This can have the values :before or :after.
options	There will be times when you might want to pass additional options to apt, yum, and so on. You can pass those options through the options attribute.
package_name	If your package name is weird and you don't want to make your package resource definition look ugly, you can always specify the right name of the package to be installed through package_name.
source	This is an optional attribute used to define the path of the local file that will be used by the package manager for installation purposes.

Attribute	Description
version	The version attribute helps us define a particular version of the package that should be installed on the machine.
gem_binary	This is very specific to the gem_package resource and it is used to specify which gem command should be used to set up a Ruby gem. This is most useful in cases where we have multiple versions of Ruby and RubyGems lying around.

We've already seen the package resource example earlier with the default option. Let's see how can we make use of other actions and available attributes to fine-tune our installation requirements if needed.

Case 1: We want to install a specific version of MongoDB, and if any other version is installed, we should just remove it and install this specific version:

```
package "mongodb" do
  action :upgrade
  allow_downgrade true
  version "xxxx"
end
```

Case 2: A new version of Git has appeared in the RPMForge repository and it's available in the rpmforge-extras repo. However, this repo is not enabled and you don't want to enable it forever. You also don't want to use the base repository while installing Git. If Git is already installed on the machine, you want to ensure that it's upgraded to the latest version available on the RPMForge repository. (The assumption is that you have RPMForge set up on your machine):

```
package "git" do
  action :upgrade
  flush_cache :before
  options "--enablerepo=rpmforge-extras --disablerepo=base"
end
```

Case 3: You've accidentally installed two versions of a package, namely version-1 and version-2. Now you want to get rid of version-1 completely from the machine:

```
package "package_name" do
  action :purge
  version "version-1"
end
package "package_name" do
  action :reconfig
end
```

Case 4: You have an RPM package on your machine and want to install it through Chef:

```
package "package_name" do
  source "/tmp/package.rpm"
end
```

This will pick up the default provider for your system type. If it's RHEL/CentOS, yum will be used. However, you might want to make use of the RPM provider for installation purposes. You can do that as well as follows:

```
package "package_name" do
  source "/tmp/package.rpm"
  provider Chef::Provider::Package::RPM
end
```

The package resource can be considered as a wrapper over several other resources that are also meant to install different software. There are quite a few such resources, for example, gem_package, easyinstall_package, dpkg_package, yum_package, and rpm_package. Unless you are trying to install a software that is specifically meant to be installed through these resources, it's always good to make use of the generic package resource.

For more details, refer to http://docs.getchef.com/resource_package.html.

The cookbook_file resource

Most of the time, the job of systems administrators is confined to the installation of software and eventually configuring them. The configuration is mostly done by means of files: be it your web server configuration, your database server configuration, or the management of users. Most of the time, everything is just manageable by modifying the concerned files. This is especially true for Unix/Linux/BSD systems. In fact, there is a famous phrase, "Everything is a file", for such systems. Chef allows us to maintain the right and consistent version of configuration files across a large set of systems through the cookbook_file resource.

Using the cookbook_file resource, we can transfer files to the concerned machine running chef-client. The files are initially kept in the COOKBOOK_NAME/files folder. We'll learn more about the organization of cookbooks later in the book.

The cookbook_file resource has the following syntax:

```
cookbook_file "name" do
  attribute "value"
```

```
    . . .
    action :action
  end
```

Here, `name` refers to the name of the file we wish to manage. If the `path` attribute is not defined in the resource, then the `name` attribute is referred to as the path to the file.

Chef makes use of the `Chef::Provider::CookbookFile` provider to manage files through the `cookbook_file` resource.

The following actions can be associated with the `cookbook_file` resource:

Action	Description
`:create`	This is used to create a file. This is the default action.
`:create_if_missing`	This is used to create a file only if it does not exist.
`:delete`	This is used to remove a file.
`:touch`	This is used to update the access time and modification time for a file.

The following attributes can be associated with the `cookbook_file` resource:

Attribute	Description
`atomic_updates`	This is used to perform atomic updates on a per-resource basis. The default value is `true`.
`backup`	This defines the number of backups to keep for a file. The default value is 5.
`cookbook`	This defines the name of the cookbook where the file can be found. This defaults to the current cookbook.
`force_unlink`	If the target file is a symlink, then this attribute if set to `true` will unlink the file and create a new file. The default value is `false`.
`group`	This is a string or ID to identify the group owner.
`owner`	This is a string or ID to identify the user.
`mode`	This is a quoted string specifying the octal mode of a file.
`path`	This is the path to the location where the file will be created.
`source`	This is the location of file in the `/files` directory in the cookbook located in the Chef repository.
`manage_symlink_source`	This is used to detect and manage the source file associated with a symlink. When set to `true`, chef-client will manage the source file associated with symlink. If set to `nil`, chef-client will manage the source file but will throw a warning. If set to `false`, chef-client will not manage the source file. The default value is `nil`.

As we saw earlier, the file is picked up from the `/files` directory in the cookbook located in chef repository. Let's say we have a cookbook called `nginx` that is used to manage the Nginx web server. The configuration file for Nginx is called `nginx.conf` and we want to use our cookbook to set up Nginx on RHEL/CentOS and Ubuntu/Debian boxes. Now there is catch, as the Nginx configuration uses a different user to start the Nginx worker process. On Ubuntu, the user is `www-data` while on RHEL, the user is `nginx`. So how do we keep two versions of the same file and yet tell Chef to set it up correctly? There are two ways to do this.

The following is not the right way (though it works just fine):

1. Create two folders `nginx/files/default/debian` and `nginx/files/default/redhat` and keep `nginx.conf` for Debian/Ubuntu in `nginx/files/default/debian` while keeping `nginx.conf` for RHEL/CentOS in `nginx/files/default/redhat`.

2. Now declare the `cookbook_file` resource as follows:

```
cookbook_file "/etc/nginx/nginx.conf" do
  case node[:platform]
  when "centos","redhat"
    source "redhat/nginx.conf"
  when "ubuntu","debian"
    source "debian/nginx.conf"
  end
  mode "0644"
  owner "root"
  group "root"
end

OR
cookbook_file "/etc/nginx/nginx.conf" do
  source "#{node[:platform_family]}/nginx.conf"
  mode "0644"
  owner "root"
  group "root"
end
```

So here we've made use of the `case` statement to decide which platform we are working on and decide the source for the `cookbook_file` resource accordingly. This will work just fine; however, there is a more elegant and correct way to accomplish the same thing.

The correct way is as follows:

1. Create the following folders: `nginx/files/centos`, `nginx/files/ubuntu`, `nginx/files/redhat`, and `nginx/files/debian` and push the correct `nginx.conf` file into the concerned folders.

2. Declare the `cookbook_file` resource as follows:

```
cookbook_file "/etc/nginx/nginx.conf" do
  source "nginx.conf"
  mode "0644"
  owner "root"
    group "root"
end
```

This will ensure that the correct `nginx.conf` file is picked up due to a concept called file specificity. In Chef, you can ensure the specificity of a file by keeping files under different folders. The precedence order is as follows in decreasing order of specificity:

1. `host-node[:fqdn]`
2. `node[:platform]-node[:platform_version]`
3. `node[:platform]-version_components`
4. `node[:platform]`
5. `default`

It's sad that there is no way to ensure that you can keep `node[:platform_family]` in this precedence order as of now, and hence we have to create `nginx/files/centos` and `nginx/files/redhat`, though both have `redhat` as a value for `node[:platform_family]`. A request has been made to get this feature soon; however, till then, you might want to modify the `preference_for_path` method in `cookbook_version.rb`, which can be found in `$GEM_PATH/chef-$CHEF_VERSION/lib/chef`.

For more details, refer to `http://docs.getchef.com/resource_cookbook_file.html`.

The directory resource

The `directory` resource is used to manage directories on concerned machines.

The syntax for using the `directory` resource is as follows:

```
directory "name" do
  attribute "value"
  ...
  action :action
end
```

Here, `name` is used to define the name of the `directory` resource. If the `path` attribute is not present in the definition of the `directory` resource, the "name" is considered to be the path as well.

The following actions are associated with the `directory` resource:

Action	Description
:create	This is used to create a directory. This is the default action.
:delete	This is used to delete a directory.

The following attributes can be associated with the `directory` resource:

Attribute	Description
path	This is used to specify the path of the directory.
owner	This is a string or ID used to specify the owner of the directory.
group	This is a string or ID used to specify the group owner of the directory.
mode	This is a string to define the permissions associated with the directory using octal mode. Generally, a directory should have the execute permission associated with it in order for it to be browsable.
recursive	This is used to create or delete parent directories recursively. The owner, group, and mode attribute values hold true only for leaf directories. The default value is `false`.

Consider the following as an example:

```
directory "/tmp/a/b" do
  owner "user"
  group "user"
  mode "0755"
  recursive true
end
```

This will create a directory, /tmp/a/b, on the concerned machine. However, the group, owner, and mode attributes will only apply to directory b. There are times when you'll want them to be applied to the entire directory tree or part of it. For such cases, you can do something like this:

```
["/tmp/a", "/tmp/a/b"].each do |dir|
  directory dir do
    owner "user"
    group "user"
    mode "0755"
  end
end
```

The following example will delete directories recursively:

```
directory "/tmp/a" do
  action :delete
  recursive true
end
```

For more details, refer to http://docs.getchef.com/resource_directory.html.

The file resource

The file resource can be used to manage the files present on a node. We can use this resource to even modify the contents of a file. It should be noted, however, that Chef provides no way to update the existing files using this resource. The original file will be overwritten if any changes are pushed. This is among the most basic resources to manage a file on a node. This should only be used if the file contents are not required to be pushed from some external source other than some strings.

The syntax of the file resource is as follows:

```
file "name" do
  attribute "value"
  ...
  action :action
end
```

The following actions can be associated with this resource:

Action	Description
:create	This is used to create a file. This is the default action.
:create_if_missing	This is used to create a file only if it's missing.

Action	Description
`:delete`	This is used to delete a file.
`:touch`	This is used to update the access time and modification time of the file.

The `file` resource can have the following attributes associated with it:

Attributes	Description
`atomic_update`	This is used to perform atomic updates on a per-resource basis. The default value is `false`.
`backup`	This determines the number of backups to keep for the file. The default value is `5`.
`content`	The value for this attribute is a string that will be written to the file.
`owner`	This is a string or ID that will determine the owner of the file.
`group`	This is a string or ID that will determine the group owner of the file.
`mode`	This is a string containing permissions for the file in octal mode.
`force_unlink`	If the concerned file is a symlink and the value for this attribute is `true`, then the chef-client run will unlink the file and create a new file. The default value is `false`.
`manage_symlink_source`	If the value of this attribute is `nil`, Chef will manage the source file associated with symlink and throw a warning. If the value is `true`, Chef will manage the source file associated with symlink quietly. If the value is `false`, Chef will not manage the source file. The default value is `false`.
`path`	This attribute determines the path to the file. If not present, the name of the resource is considered for determining the path of the file.

Consider the following as an example:

```
file "/tmp/somefile" do
  content "Hey ya !"
  owner "user"
  group "user"
  mode "0640"
end
```

This will create a file called `somefile` in the `/tmp` directory with the content `Hey ya!`. The file will be owned by a user called `user` and group ownership of the file will be associated with the group called `group`. The file will be created with mode `640`, which means read/write for owner, read-only for group, and no permissions for others.

For more details, refer to `http://docs.getchef.com/resource_file.html`.

The execute resource

The `execute` resource can be used to execute a command. Commands executed by the `execute` resource aren't generally idempotent. One must make use of `not_if` and `only_if` to guard this resource for idempotence.

The syntax of the `execute` resource is as follows:

```
execute "name" do
  attribute "value"
  ...
  action :action
end
```

The following actions can be associated with the `execute` resource:

Action	Description
`:run`	This is used to execute the command. This is the default action.
`:nothing`	This is used to prevent a command from running. It's primarily meant to ensure that the command is executed only when the `execute` resource is notified by some other resource.

The following attributes can be associated with the `execute` resource:

Attribute	Description
`command`	This defines the name of the command to be executed. If not mentioned, the name of the resource is considered to be the name of the command by default.
`path`	This is a list containing different strings with each string corresponding to a location in which to search for the command. The default value uses the system path.
`user`	This is the username or ID used to execute the command.
`group`	This is the group name or ID used to execute the command.
`timeout`	This is the amount of time the command will wait before getting timed out.

Attribute	Description
cwd	This specifies the current working directory from which to run the command.
creates	This is used to prevent a command from creating a file if the file already exists.
returns	This is the return value of the command. This is an array of acceptable values. This is especially useful in cases when the command doesn't return 0 upon successful execution.
environment	This is a hash of environment variables.
umask	This specifies the file creation mask.

As we discussed earlier, we must make use of the guard attributes not_if and only_if to ensure the idempotency of the command being executed by the execute resource or we can use the creates attribute. Let's see a few examples.

Example 1: Run a script to test the Nginx config:

```
execute "test-nginx-config"
  command "nginx -t -c /etc/nginx/nginx.conf"
  path ["/opt/nginx/sbin"]
  action :nothing
  subscribes :run, "cookbook_file[/etc/nginx/nginx.conf]",
    :immediately
end
```

Example 2: Extract a tar ball archive:

```
execute "package_xyz" do
  cwd "/opt"
  command <<-EOH
    curl <URL> | tar zxf -
  EOH
  not_if { ::File.exists?("/opt/package_xyz") }
end
```

Instead of using a guard attribute, we could've also made use of the creates attribute associated with the execute resource as follows:

```
execute "package_xyz" do
  cwd "/opt"
  command <<-EOH
    curl <URL> | tar zxf -
  EOH
  creates "opt/package_xyz"
end
```

The `creates` attribute here ensures that the command doesn't re-run the next time as the file will already be present.

For more details, refer to `http://docs.getchef.com/resource_execute.html`.

The cron resource

The `cron` resource is used to handle cron entries that are used for scheduling jobs to run at a particular time. The `cron` resource requires crontab to be present on the concerned machine.

The syntax for the `cron` resource is as follows:

```
cron "name" do
  attribute "value"
  ...
  action :action
end
```

The following actions can be associated with the `cron` resource:

Action	Description
:create	This is used to create a new cron job. If an entry already exists with the same name, then this will update the job settings. This is the default action.
:delete	This is used to remove a cron job.

The `cron` resource can have the following attributes:

Attributes	Description
command	This attribute defines the command or script that will need to be executed.
day	This is the day of the month when the cron job will execute. The acceptable values for this attribute are integers between 1 and 31. The default value for this attribute is *.
hour	This is the hour at which the cron job will execute. The acceptable values are 0 to 23. The default value is *.
minute	This is the minute at which the cron job will execute. The acceptable values are 0 to 59. The default value is *.
month	This is the month in the year when the cron job should run. The acceptable values are 1 to 12. The default value is *.
weekday	This is the day of the week when the cron job should run. The acceptable values are 0 to 6 with Sunday = 0. The default value is *.
path	This is used to set the PATH environment variable.

Attributes	Description
shell	This is used to set the SHELL environment variable.
user	This specifies the name of the user under whose account the cron job will be set up.
mailto	This sets the MAILTO environment variable.
home	This is used to set the HOME environment variable.

A * as a value for the day, hour, minute, month, and weekday attributes should be interpreted as "every". For example, if the value for the day attribute is *, it means every day.

Cron jobs, unlike daemons, can only execute a set of instructions every minute at a minimum. If you need to run commands at intervals that are less than 60 seconds, make use of a daemon. The following are some examples of cron jobs:

Example 1: Run a command every day at 1 AM as a user named user1:

```
cron "GIVE_ANY_USEFUL_NAME" do
  command "SPECIFY_COMMAND_HERE"
  user "user1"
  hour "1"
  minute "0"
end
```

Example 2: Run a command every 5 minutes:

```
cron "GIVE_ANY_USEFUL_NAME" do
  command "SPECIFY_COMMAND_HERE"
  user "user1"
  minute "*/5"
end
```

Example 3: Run a command every Sunday at 8 AM:

```
cron "GIVE_ANY_USEFUL_NAME" do
  command "SPECIFY_COMMAND_HERE"
  user "user1"
  hour "8"
  minute "0"
  weekday "0"
end
```

Users can verify the sanity of the cron entries by manually inspecting the crontab entry using the command crontab -l. This command will list all the cron jobs set for the concerned user.

For more details, refer to `http://docs.getchef.com/resource_cron.html`.

The service resource

Most of the daemons and startup scripts are generally managed through the concept of services. The `service` resource is useful for managing such scripts. Different operating systems have different mechanisms to manage services. Most of Unix and its variants make use of an init daemon to manage services; many modern-day systems on the other hand have started using an event-based replacement called upstart. Mac OS X makes use of launchd and so on. Chef provides us with a wrapper resource called `service` that allows us to manage the startup scripts in a convenient way.

The syntax of the `service` resource is as follows:

```
service "name" do
  attribute "value"
  ...
  action :action
end
```

When the `service_name` attribute is not specified, `name` is also the name of the service on the concerned machine.

The following actions can be associated with the `service` resource:

Action	Description
`:enable`	This ensures that the service starts up at boot time
`:disable`	This ensures that the service never starts up at boot time
`:start`	This starts the concerned service
`:stop`	This stops the concerned service if running
`:restart`	This restarts the concerned service
`:reload`	This reloads the configuration for the service

The `service` resource can have the following attributes associated with it:

Attribute	Description
`init_command`	This is the path to the init script associated with the service. In general, it's usually `/etc/init.d/SERVICE_NAME`. Its default value is `nil`.
`pattern`	This is the pattern to look for in a process table.
`priority`	This attribute determines the relative priority of the program for start and shutdown ordering. It can be an integer or a hash.

Attribute	Description
`reload_command`	This specifies the command used to reload the configuration.
`stop_command`	This specifies the command used to stop the service.
`start_command`	This specifies the command used to start the service.
`restart_command`	This specifies the command used to restart the service.
`status_command`	This specifies the command used to get the status of the service.
`supports`	This specifies a list of attributes that control how chef-client will attempt to manage a service – `:status`, `:restart`, or `:reload`. If the service supports these actions, then set `true` against these; if not, say `false`.
`service_name`	This is used to specify the name of the service. If it's not specified, the name of the `service` resource is used by default.

There is no fixed provider meant for the `service` resource and this is quite obvious too, because we have so many different kinds of systems. The following is a list of providers for the `service` resource:

Provider	Description
`Chef::Provider::Service::Init::Debian`	This is used on Debian/Ubuntu platforms
`Chef::Provider::Service::Upstart`	This is used on platforms where upstart is available
`Chef::Provider::Service::Init::Freebsd`	This is used on the FreeBSD platform
`Chef::Provider::Service::Init::Gentoo`	This is used on the Gentoo platform
`Chef::Provider::Service::Init::Redhat`	This is used on Red Hat and CentOS platforms
`Chef::Provider::Service::Init::Solaris`	This is used on the Solaris platform
`Chef::Provider::Service::Init::Windows`	This is used on the Windows platform
`Chef::Provider::Service::Init::MacosX`	This is used on the Mac OS X platform

Let's see some examples of the `service` resource in action.

Example 1: Manage the `nginx` web server service:

```
service "nginx" do
  supports :status => true, :restart => true, :reload => true
  action [ :enable, :start ]
end
```

Example 2: We want to manage a service using upstart if we are on a system running Debian or its variants and the OS version is > X; otherwise, we want to use the default init daemons to manage a service:

```
service "example_service" do
  if node["platform_family"] == "debian"  and node["platform_
version"].to_f > X
        provider Chef::Provider::Service::Upstart
  end
  action :start
end
```

Example 3: Do not start the service unless its configuration file has been pushed. Till then just enable the service:

```
service "example_service" do
  action :enable
end
cookbook_file "example_service_config" do
  source "example_service_config"
  owner "root"
  group "root"
  mode "0644"
  notify :start, "service[example_service]", :immediately
end
```

For more details, refer to http://docs.getchef.com/resource_service.html.

The bash resource

If you are working on any Unix or its variants and the service/execute/cookbook_file combo wasn't good enough for you, you can use the bash resource, which is like the mother of all solutions! The bash resource is used to execute scripts using the bash interpreter. This resource can also use all the actions and attributes associated with the execute resource. As with execute, the commands that are executed using the bash resource aren't idempotent by nature and hence we should make use of not_if and only_if to ensure idempotency.

The syntax of the bash resource is as follows:

```
bash "name" do
  attribute "value"
  ...
  action :action
end
```

When the `command` attribute is not specified while declaring the `bash` resource, then the name of the resource is considered to be the command to be executed.

The following actions can be associated with the `bash` resource:

Action	Description
`:run`	This runs the script. This is the default action.
`:nothing`	This means don't run the script. This is useful in cases where we want some other resource to trigger the run action for this `bash` resource.

The following attributes can be associated with the `bash` resource:

Attributes	Description
`code`	This is a quoted string containing the code to be executed.
`command`	This is the name of the command to be executed.
`creates`	This is used to prevent a file from being created if it already exists.
`cwd`	This changes the current working directory. The code concerned with the `bash` resource will run from within this directory.
`user`	This is the username or ID that will be used to execute the code.
`timeout`	This is the amount of time (in seconds) a command will wait before timing out. The default value is one hour or 3,600 seconds.
`path`	This is an array of paths to be used for searching the command.
`flags`	These are one or more flags that are passed on to the bash interpreter.
`environment`	This is a hash of environment variables.
`returns`	This can be an array of accepted values. By default, if the command exits with 0, it's considered to be a success.
`group`	This is the group name or group ID to be used while executing the command.
`umask`	This is the file creation mask.

In general, if you have a bunch of commands that need to be executed along with some logic to be placed in between, you are better off using the `bash` resource rather than trying to fit in everything under a command inside the `execute` resource. However, it has some pitfalls, because the `bash` resource generally has a set of instructions to execute and, if one of the instruction misbehaves, it's quite hard to diagnose the problem very quickly. Let's see a few examples of the `bash` resource in action.

Example 1: Set up HAProxy from source:

```
bash "setup_haproxy" do
  user "root"
  cwd "/tmp"
  code <<-EOH
  wget "http://www.haproxy.org/download/1.5/src/haproxy-
    1.5.2.tar.gz"
   tar -zxf haproxy-1.5.2.tar.gz
   cd haproxy-1.5.2
   ./configure
   make
   make install
   EOH
end
```

In this example, we are downloading the 1.5.2 version of HAProxy and trying to build it rather than installing it through packages.

This example will keep on repeating itself during every chef-client run. In order to avoid that, let's add a not_if guard:

Example 2: Set up HAProxy from source with idempotency:

```
bash "setup_haproxy" do
  user "root"
  cwd "/tmp"
  code <<-EOH
  wget "http://www.haproxy.org/download/1.5/src/haproxy-
    1.5.2.tar.gz"
   tar -zxf haproxy-1.5.2.tar.gz
   cd haproxy-1.5.2
   ./configure
   make
   make install
   EOH
   not_if  { ::File.exists?("/usr/local/sbin/haproxy") }
end
```

Example 3: Set up a Java application from a tar ball and run it as a user named user1:

```
bash "setup_javaapp" do
  user "user1"
```

```
      cwd "/apps"
      path "/usr/default/java/bin"
      environment {"JAVA_HOME" => "/usr/default/java"}
      code <<-EOH
      wget "http://www.example.org/javaapp.tgz"
      tar -zxf javapp.tgz
      cd javaapp
      java app &
      EOH
      not_if { ::File.exists?("/apps/javaapp") }
    end
```

Here, we've ensured that the JAVA_HOME environment variable is set and the Java command is found in the path /usr/default/java/bin. This example obviously requires write permission for user1 on the path /apps.

For more details, refer to http://docs.getchef.com/resource_bash.html.

The template resource

So we've understood how to push the configuration files through the cookbook_file resource. We know how to manage other resources like start, stop, restart, or reload if a configuration file changes. However, as we were happily going about managing our infrastructure using these known resources, one day we realized that now we have multiple files lying around in our chef-repository. Maybe they are different versions of configurations for different operating systems or different versions of the same operating system. Mostly, these configuration files won't greatly differ. Often, we see that there is just one change between configuration files across different operating systems. Considering this, it seems like a waste to duplicate our efforts in maintaining different configuration files. Templates are just the right choice in such cases.

Templates are **Embedded Ruby (ERB)** templates that can be used to generate files on-the-fly based on the logic and variables contained within the template. Templates are allowed to contain Ruby expressions and they are the best way to manage configurations across different environments in an organization. The templates should be placed inside the /templates directory of your cookbook.

The template resource has two components:

- The template resource, declared in the recipe itself
- The template file itself

The syntax for declaring the `template` resource is as follows:

```
template "name" do
  source "template_file.erb"
  attribute "value"
  ...
  action :action
end
```

The `source` attribute points to the file in the Chef repository inside the `templates/default` directory of the cookbook where the recipe is loaded from.

The following actions can be associated with the `template` resource:

Action	Description
`:create`	This creates the file using the ERB template. This is the default action.
`:create_if_missing`	This creates the file using the ERB template only if the file to be managed is not already created.
`:delete`	This deletes the file.
`:touch`	This updates the access and modification time for the file.

The `template` resource can have the following attributes:

Attributes	Description
`atomic_update`	This is used to perform atomic updates on a per-resource basis. The default value is `true`.
`backup`	This is used to specify the number of backups to keep. The default value is `5`.
`cookbook`	This is used to specify the name of the cookbook where the file is located. The default value is the current cookbook.
`force_unlink`	If the file to be managed is symlink, this attribute if set to `true` will unlink the symlink and create a file.
`manage_symlink_source`	If set to `true`, the source file associated with symlink will be managed. This is only relevant if the concerned file to be managed is a symlink.
`owner`	This is a string or an ID used to specify the owner of the file.
`group`	This is a string or an ID used to specify the group owner of the file.
`mode`	This is a string containing the permissions for the file in octal mode.

Attributes	Description
path	This is the path to the file. If this attribute is not present, the name of the resource is used to identify the path.
source	This is the location of the template file. By default, chef-client will look in the /templates directory. When the local attribute is set to true, we can use this attribute to specify the path to an ERB template on the node.
variables	This is where things become different with the cookbook_file resource. We can pass variables along with the concerned values to the ERB template using a hash containing the list of variables. The variables in the ERB template are replaced with the values passed on from the template resource.
helper	This is used to define an inline helper module or function. The default value is { }.
helpers	This is used to define an inline helper module or a library. The default value is [].
local	This is used to load a local template. This will allow us to use ERB templates residing on the node where chef-client is running.

As with cookbook_file, the template resource also follows the same order of file specificity:

1. host-node[:fqdn]
2. node[:platform]-node[:platform_version]
3. node[:platform]-version_components
4. node[:platform]
5. default

Let's examine a quick example to understand the concept behind the template resource.

Configure the Nginx web server config. We are assuming that only the config change between Debian/Ubuntu and RedHat/CentOS is the user used to execute the Nginx worker. And hence it's a one-line change as shown here.

The following is the Debian/Ubuntu Nginx config:

```
user www;
worker processes 1;
events {
  worker connections 1024;
}
http {
```

```
}
...
```

The following is the CentOS/RedHat Nginx config:

```
user nginx;
worker processes 1;
events {
  worker connections 1024;
}
http {
}
...
```

As you can see, the only difference is on the first line and we should make use of templates here to avoid keeping two copies of this configuration.

First create an ERB template file in `templates/default` named `nginx.conf.erb`:

```
user <%= @user %>;
worker processes 1;
events {
  worker connections 1024;
}
http {
}
...
```

Next, in your recipe, add the `template` resource as follows:

```
if node[:platform_family] == "debian"
  nginx_user = "www"
elsif node[:platform_family] == "redhat"
  nginx_user = "nginx"
else
  nginx_user ="nobody"
end
template "/etc/nginx/nginx.conf" do
  source "nginx.conf.erb"
  owner "root"
  group "root"
  mode "0644"
  variables ({
    :user => nginx_user
  )}
end
```

Helper modules

Chef even allows us to extend the functionality of templates by means of helper modules. We can adopt one of the following three approaches to implementing helper modules:

- An inline helper method
- An inline helper module
- A cookbook library module

One can use the `helper` attribute in a recipe to define an inline helper method. One can make use of the `helpers` attribute to define an inline helper module or a cookbook library module.

Let's see a few examples of each.

Inline methods

First of all, embed the `helper` attribute in your `template` resource:

```
template "/tmp/myfile" do
  helper(:print_greeting) { "Hey there !" }
end
```

Next use the `helper` method in your template file:

```
Greetings : <%= print_greeting %>
```

Inline modules

First of all, declare the helper modules inline or on a per-resource basis as follows:

```
template "/tmp/myfile" do
  helpers do
    def print_greeting
      "Hey there !"
    end
    def print_goodbye
      "Bye my friend !"
    end
  end
end
```

Now we can use these helper methods anywhere in our template file.

Library modules

We can even keep these helper modules in a library. To do so, create a file {cookbook_name}helper.rb in the libraries folder of your cookbook and define all the concerned helper methods there as follows:

```
helpers do
  def print_greeting
    "Hey there !"
  end
  def print_goodbye
    "Bye my friend !"
  end
end
```

Once done, you can use these helper methods in your template by first including the library in your template resource as follows:

```
template "/tmp/myfile" do
  helpers({cookbook_name}helper)
end
```

Partial templates

A template can be built in such a way that it allows several other smaller templates to be referenced. These smaller template files are referred to as partials. A partial can be referenced in a template by using the render method as follows:

```
<%= render "partial_file.erb", :options => { } %>
```

Here, partial_file.erb is the name of the partial template file and options can be one of the following:

Option	Description
:cookbook	By default, the partial template is searched in the same cookbook where the top-level template was loaded from. This can be used to load the partial templates from different cookbooks.
:local	This can be used to load the partial template from the local node where chef-client is executing.
:source	By default, the partial template is identified by its filename. This can be used to specify a different name or local path to use.
:variables	This is a hash of the variable_name => value that will be used by the partial template file.

One can perform quite a lot of computations and use lots of logic inside ERB templates, which make them an indispensable tool for managing configuration files; however, one shouldn't just go about doing all the heavy logic lifting inside the templates and instead should rely on helper modules or recipes.

For more details, refer to `http://docs.getchef.com/resource_template.html`.

There are plenty of other resources like `git`, `gem_package`, `link`, `ohai`, `mount`, `python`, `perl`, and so on that can be put to effective use for managing almost every aspect of system configuration.

Recipes

So we saw how we can make use of resources to manage different components of the system configuration. Now let's see how to make use of recipes to arrange these resources in a way that allows us to manage our infrastructure efficiently.

A recipe is nothing but a collection of resources with a stir of Ruby code along with attributes as spices. Once you've chosen the right attributes, added them in the right order along with resources, and stirred everything together well using custom Ruby code, you have a wonderful recipe in your hand that can be happily fed to the underlying infrastructure.

We have already learned a lot about resources; let's see what attributes are and how to make good use of them.

Attributes

An attribute is nothing but a key-value pair. We have a whole bunch of attributes to deal with when working with Chef. Ohai, for example, generates tons of attributes for us to consume and play around with. Then we can specify the attribute at node level while running chef-client. Those attributes are referred to as node attributes. The attributes used in recipes are referred to as recipe attributes. These recipe attributes can either add to an already large list of attributes or they can override certain preexistent attributes. When recipe attributes take precedence over default attributes, the chef-client applies new settings and values during the chef-client run on the concerned node.

Types of attributes

An attribute can be of one of the following types:

Type	Description
`default`	This attribute has the lowest precedence and cookbooks should make use of these attributes as often as possible.
`force_default`	If an attribute is already defined in a role or environment and the cookbook specifies the attribute with the same name but with the `force_default` type, then the attribute defined in the cookbook will take precedence.
`normal`	This attribute persists in the node object. It has higher precedence than the `default` attribute.
`override`	This attribute takes precedence over the `default`, `force_default`, and `normal` attribute. It is most often specified in a recipe but can be specified in the attribute file, role, or environment too. It should be used only if required.
`force_override`	This attribute ensures that the `override` attribute in the cookbook takes precedence over the `override` attribute defined in the role or environment.
`automatic`	This attribute is usually defined by Ohai during the chef-client run. These attributes have the highest precedence and they can't be overridden.

Including recipes

A recipe need not work all alone on its own. Chef provides us with a way to include other recipes through the `include_recipe` method. When a recipe is included in another recipe, then the resources are loaded in the exact order as specified.

The syntax for including a recipe is as follows:

```
include_recipe "recipe"
```

Any recipe that is included needs to be mentioned as a dependency in the metadata definition as well.

Say we have a cookbook called x having a default recipe and there is another cookbook called y having a default recipe. We now want to include y in x. To do so, we'll need to mention `include_recipe "Y"` in the default recipe of the cookbook x and along with that we'll also need to add y as a dependency in the metadata associated with the cookbook x.

To do so, edit the `metadata.rb` file associated with the cookbook X and add the following code:

```
depends "Y"
```

The run_list

Finally, in order to execute a recipe, it has to be added to `run_list`. Let's say we have a cookbook with the following structure:

```
cookbooks/
  nginx/
    recipes/
      default.rb
      mod_ssl.rb
```

Now, as you can see, we have two recipes associated with the cookbook called `nginx`. One of them is the default recipe and it can be loaded into `run_list` just by using the name of the cookbook. The other recipe, called `mod_ssl.rb`, can be loaded into `run_list` by using the name `nginx::mod_ssl` as shown here:

```
{
  "run_list": ["recipe[nginx]","recipe[nginx::mod_ssl]"]
}
```

We can use Knife to add a recipe to `run_list` associated with a node as follows:

```
knife node run list add NODENAME recipe[nginx], recipe[nginx::mod_ssl]
```

Recipe DSL methods

Recipe DSL is a Ruby DSL and hence anything that can be done using Ruby can also be done in a recipe. Other than Ruby code, recipe DSL provides support for using attributes, data bags, and search results in a recipe. It also provides four helper methods to check for the node's platform from within the recipe.

The helper methods are as follows.

The platform method

The `platform` method can be used to identify the platform on which the chef-client run is executing. For example:

```
if platform?("redhat","centos")
  # Write code for systems which have platform as redhat or centos
end
```

The platform_family method

The `platform_family` method can be used to identify the platform family on which the chef-client run is happening. For example:

```
if platform_family?("debian")
   # Write code for systems which have platform family as debian.
   # These include systems running Debian/Ubuntu etc.
end
```

The value_for_platform method

The `value_for_platform` method can be employed to use a hash to select a particular value depending on the value of `node['platform']` and `node['platform_version']`. For example, we may want to set a variable with a certain value if `node['platform']` is redhat or centos and a different value if `node['platform']` is debian or ubuntu. This can be easily achieved using the `value_for_platform` method. For example:

```
package_name = value_for_platform(
   ["centos","redhat"] => "httpd",
   ["debian","ubuntu"]  => "apache2"
)
```

This will set the value for the `package_name` variable to either `httpd` or `apache2` depending on which platform the chef-client run is happening on.

The value_for_platform_family method

Just like `value_for_platform`, the `value_for_platform_family` method uses a hash to select a particular value depending on the value of `node['platform_family']`. We could've rewritten the last example in `value_for_platform` more compactly, using `value_for_platform_family`, provided we want to encompass all operating systems belonging to a particular operating system family. For example:

```
package_name = value_for_platform_family (
"centos" => "httpd",
"debian" => "apache2"
)
```

There are a few other methods that might be useful while writing recipes.

The attribute method

The `attribute` method will return `true` if one of the listed arguments to this method belongs to the list of attributes returned by Ohai. For example:

```
if node.attribute?('ipaddress')
```

```
    #Write code that you wanted to execute if node has an ipaddress
end
```

The resources method

The `resources` method can be used to search for a resource in a collection of resources. The return value of this method is the resource object found in the collection or nil.

Let's say we have a file resource declared as follows:

```
file "/tmp/testing" do
  owner "root"
end
```

Maybe after the execution of a few blocks of code, we want to set the content of the file resource that we declared earlier. We can do this as follows:

```
f = resources("file[/tmp/testing]")
f.content "Hey there"
```

Other than these methods, there are ones that allow us to search data bags and then there are search methods that allow us to search data that is indexed by the Chef server. We'll cover those later when we look into data bags and the Chef API in detail.

Best practices when writing recipes

As with any coding practice, there are some good practices that, when adopted, lead to better code quality:

1. *Don't repeat yourself.* This is especially important because generally system administrators have the habit of working in silos. Every other system administrator feels some sense of pride in having a repository full of tools of trade that he/she has written himself/herself. Now, there is nothing wrong with that; however, almost 95 percent of tools are rewrites. Avoid doing so with your recipes. Reusability is a wonderful concept and rather than wasting time in writing recipes from scratch, make use of recipes that are already available within the community. If you are really feeling the itch, write a wrapper, work with the community to improve features in a cookbook, or extend the available set of cookbooks by writing recipes for things for which there isn't any cookbook currently available.

2. *Don't feel stupid when using the include_recipe method.* It's a wonderful method and you are encouraged to use it as much as possible. In fact, a long recipe is not a great idea if the functionality associated with it can be broken down into different smaller entities. For example, consider a recipe to handle the Nginx web server installation. Now, we can do everything like managing SSL certificates and so on inside the `default.rb` file. However, it's not wise to do that because, as soon as you go down that route, you give up on reusability as the recipe is no longer reusable.

3. *Don't specify versions of packages directly in the recipe.* Rather, make good use of attributes and declare an attribute like `node["app_name"]["version"]` and use it in your recipe. The same goes for the specification of ports, log file locations, PID file locations, and so on.

4. *Try to ensure idempotency*, especially with the `execute` and `bash` resources.

Summary

This pretty much sums up our journey into the world of recipes. In this chapter, we learned about resources, the two-phase model used by chef-client, and the use of guard attributes. We also saw lots of resources and eventually we learned about using them in recipes. We also learned about DSL methods and run lists. With knowledge about the best practices you should follow, you should now be able to write a recipe with all the different resources and attributes.

In the next chapter, we'll look at cookbooks and LWRPS in more detail.

6
Cookbooks and LWRPs

So, we have learned how to manage different components of our infrastructure using the concept of resources. We also learned what a recipe is and how to handle attributes.

Recipes are nothing but simple Ruby code that defines how the system is going to get to a particular state. A system is comprised of multiple components and each of these components is handled by means of resources.

A resource is a statement of configuration policy. It describes the desired state of an element in our system. It also describes how that state can be achieved. Each resource statement in a Chef recipe corresponds to a specific part of infrastructure: a file, a cron job, a package, a service, and so on.

Recipes group together these resource statements and describe the working configuration of the entire system.

The recipes by themselves aren't good enough to configure a concerned host and we need to manage configuration files, along with packages, services, users, and so on. For this purpose, we rely on resources like `cookbook_file`, `template`, and so on. All these components, along with attributes, are eventually stored collectively in a container called `Cookbook`. In this chapter, we'll see how a cookbook is authored, how is it pushed to the Chef server, and so on.

In the previous chapter, we learned about the different resources that can be used to manage the different aspects of a system configuration, but there are times when the existing resources aren't sufficient for our purpose. This is when we need to create custom resource providers, also known as LWRPs or lightweight resource providers. A LWRP is a piece of code written using Chef DSL that can be used to define a new resource and provider. A LWRP provides the steps needed to bring a system from the current state to a desired state. It constitutes two parts – a lightweight resource and a lightweight provider. In this chapter, we'll see how to make use of LWRPs to extend Chef. We'll write our own custom LWRP as well.

Cookbooks

While recipes in the world of Chef are a fundamental unit of execution, a cookbook is the fundamental unit of configuration and policy distribution. A cookbook is a container that is responsible for holding everything. It is needed to configure a component of a system, be it the attributes, configuration files, templates, custom resources (more about resources later in this chapter), recipes, versions, metadata, or libraries/helper functions; everything is packed into a cookbook and is used later on during the execution of Chef code when `run_list` is expanded during the chef-client run on the concerned machine.

Authoring a cookbook

A cookbook has the following directory structure:

```
|-- CHANGELOG.md
|-- README.md
|-- attributes
|-- definitions
|-- files
|    `-- default
|-- libraries
|-- metadata.rb
|-- providers
|-- recipes
|    `-- default.rb
|-- resources
`-- templates
     `-- default
```

The `attributes` folder is meant to contain a list of attributes that can be used within the recipes contained in the cookbook.

The `definitions` folder is meant to contain definitions that can be reused across recipes. This is very similar to compile-time macros. The definitions are very useful in cases where we have repeating patterns in our code.

For example, we might have a web server running Nginx along with Passenger and php-fpm. We would like to have a definition that can help us build the Nginx configuration for Rails and PHP apps. We can go about doing this by first creating a definition, say `nginx_config`, as follows:

```
define :nginx_config,  :type => nil, :base => "/var/www/html",
    :port => 80, :log_file_prefix => nil,
```

```
    template "/etc/nginx/conf/#{params[name]}" do
      source "/etc/nginx/conf/#{params[name]}"
      owner "root"
      group "root"
      mode "0644"
      variables ({
          :root_dir => params[base],
          :type => params[type],
          :port => params[port],
          :log_file => params[log_file_prefix]
      })
    end
  end
```

Now you can use this definition in your recipes to create a new configuration, as follows:

```
nginx_config "foobar.conf" do
   base "/apps/foobar/public"
   type "rails"
   port "80"
   log_file_prefix "foobar"
end
```

The `files` folder is meant to hold up files that are meant to be distributed using the `cookbook_file` or `remote_directory` resource.

The `libraries` folder is meant to contain files that essentially contain Ruby code that is meant to be used as a helper method.

The `metadata.rb` file contains metadata information about the concerned cookbook. It is used to define the version and dependency to other cookbooks as well.

The `recipes` folder is where the recipes are kept. By default, we have a file called `default.rb`. We refer to a cookbook in `run_list` as follows:

```
run_list "cookbook_name"
```

Whenever we do this, we are in effect calling up the default recipe in the concerned cookbook.

One can store as many recipes as required in a cookbook. However, as a good practice, it's always nice to store related recipes in a cookbook. For example, you might not want to store recipes for Nginx and MySQL in the same cookbook.

There are times when a single software component might require different recipes for different modes of operations. For example, MySQL comes with server, client, and development libraries. You might want to only install the MySQL server and client on the server, while on desktop workstations, you might only want to have development libraries. In such cases, it's wise to separate out recipes for the management of MySQL server, client, and development libraries, and include the necessary recipes in `run_list`.

For example, we might choose to have three different recipes called `server.rb`, `client.rb`, and `dev.rb` in a cookbook called `mysql`. For a machine with the role of SQL server, we would have `mysql::server` and `mysql::client` in the `run_list`, while for a developer workstation, we would keep `mysql::client` and `mysql::dev` in the `run_list`.

The `resource` folder is meant to keep any custom resource provider that we might create. We'll see more about this later in the chapter.

The `templates` folder is meant to contain dynamic templates that can be used to create configuration files dynamically.

This directory structure can either be created manually or you can make use of Knife to create it automatically for you:

```
knife cookbook create <cookbook_name>
```

You may add details like copyright, license, and e-mail into `knife.rb` and whenever you issue this command, the required information will be automatically filled up for you. The following are the concerned values that need to be filled up in `knife.rb` for this to work:

```
cookbook_copyright "Your Company, Inc."
cookbook_license "apachev2"
cookbook_email "me@foobar.com"
```

Knife, by default, will create version 0.1.0 of the cookbook. If you want to change it, edit the `metadata.rb` file associated with the concerned cookbook.

Uploading a cookbook to the Chef server

Once you've authored a cookbook on a developer workstation, you can upload it to the Chef server using Knife as follows:

```
knife cookbook upload <cookbook_name>
```

This command will search for a cookbook called `cookbook_name` in the `cookbooks/` folder of your Chef repository on your workstation and will eventually upload the contents to the concerned Chef server.

The uploaded cookbook is stored on the Chef server in a bookshelf. The content is stored as flat files as part of a cookbook version. The cookbook content is stored by content checksum. If two different cookbooks or different versions of the same cookbook include the same file or template, the bookshelf will store the file just once.

Deleting a cookbook

A cookbook can be deleted from the Chef server using Knife as follows:

```
knife cookbook delete <cookbook_name> [<version>]
```

If there are multiple versions of a cookbook, it'll ask, "which version do you want to delete?" If you want to delete all versions of a cookbook, you may use the following command:

```
knife cookbook delete <cookbook_name> -a
```

If you are sure that no file in the existing cookbook is being referenced by any other cookbook, you may even choose to purge the cookbook:

```
knife cookbook delete <cookbook_name> -p
```

This will entirely remove a cookbook from the Chef server. Purging a cookbook will disable any cookbook that references one or more files from a cookbook that has been purged.

Testing a cookbook

So, you've authored the cookbook and are now eager to push it to the Chef server. However, before you go ahead, you might want to test it for any syntax errors. You can use Knife to do this job for you, as follows:

```
knife cookbook test <cookbook_name>
```

This will check all `.rb` and `.erb` files for syntax errors in a specified cookbook.

Cookbook versioning

The cookbooks on the Chef server are versioned. A cookbook version represents a set of functionalities that are different from the cookbook on which it is based. One might keep different versions of a cookbook due to many different reasons – adding an improvement, updating a bug fix, and so on. This concept of versioning is referred to as semantic versioning (http://semver.org). A cookbook version can even be frozen to ensure that no further updates are allowed in the concerned version of the cookbook.

Cookbook versions follow a format of x.y.z, where x, y, and z are decimal numbers and are used to represent major (x), minor (y), and patch (z) versions.

Operators available for use with versioning

The following operators can be used along with cookbook versions:

Operator	Description
=	Equal to
>	Greater than
<	Less than
>=	Greater than or equal to
<=	Less than or equal to
~>	Approximately greater than

Say you have two cookbooks, A and B. There are two versions of cookbook A available on Chef server – 0.1.0 and 1.2.0. If you want to have the dependency set to A@0.1.0 for cookbook B, then you can say so in metadata.rb by issuing the following statement:

```
depends "A", "= 0.1.0"
```

However, say you are going to push some patches to the 0.1.0 version of cookbook A, and you want to ensure that B is always dependent on the 0.1.x version, where x denotes the latest patch number. In such cases, you can specify the dependency as follows:

```
depends "A", "< 0.2.0"
```

If you want to use a particular version of a cookbook in your node's run_list, you can do so by using @ as follows:

```
{"run_list": ["recipe[cookbook_name@version_number]"]}
```

For example, the following statement will set `run_list` with the cookbook version 0.1.1:

```
{"run_list": ["recipe[cookbook_name@0.1.1]"]}
```

Freezing versions

After you've pushed all the different patches to a particular version of the cookbook, you will eventually land in a situation where you'll not want any further updates to be pushed to a particular version of a cookbook. In such a an instance, a cookbook version can be frozen, which will prevent any further updates being pushed to that version. This is extremely useful in ensuring that accidental updates aren't pushed to the production environment, and it also helps maintain the reliability of the production environment.

A cookbook version can be frozen using Knife as follows:

```
knife cookbook upload cookbook_name –freeze
```

Once a version has been frozen, it can only be updated by making use of the `–force` option while uploading the cookbook, or else it'll throw an error saying `Version x.y.z of cookbook cookbook_name is frozen. Use –force to override.`

Maintaining multiple versions of cookbooks

There are two strategies to choose when using version control as part of the process of managing cookbooks:

- Use maximum version control when it is important to keep every bit of data within version control
- Use branch tracking when cookbooks are being managed in separate environments using Git branches and when versioning information is already stored in `metadata.rb`

Maximum version control strategy

This approach is useful if we want to version control everything. In the development environment, follow these steps:

1. Bump up the version number of the cookbook as appropriate.
2. Hack.
3. Upload and test.

When we are ready to move the cookbooks to production, we need to do the following:

1. Upload and freeze the cookbooks:

    ```
    knife cookbook upload <cookbook> --freeze
    ```

2. Modify the environment to specify the new version by editing the `environments/production.rb` file.

3. Update the environment:

    ```
    knife environment from file production.rb
    ```

Branch tracking strategy

In the branch tracking strategy approach, we have a branch in our repository for each environment, and the cookbook versioning policy tracks whatever is at the tip of the branch. In this case, we have to ensure that the version is always upgraded before the cookbook is uploaded for testing. For environments that need special protection, we can upload cookbooks using the `-E ENVIRONMENT` and `-freeze` flags. To adopt this approach, follow these steps in a development environment:

1. Bump up the version number of the cookbook as appropriate.

2. Hack.

3. Upload and test.

When we are ready to move the changes to production, just upload the cookbook with automatic version constraints, as follows:

```
knife cookbook upload <cookbook> -E production freeze
```

Custom resources

There are two ways to define custom resources – via LWRPs (lightweight resource providers) or HWRPs (heavyweight resource providers). Before LWRPs were introduced, all extensions to Chef were written using Ruby, and these are referred to as HWRPs. While LWRPs are simple, a HWRP is extremely flexible. The HWRPs reside in the `libraries` folder of the cookbook repository. Chef tries to import anything residing there at runtime and is interpreted as code, rather than a Chef DSL. We'll mostly be concerned with LWRPs in this chapter.

A LWRP is meant to extend chef-client so that custom actions can be defined and eventually used in a recipe.

A LWRP has two main components. They are as follows:

- A lightweight resource that defines a set of actions and attributes
- A lightweight provider that tells the chef-client how to handle each action

One may use existing resources or custom Ruby code to build a new LWRP. Once a LWRP is ready, it's read every time during the chef-client run and processed alongside all of the other resources. During the chef-client run, each lightweight resource is identified and associated with a lightweight provider. A lightweight provider does the job of completing actions that are required by the lightweight resource.

In addition to using a lightweight resource/provider, a custom resource can also be defined using libraries. These resources cannot make use of the recipe DSL and must make use of a specific syntax to call core chef-client resources.

Setup

The lightweight resources and providers are loaded from files that are saved in the following directories inside a cookbook:

- `providers/`: The subdirectory where lightweight providers are located
- `resources/`: The subdirectory where lightweight resources are located

You may find files like `default.rb`, `xyz.rb`, and so on, and the names of lightweight resources and providers will be decided by these filenames. For example, if there is a cookbook called `cookbook_name` and it has a `default.rb` file in the `providers` and `resources` folder, then the provider and resource can be referred to as `cookbook_name`. However, for a resource or provider in a file called `xyz.rb`, the resource and provider will be referred to as `cookbook_name_xyz` and `xyz` respectively.

Let's see an example to understand what elements are required to build our first custom LWRP. We have been entitled with the responsibility to come up with a cookbook to set up Node.js and a few npm packages. We would like to make use of a LWRP called `nodejs_npm` in our recipe to install the npm packages. This new resource should be able to accept the name of the package to be installed, the version of package, and the type of package (`local` or `global`) as an argument. If the package is local, we should be able to specify the path where the package will be installed. Our cookbook is known as `nodejs`.

Resource

The resource is created under the file `resources/npm.rb`:

```
#
# Cookbook Name:: nodejs
# Resource:: npm
#
# Copyright 2014, Sychonet
#
# All rights reserved - Do Not Redistribute
#

actions :install, :uninstall
default_action :install

attribute :package, :name_attribute => true
attribute :type, :kind_of => String
attribute :path, :kind_of => String
```

Our resource has two actions, namely `install` and `uninstall`. Actions determine what can be done by the concerned resource. The next line determines the default action associated with a resource. In our case, the default action is `install`. If we don't specify any action while using our custom resource, the default action that will be triggered would be `install`.

Next, we define a set of attributes associated with our resource. We would like to be able to specify a version, a type, and a path along with the package name. The type would determine if the package is global or local. If a package is local, we can specify a path where we want the package to be installed.

As you can see, the resource is meant to define what to expect from our new LWRP; it doesn't deal with the implementation. For example, nowhere in the resource does it say what the `install` or `uninstall` action is supposed to do. We've defined our resource in a file named `npm.rb`, and hence it'll be referred to as `nodejs_npm`.

Provider

The provider is created under the file `providers/npm.rb`:

```
require 'json'

def package_is_installed?
  if new_resource.type == "global"
```

```
      installed_packages_hash = JSON.parse(`npm list -global -
         json`)['dependencies']
   else
      installed_packages_hash = JSON.parse(`npm list -json`)
         ['dependencies']
   end
   installed_packages = Array.new
   if (new_resource.version.nil?)
      installed_packages_hash.each do |key,value|
         installed_packages << key
      end
      installed_packages.nil? ? false : installed_packages.include?
         (new_resource.name)
   else
      installed_packages_hash.each do |key,value|
         installed_packages << key+"@"+value["version"]
      end
      installed_packages.nil? ? false : installed_packages.include?
         (new_resource.name+"@"+new_resource.version)
   end
end


def setup
   if new_resource.type == "global"
      path="/tmp"
      if new_resource.version.nil?
         command="npm install #{new_resource.package} -g"
      else
         command="npm install #{new_resource.package}
            @#{new_resource.version} -g"
   else
      path=new_resource.path
      if new_resource.version.nil?
         command="npm install #{new_resource.package}"
      else
         command="npm install #{new_resource.package}@#
            {new_resource.version}"

      directory "#{new_resource.path}" do
         action :create
         recursive true
      end
   end
```

```ruby
  end

  def whyrun_supported?
    true
  end

  action :install do
    setup
    description = "Install #{new_resource.package}"
    converge_by(description) do
      execute "Install NPM package #{new_resource.package}" do
        cwd "#{path}"
        command "#{command}"
        not_if { package_is_installed? }
      end
    end
  end

  action :uninstall do
    setup
    description = "Uninstall #{new_resource.package}"
    converge_by(description) do
      execute "Uninstall NPM package #{new_resource.package}" do
        cwd "#{path}"
        command "npm uninstall #{new_resource.package}"
        only_if { packge_is_installed? }
      end
    end
  end
```

The provider is meant to take care of defining these actions. Our provider is created under the file `providers/npm.rb`. It is mandatory for the provider to define all actions declared in the resource. Since we had declared two actions, `install` and `uninstall`, in our resource, we'll need to define both of them in our provider here.

The actions can be written using Ruby and hence allow you the flexibility to write highly customized code to handle a particular action. In our case, we have used the attributes associated with the resource to build some logic that we can use to install or uninstall a given npm package.

Apart from the definition of actions that are defined inside the action block, we've used two functions in our code to help us modularize our code. We have also used a function called `whyrun_supported?`. If this function returns `true`, then the provider can be executed in why-run mode.

Provider DSL

The following methods come packaged with the provider DSL in Chef:

- `converge_by`: This method is used to define what needs to be done when a provider is executed in why-run mode.

- `new_resource`: This method is used to represent a resource as loaded by chef-client during a chef-client run.

- `action`: This method is used to define the steps that need to be taken to define all possible actions that are declared in the resource. Each action must be defined in a separate action block.

- `converge_by`: This method is a wrapper used to tell chef-client what to do if a resource is run in why-run mode. The syntax of the `converge_by` method is:

  ```
  converge_by("message")
  ```

  The code in the `converge_by` method will actually be executed in the execution phase and finally the "updated" state of resource will be updated.

- `current_resource`: This method is used to represent a resource as it exists on the node at the beginning of the chef-client run. The chef-client compares the resource as it exists on the node and tries to execute the steps to allow it to be brought to the desired state. This method is often used as an instance variable (`@current_resource`). For example:

  ```
  action :install do
    unless @current_resource.exists
      <code to install>
    else
      Chef::Log.debug("#{@new_resource} already exists.")
    end
  end
  ```

- `load_current_resource`: This method is used to find a resource on the basis of a collection of attributes. This method asks chef-client to see if a resource exists with matching attributes on the node.

- `updated_by_last_action`: This method is used to notify a lightweight resource that a node was successfully updated.

- `whyrun_supported?`: The why-run mode is used to see what chef-client would've configured on the node without actually modifying the concerned resources. This is very similar to the no-op mode. The why-run mode is very helpful in verifying if everything will be configured in the manner we want. With the `whyrun_supported?` method, the resource can be configured to support the why-run mode. The syntax of this method is as follows:

```
def whyrun_supported?
   true
end
```

When the why-run mode is supported by a lightweight provider, the `converge_by` method is used to define strings that are logged by the chef-client when it is run in why-run mode.

Logging

One can make use of the `Chef::Log` class in a lightweight provider to define log entries that are created during the chef-client run. The syntax for a log message is as follows:

```
Chef::Log.log_type("message")
```

Here, `log_type` can be debug, info, warn, error, or fatal, while message is what we want to log.

One should make use of exception handling to ensure that a log message is always provided. For example:

```
action :some_action
   ...
   begin
      ...
   rescue
      Chef::Log.debug("Some log message in event of failure")
   end
   ...
end
```

With this information in your hands, you should be comfortable in creating your own custom lightweight resources and providers and extend Chef. For more details, you might want to check out http://dougireton.com/blog/2012/12/31/creating-an-lwrp/.

Summary

In this chapter, we went through how cookbooks are structured and how to manage recipes stored in a cookbook. We also learned about versioning and its uses. Finally, we went on to create custom resource providers that can help extend the chef-client by providing new resources.

In the next chapter, we'll move into the world of roles and environments and see how we can group together all these cookbooks under a hood to bootstrap machines with a particular role or in a particular environment.

7
Roles and Environments

We now know how to manage a particular component of our infrastructure using a resource, how to group together resources, and how to manage interactions between different resources by getting them grouped together in a recipe. We also know how to group recipes and attributes together in a cookbook.

However, in most practical use cases, you'll find that no single cookbook is useful for the purpose of configuring a system. This problem can be handled in two ways. One way to handle this issue is to get everything required to be configured on a machine inside one cookbook. Now this approach has a very fundamental flaw, as these recipes/cookbooks won't be reusable to a great extent and they'll be very bulky too. As we all know, a good development practice is to break down things into smaller chunks and include whatever is required when required. Roles specifically allow us to do this.

A role in Chef is a way to group together attributes and cookbooks to facilitate the accomplishment of a particular function. Each role comprises zero or more attributes and a run list. Once we have a role in place, we can use it in the run list associated with the node and then, during the chef-client run, the run list will be expanded and all the attributes and recipes defined in the role's run list are merged into those associated with the node.

The following example case will help you understand this better. Let's say you are a Chef coder at a company and you decide to write a recipe that will help set up a barebones machine with the setting up of a few packages such as iptraf, htop, and so on along with the configuration of the SSH server; let's further say you decide to keep this recipe in a cookbook called base. Now you will be using this recipe on all machines in your infrastructure; however, you'll also want to set up machines individually according to their assigned tasks.

For example, you might have a web server, a database server, and so on. You'll use recipes such as nginx, mysql, and so on to configure a web server or a database server. So, an ideal way to go about bootstrapping a machine with the base recipe and a specific recipe would be to keep the base recipe and the specific recipe in a role and eventually use that role in the run list of the machine. The following is a typical example of a role:

```
webserver.rb
name "webserver"
description "Webserver Role"
run_list "recipe[base]","recipe[passenger]","recipe[nginx]"
override_attributes (
    :app => { :user => "application", :group => "application" }
)
```

This role is meant to configure a web server and, as you can see, it has three recipes in its run list and it's overriding two attributes: node[:app][:user] and node[:app][:group]. I use these two attributes to identify the credentials under which the application will be running.

Once a role is created, it can be used in a node's run list as follows:

```
run_list "role[webserver]"
```

Also, it's a general practice in software development to split infrastructure into different environments. Generally, you will find at least three environments: development, staging, and production. Developers write their code in the development environment; once the code is developed and has passed unit tests, it progresses to the staging environment, where it undergoes integration testing and only when the software has been thoroughly tested in the staging environment does it move to the production environment, where it's exposed to end users.

This practice allows for rapid development without bothering about breaking the impact of changes on functionality of the final product. In some cases, you might even find a functional testing environment or a user acceptance testing environment within your infrastructure. Whatever the number of different environments, one thing that is prominent here is the fact that the configurations of environments tend to vary and hence it becomes important to manage different configurations across different environments. Chef allows us to manage different environments through the concept of "environment".

An **environment** in Chef is a way to map an organization's environments to what can be configured and managed using Chef server. Chef server comes with a default environment called _default and this environment can't be modified or removed.

In this chapter, we'll see how to manage our infrastructure by classifying it into different environments along with ways to make use of roles to group multiple cookbooks together and apply them to a node.

We'll start of by understanding how to manage roles, followed by understanding how Chef handles environment-specific configurations. Once we have an understanding of how roles and environments are managed, we'll look into different types of attributes that can be used with a role or environment and how their precedence is evaluated.

Managing roles

There are multiple ways to manage roles in the Chef ecosystem.

Using Knife

Knife can be used to create, edit, delete, edit, or show a particular role; alternatively, it can be used to push a role file created using Ruby DSL to the Chef server. Knife can also be used to get a list of all roles defined on the Chef server.

Creating a new role

The `knife role create ROLE` command can be used to create a new role. Let's use it to create a role called `webserver` and see the command in action:

```
$ knife role create webserver
```

As soon as you issue this command, an editor will open up. The choice of which editor to make use of can be specified by editing the value of the `knife[:editor]` attribute in your `knife.rb` file.

The file will look like the following:

```
{
    "name": "webserver",
    "description": "",
    "json_class": "Chef::Role",
    "default_attributes": {
    },
    "override_attributes": {
    },
    "chef_type": "role",
```

```
    "run_list": [
    ],
    "env_run_list": [
    ]
}
```

This is a simple JSON file containing various key-value pairs. The following is a description of the different keys and expected values:

Key	Expected value
name	This is the name used to identify this role
description (optional)	This is a description associated with this role
json_class	Chef::Role
default_attributes (optional)	This is a hash containing the different default attributes
override_attributes (optional)	This is a hash containing the different override attributes
run_list	This is a list containing the recipes and roles that should be applied on the machine when this role is expanded during a chef-client run
env_run_list (optional)	This is an environment-specific run list
chef_type	role

Let's add some meaningful values to this file:

```
{
    "name": "webserver",
    "description": "Webserver Role",
    "json_class": "Chef::Role",
    "chef_type": "role",
    "run_list": [
        recipe["base"],"recipe[nginx]"
    ]
}
```

Now save this file and exit your editor. As soon as you exit your editor, you'll see that Knife will contact Chef server and create a new role there corresponding to this JSON file.

Editing an existing role

The `knife role edit ROLE` command can be used to edit an existing role on Chef server. We created our role, `webserver`, earlier. However, between then and now, we managed to create a cookbook to set up logstash, which will allow us to push `webserver` logs to a central server. Let's edit our role to include this recipe into the run list associated with the `webserver` role:

```
$ knife edit role webserver
```

This command will once again open up the JSON associated with the `webserver` role. Edit the concerned values and exit the editor:

```
{
    "name": "webserver",
    "description": "Webserver Role",
    "json_class": "Chef::Role",
    "chef_type": "role",
    "run_list": [
        recipe[base],"recipe[nginx]","recipe[logstash]"
    ]
}
```

Deleting an existing role

The `knife role delete ROLE` command can be used to delete an existing role on Chef server. If you are managing roles through Ruby DSL, then note that this command won't remove the DSL file from the Chef repository but will only remove the role from Chef server.

Let's try and delete the `webserver` role we created earlier:

```
$ knife role delete webserver
Do you really want to delete webserver? (Y/N)y
Deleted role[webserver]
```

As you can see, Knife prompted you to confirm the deletion of the concerned role. If you are very sure about your actions, you can append the command with `-y` and now you won't be asked for confirmation.

Showing details about an existing role

The `knife role show ROLE` command can be used to see the details associated with a particular role on Chef server.

Let's see the details of the `webserver` role we created earlier:

```
$ knife role show webserver
chef_type:          role
default_attributes:
description:        Role to manage webserver
env_run_lists:
json_class:         Chef::Role
name:               webserver
override_attributes:
run_list:
      recipe[base]
      recipe[nginx]
      recipe[logstash]
```

Listing all roles on the Chef server

The `knife role list` command can be used to see a list of all the roles defined on Chef server:

```
$ knife role list
webserver
```

As we had just one role, `webserver`, on the Chef server, we can see that the command returned the name of the role.

Using Ruby DSL

Instead of directly using Knife to create and edit roles, one can make use of Ruby DSL to create files that can later be used to set up the concerned role on Chef server. The benefit of this approach is that we can store these files in the version control system and hence maintain the history of changes we've been making to our roles.

To create a role using Ruby DSL, you have to create Ruby files in a directory called `roles` in your chef-repository. The structure of your repository should look somewhat like this:

```
code/chef-repo [master] " tree -L 1 -d
.
|-- cookbooks
|-- data_bags
|-- environments
'-- roles
```

Once you have the directory created, you can store all your role-related files there and version them in your version control system.

You can specify the following properties in your `roles` file:

- `name`: This is a string used to define the name of your role
- `description`: This is a string used to give a human-friendly description to your role
- `run_list`: This is a comma-separated list of recipes and roles
- `env_run_lists`: This is again a comma-separated list of recipes and roles
- `default_attributes`: This is a hash used to define default attributes
- `override_attributes`: This is a hash used to define override attributes

Let's create our `webserver` role once again. Only this time, we'll make use of Ruby DSL to create a role file first and eventually upload it to Chef server using Knife:

```
roles/webserver.rb
# Role Name:: webserver
# Author: maxc0d3r@sychonet.com
name "webserver"
description "Role to manage webserver"
run_list "recipe[base]","recipe[nginx]"
```

With the file in place, now you can create the role on Chef server using the Knife command `knife role from file FILENAME`:

```
$ knife role from file roles/webserver.rb
Updated Role webserver!
```

Knife responds back with a message saying `Updated Role webserver!`. This means that the role was successfully created on Chef server.

Remember that the role is created on Chef server with the name you specify as the property name in your Ruby file and this has nothing to do with the name of the file itself. So you can create a file `test.rb` with the name of the role specified as `webserver`, use the command `knife role from file test.rb`; and you'll still get the role created under the name `webserver`.

So now we have our role created on Chef server and we just realized that we forgot to add the `logstash` recipe to the run list. No worries, just edit the Ruby DSL file and add `recipe[logstash]` to the `run_list`:

```
roles/webserver.rb
# Role Name:: webserver
# Author: maxc0d3r@sychonet.com
name "webserver"
description "Role to manage webserver"
run_list "recipe[base]","recipe[nginx]","recipe[logstash]"
```

Now use Knife to update the role once again:

```
$ knife role from file roles/webserver.rb
Updated Role webserver!
```

And voilà! Your role is updated with a run list containing the `logstash` recipe.

Always remember that, if you want to make good use of Chef, you should commit everything to a version control system in order to track changes being made to your infrastructure code.

Using a JSON file

As was the case with Ruby DSL, you can make use of a JSON file to manage roles too. The only difference is that you have to specify the additional property called `json_class` with the value `Chef::Role` in your JSON file.

Let's create our `webserver` role using a JSON file:

```
roles/webserver.json
{
    "name": "webserver",
    "description": "Role to manage webserver",
    "json_class": "Chef::Role",
    "run_list": [
        "recipe[base]",
        "recipe[nginx]",
        "recipe[logstash]"
    ]
}
```

Use the `knife role from file FILENAME` command once again to update the role on Chef server:

```
$ knife role from file roles/webserver.json
Updated Role webserver!
```

Using the Chef API

Rather than relying on Knife, you can even use the Chef API to directly manipulate roles.

For example, the following Ruby script will use the Chef API to load config from your `knife.rb` file and use it to find the list of all roles defined on the Chef server:

```
#!/usr/bin/env ruby
require 'chef'
Chef::Config.from_file(File.expand_path("PATH_TO_knife.rb"))
Chef::Role.list.each do |role|
  puts role
end
```

Run this script and you'll get a list of all roles that you've created so far on your Chef server:

```
$ruby list_roles.rb
webserver
http://chef-server.sychonet.com:4000/roles/webserver
```

Similarly, you can use POST requests to create a new role or delete a role. For example, the following piece of Ruby code will delete the role `webserver` from Chef server:

```
#!/usr/bin/env ruby
require 'chef'
Chef::Config.from_file(File.expand_path("PATH_TO_knife.rb"))
role = Chef::Role.load("webserver")
role.destroy
```

Though you'll be using Knife to manipulate roles most of the times, it's useful to know that you can accomplish the same task using the Chef API too. We'll look into this in more detail when we cover the Chef API.

Using the Chef server WebUI

You can also create a new role or edit or delete an existing role by making use of the Chef server web interface. Connect to your Chef server's web interface (usually over port 4040). Once you've logged in to the system, navigate to the section called **Roles** and choose to create a role. You'll be presented with a window as follows:

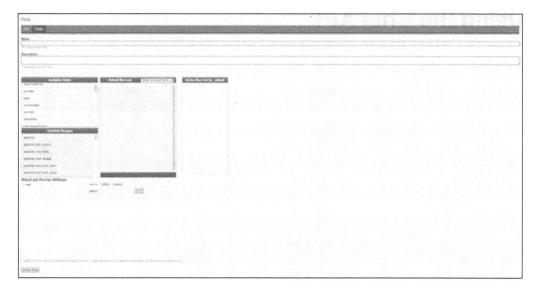

Enter the required details such as the name of the role, description, applicable default, and override attributes and choose the recipes/roles to be added to the run list corresponding to this new role. Once you are done with it, click on the **Create Role** button.

To edit/delete an existing role, you can simply select the concerned role and choose the appropriate action.

Whatever approach you take, it's wise to stick to one or else there is a very high risk of messing things up. For example, if you are maintaining roles through Ruby DSL scripts or JSON files and later you go about editing them through Knife, then you won't be able to find out about the changes without comparing what's on Chef server against what's present on the version control system.

Managing environments

There are multiple ways to manage environments in Chef. They are described in the following subsections.

Using Knife

Knife can be used to create, edit, delete, show information about a particular environment, or list all available environments. It can be used to push the configuration concerned with an environment through a file containing code written using Ruby DSL and eventually this file can be maintained in the version control system.

Creating a new environment

The `knife environment create ENVIRONMENT_NAME` command can be used to create a new environment. Let's use it to create a new environment called `production` and see the command in action:

```
$ knife environment create production
```

As soon as you execute this command, an editor will open up. The choice of which editor to make use of can be configured by editing the value of `knife[:editor]` in your `knife.rb` file.

The file will look something like this:

```
{
    "name": "production",
    "description": "Production Environment",
    "cookbook_versions": {
    },
    "json_class": "Chef::Environment",
    "chef_type": "environment",
    "default_attributes": {
    },
    "override_attributes": {
    }
}
```

This is a simple JSON file containing the following key-value pairs:

Key	Value
name	This is the name used to identify the environment
description	This is the description associated with the environment
json_class	This should be Chef::Environment
chef_type	This should be environment

Key	Value
`default_attributes`	This is a hash containing the different default attributes
`override_attributes`	This is a hash containing the different override attributes
`cookbook_versions`	This is a hash containing a list of cookbooks along with the versions to be used in the concerned environment
`cookbook`	This is a version constraint for a single cookbook

Let's say you are a developer who loves to be on the cutting edge of technology and you want to be sure to keep the latest version of Ruby in the development environment; in the production environment, on the other hand, you want to keep the stable version of Ruby to ensure that things don't break down. This can be accomplished with great ease by using the concept of environments.

Let's presume that your environment files are called `dev.rb` and `prod.rb` and you have a default attribute called `default['ruby']['version']` in your Ruby cookbook's attribute file.

We'll create an `override_attribute` called `['ruby']['version']` with different values for different environments and this will help us deploy different versions of Ruby across the development and production environments.

The `dev.rb` file will be as follows:

```
name "dev"
override_attribute("ruby"=>{"version"=>"2.1-head"})
```

The `production.rb` file will be as follows:

```
name "prod"
override_attribute("ruby"=>{"version"=>"2.1.2"})
```

Now if we do a chef-client run on a machine in the `dev` environment, the `2.1-head` version of Ruby will get installed; for machines in the `prod` environment, the `2.1.2` version will be installed.

Editing an environment configuration

The `knife environment edit ENVIRONMENT_NAME` command can be used to edit the configuration associated with an environment. Let's use this command to edit the configuration of the `production` environment we created earlier:

```
$ knife environment edit production
```

As soon as this command is executed, a JSON file will open up in the editor of your choice:

```
{
    "name": "production",
    "description": "Production Environment",
    "cookbook_versions": {
    },
    "json_class": "Chef::Environment",
    "chef_type": "environment",
    "default_attributes": {
    },
    "override_attributes": {
    }
}
```

Now make the concerned change to the configuration and save the contents and exit the editor. Finally, you'll get confirmation about the environment configuration being saved to Chef server.

Deleting an environment

The `knife environment delete ENVIRONMENT_NAME` command can be used to delete an existing environment:

```
$ knife delete environment production
Do you really want to delete production? (Y/N)y
Deleted production
```

If you don't want to be bothered about the confirmation, add the `-y` argument to the last command:

```
$ knife delete environment production -y
Deleted production
```

Displaying all the environments configured on the Chef server

The `knife environment list` command can be used to get a list of all environments configured on the Chef server:

```
$ knife environment list
_default
production
```

As you can see, we have two environments on our Chef server. The `production` environment was created by us; however, the `_default` environment is provided by default with Chef server.

Showing details associated with an environment

The `knife environment show ENVIRONMENT_NAME` command can be used to show the details associated with an environment on Chef server. This will output the following results:

```
$ knife environment show production
chef_type:          environment
cookbook_versions:
default_attributes:
description:        Production Environment
json_class:         Chef::Environment
name:               production
override_attributes:
```

You may also choose to get the output for this command in other formats such as JSON, using the `--format` argument as follows:

```
$ knife environment show production --format json
{
  "name": "production",
  "description": "Production environment",
  "cookbook_versions": {
  },
  "json_class": "Chef::Environment",
  "chef_type": "environment",
  "default_attributes": {
  },
  "override_attributes": {
  }
}
```

Comparing cookbook versions across environments

The `knife cookbook compare` command can be used to compare cookbook versions across different environments.

Let's say we have two environments in our setup. The `production` environment is as follows:

```
{
  "name": "production",
  "description": "Production environment",
  "cookbook_versions": {
      "nginx": "= 1.0.2"
  },
  "json_class": "Chef::Environment",
  "chef_type": "environment",
  "default_attributes": {
  },
  "override_attributes": {
  }
}
```

And the `development` environment is as follows:

```
{
  "name": "development",
  "description": "Development environment",
  "cookbook_versions": {
      "nginx": "= 2.1.1"
  },
  "json_class": "Chef::Environment",
  "chef_type": "environment",
  "default_attributes": {
  },
  "override_attributes": {
  }
}
```

To know the cookbook versions corresponding to an individual environment, use this command:

```
$ knife environment compare development
        development
nginx   2.1.1
```

To compare cookbook versions between the `development` and `production` environment, use this command:

```
$ knife environment compare development production
        development    production
nginx   2.1.1          1.0.2
```

To compare cookbook versions across all environments, use this command:

```
$ knife environment compare --all
        development    production
nginx   2.1.1          1.0.2
```

Creating or editing an environment using the configuration specified in a file

Rather than directly modifying the environment specification using the `knife create` or `knife edit` commands, we can instead keep the environment-specific configuration in a file and use it for the purpose of setting up the environment. These files can be written either in JSON format or using Ruby DSL.

This is especially useful as it allows us to maintain the configuration file in a version control system. Once we have the files, we can just set up the environment using the `knife environment from file` command as follows:

```
$ knife environment from file production.rb
Updated environment production
```

Using Ruby DSL

Instead of directly editing the environment configuration using the `knife environment create/edit` commands, we can create the configuration files using Ruby DSL or in JSON format and store them in the Chef repository. This allows us to maintain versions of the configuration in a version control system such as Git/SVN. As we saw earlier, this approach can be used to create/edit an environment using the `knife environment from file` command.

To create an environment using Ruby DSL, we have to create Ruby files for each environment in a directory called `environments` inside the Chef repository. The structure of the Chef repository will look something like this:

```
code/chef-repo [master] " tree -L 1 -d
.
|-- cookbooks
|-- data_bags
|-- environments
'-- roles
```

We can specify the following properties in the Ruby files:

- `name`: This is a string used to define the name of the environment. This has to be unique for an organization.

- `description`: This is a string used to provide a description for the concerned environment.

- `cookbook_versions`: This is a hash containing the list of cookbooks along with the versions to be used in the concerned environments.

- `default_attributes`: This is a method comprising a hash containing different default attributes.

- `override_attributes`: This is a method comprising a hash containing different override attributes.

Let's create an environment called `production` using Ruby DSL:

```
environments/production.rb
name "production"
description "Production Environment configuration"
cookbook_version ({
  "nginx"=>"= 1.0.2"
)}
default_attributes "nginx" => { "ports" => ['80','443'] }
override_attributes "nginx" => { "worker_connections" => 2048 }
```

Now we can make use of the `knife environment from file` command to push this configuration to Chef server as follows:

```
$ knife environment from file environments/production.rb
Updated environment production
```

We can also specify this configuration using JSON as follows:

```
environments/production.json
{
  "name": "production",
  "description": Production Environment",
  "cookbook_versions": {
    "nginx": "= 1.0.2"
  },
  "json_class": "Chef::Environment",
  "chef_type": "environment",
  "default_attributes": {
    "nginx": {
      "ports": ["80","443"]
    }
  },
  "override_attributes": {
    "nginx": {
      "worker_connections": 2048
    }
  }
}
```

When specifying configuration as JSON, we have two additional attributes to specify, namely:

- `json_class`: This is always set to `Chef::Environment`
- `chef_type`: This is always set to `environment`

We can also manage environments using the Chef API or the web interface. We'll see more about the Chef API in later chapters and I'll leave exploring the web interface for environment management as an exercise for you.

Setting up an environment on a node

Once environments have been created, we will need to ensure that the nodes are correctly associated with the environments. Again, as with the management of environments, there are multiple ways to associate a node with an environment.

Using Knife

We can make use of the `knife node` command with the `environment_set` argument to set the environment for a node without editing the node object:

```
$ knife node environment_set node01 production
```

This will set the environment for `node01` as `production`. The next time chef-client executes on the node, it'll apply the configuration corresponding to the `production` environment on `node01`.

We can also edit the node object itself and set the `chef_environment` property with the required environment name as follows:

```
$ knife node edit node01
```

This will open up the corresponding `node01` object's JSON in the text editor. Add/edit the `chef_environment` property with the right environment name and save the file to apply the changes:

```
{
    "normal": {
    },
    "name": "node01",
    "override": {
    },
    "default": {
    },
    "json_class": "Chef::Node",
    "automatic": {
    },
    "run_list": [
        "recipe[devops]",
        "role[webserver]"
    ],
    "chef_type": "node",
    "chef_environment": "production"
}
```

We can also move nodes from one environment to another using the `knife exec` subcommand as follows:

```
$ knife exec -E 'nodes.transform("chef_environment:_default") { |n|
n.chef_environment("production")}'
```

This will move all nodes in the development environment to the production environment.

The knife exec subcommand uses the Knife configuration file to execute Ruby scripts in the context of a full-fledged chef-client. For more details, please refer to https://docs.chef.io/knife_exec.html.

Editing the client.rb file on the node

We can add an environment configuration entry into the client.rb file on the machine that is associated with the node object. Let's say our machine corresponding to the node object node01 is called node01.production.domain. To edit client.rb, SSH to node01.production.domain and edit the client.rb file by adding the property called environment as follows:

```
/etc/chef/client.rb
log_level          :info
log_location       STDOUT
chef_server_url    "http://chef-server.sychonet.com:4000"
environment "production"
```

The next time that chef-client executes on this machine, the configuration corresponding to the production environment will be applied to the node object.

If no environment configuration is supplied, then Chef picks up the configuration associated with the _default environment.

You may also associate an environment with a node object using the web UI. However, I'll leave that to you to explore as an exercise.

Once an environment has been associated with a node, you can make use of node.chef_environment to figure out the environment and take the appropriate action in your recipe. This is especially useful when you want to apply some conditional logic to the execution of Chef recipes on the basis of environment. For example, it might be the case that you run a bash script in your recipe using the bash resource; however, maybe you don't want it to be running in any environment other than production. To accomplish this, you can do something like the following in your Chef recipe:

```
if node.chef_environment == "production"
  bash "script" do
     Your chef code here ...
   end
end
```

Now, with the knowledge of how to manage roles and environments, let's see what we can do with attributes within a role or an environment.

Role and environment attributes

We can define an attribute in a role or an environment and use it to override the default settings on a node. When a role or an environment is applied during a chef-client run, the attributes defined in them are compared against those already present on the node. Finally, depending on the precedence order, the right attributes are applied to the node.

A role or environment attribute can be either a `default` attribute or an `override` attribute. It can't be a `normal` attribute.

A `default` attribute is automatically reset at every start of chef-client runs and has the lowest attribute precedence. Any cookbook should be authored to make the most of `default` attributes.

An `override` attribute, on the other hand, has higher attribute precedence over the `default`, `force_default`, and `normal` attributes. A cookbook should be authored to make use of `override_attribute` only when required.

Attribute precedence

Attributes are always applied to a machine by chef-client in the following order:

1. A `default` attribute specified in an attribute file in a cookbook.
2. A `default` attribute specified in a recipe.
3. A `default` attribute specified in an environment.
4. A `default` attributed specified in a role.
5. A `force_default` attribute specified in an attribute file in a cookbook.
6. A `force_default` attribute specified in a recipe.
7. A `normal` attribute specified in an attribute file in a cookbook.
8. A `normal` attribute specified in a recipe.
9. An `override` attribute specified in an attribute file in a cookbook.
10. An `override` attribute specified in a recipe.
11. An `override` attribute specified in a role.
12. An `override` attribute specified in an environment.
13. A `force_override` attribute specified in an attribute file in a cookbook.
14. A `force_override` attribute specified in a recipe.
15. An `automatic` attribute identified by Ohai.

This precedence order can also be visualized as a table as follows:

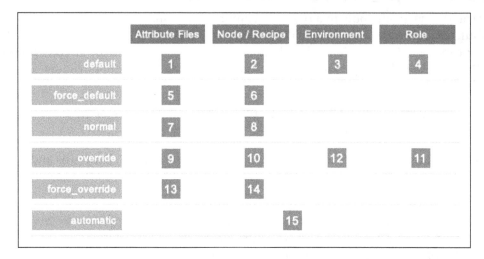

	Attribute Files	Node / Recipe	Environment	Role
default	1	2	3	4
force_default	5	6		
normal	7	8		
override	9	10	12	11
force_override	13	14		
automatic		15		

Or one can visualize it as an overview diagram as follows:

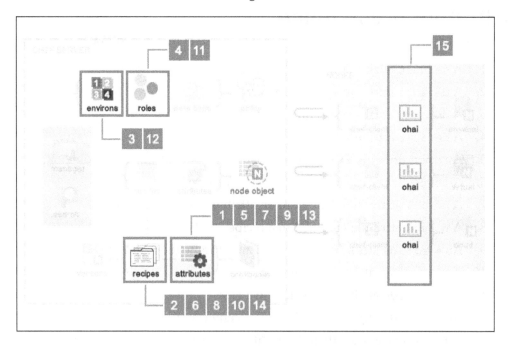

Environment run lists

One of the major reasons why roles aren't popular is due to the fact that it's hard to maintain versioned run lists. For example, you might have created web servers with the role `webserver` that had a run list containing the `base` and `nginx` recipes. Now, today you needed to add another recipe, say `logstash`, to these servers. So you went ahead and added the recipe to the run list in your role and triggered a chef-client run either automatically or manually. This is where you didn't realize that your new recipe code had a bug and now all your ten servers are in a messed-up state.

There are many ways to overcome this issue; however, I like to use environment run lists just for this very purpose. I split my infrastructure into different environments such as `dev`, `staging`, and `production`. Whenever I write a new piece of Chef code, I ensure that I push it into the run list associated with the `dev` environment initially for local testing. Once it has passed there, I add the recipe to the run list associated with the `staging` environment and only once I'm satisfied there do I go about adding it to the run list in the `production` environment.

Environment-specific run lists can be managed using the `env_run_lists` property. Let's see how we can go about adding the `logstash` recipe to the `dev` and `staging` environments while leaving the `production` environment as it is:

```
{
    "name": "webserver",
    "description": "Role to manage a webserver",
    "json_class": "Chef::Role",
    "env_run_lists": {
        "production": [ "recipe[base]", "recipe[nginx]" ],
        "staging": [ "recipe[base]", "recipe[nginx]",
          "recipe[logstash]" ],
        "dev": [ "recipe[base]", "recipe[nginx]", "recipe[logstash]" ]
    }
    "chef_type": "role",
    "default_attributes": {
    },
    "override_attributes": {
    }
}
```

Update your Chef server by pushing this role using Knife. And now, whenever you execute a chef-client run on machines within the `production` environment, only the `base` and `nginx` recipes will be applied; for the `staging` and `dev` environments, on the other hand, the `base`, `nginx`, and `logstash` recipes will be applicable.

Summary

This pretty much sums up our study of roles and environments and their uses. We learned about the different ways of managing roles and environments. We saw how we can make use of attributes in roles or environments and eventually we saw how we can make use of environment run lists and set up different run lists for different environments.

In the next chapter, we'll discuss more about attributes and their uses.

8
Attributes and Their Uses

As we've seen so far, any machine (henceforth referred to as node) can be described through Chef by means of recipes, roles, and environment that it is associated with. However, throughout all this there are a few properties associated with a node as well. A node will have properties such as name, IP address, kernel, FQDN, OS type, and so on, associated with it. All these properties help in defining a system in a more meaningful way. The more properties are associated with a node, the better the quality of its definition. Some of these properties are tightly coupled to the system—for example, OS type, kernel, IP address, and so on—while some are abstract in nature. For example, we might have different kinds of web applications in our setup, some related to finance and others perhaps related to HR. All these applications may be deployed on different machines and they all use the same underlying technology stack; hence, they all have a common role, say `web server`, associated with them. Maybe we want to enforce strict access rules on web applications meant for finance as compared to HR. In order to be able to distinguish between these different sets of instances, we can add a property called `device_class`, which will define which class the node belongs to. This property can have a value *Finance*, *HR*, and so on. Now, we can use this property in our recipes to take an appropriate action. This will also help us identify the instances associated with a particular class of an application very quickly; this will be a real help as your infrastructure grows.

All these properties that are either automatically associated with a node or assigned explicitly by you are called **attributes**. An attribute is a specific detail about the node and is used for the following purposes by Chef:

- To understand current the state of the node
- To determine which state the node was in at the end of the previous chef-client run
- To determine what state the node will be in at the end of the current chef-client run

The attribute list is built during every chef-client run, using various sources:

- Ohai collects lots of properties about the system and returns it in the form of a JSON object to chef-client
- The node object that was saved to the Chef server at the end of the previous chef-client run has attributes associated with it
- During the current chef-client run, any additional attributes or edited attributes — that might come from cookbooks (via an attribute file or recipe), roles, and environments, or due to change in node configuration itself — are gathered

Once a node object is built, all of the attributes are compared and finally the node is updated, depending on the precedence of attributes. Eventually, at the end of the chef-client run, the current state of the node is pushed to the Chef server so that it can be indexed for search.

There has been a significant change in how attributes are handled since Chef version 11; thus, if you are coming from Chef versions prior to Chef 11, pay attention as things have changed considerably.

Attribute naming

This can be confusing for some people, especially those who aren't coming from the Ruby world. You looked up two different cookbooks and, in one of them, you found something like the following in the attributes file:

```
default[:app][:user] = "web-admin"
```

On the other hand, the other cookbook had something like the following:

```
default['app']['user'] = "web-admin"
```

These are two different styles of specifying the keys in a Ruby hash. In one, you are making use of symbols; in the other, you are using strings. You can choose either of these but, for the sake of sanity, try to be consistent. There are some pitfalls in using either approach and there are some inherent benefits too. For example, symbols are immutable and are allocated just once, which is a performance gain. On the other hand, they can be pretty irritating if you are trying to include stuff such as hyphens in their names. If symbols confuse you, stick with strings or vice-versa.

One of the popular lint tools called Foodcritic will complain if symbols are used while accessing node attributes.

Different types of attributes

Chef provides six different types of attributes, as listed in the following table:

Attribute type	Description
default	This attribute is reset upon the start of every chef-client run and has the lowest attribute precedence. A cookbook should make the most use of the default attributes.
force_default	Say you've specified the same default attribute in role and environment along with a cookbook, and you want to ensure that the attribute in the cookbook takes precedence. In order to do so, one must make use of the force_default attribute type.
normal	A normal attribute is never reset and persists with the node object. It has higher precedence over the default attribute.
override	An override attribute has higher precedence over the default, force_default, and normal attributes. It can be defined in a recipe, role, or environment.
force_override	Similar to the force_default attribute, the force_override attribute specified in a recipe takes precedence over the attribute specified in a role or environment.
automatic	When data is collected by Ohai, the collected data is organized as a set of attributes called the automatic attributes. These attributes cannot be modified and have highest precedence.

When a chef-client run starts, all the default, override, and automatic attributes are reset. The chef-client rebuilds them using the data collected by Ohai (the automatic attributes) and by the attributes defined in cookbooks, roles, and environments (the default and override attributes). Finally, at the end of the chef-client run, only a list of the normal attributes is left over; these will persist until the next chef-client run. These normal attributes persist on a Chef server, and chef-client uploads it at the end of its run. We'll see a little later in this chapter how to go about declaring and consuming these different attributes.

You can also make use of custom JSON to specify a list of attributes to be applied to a node by chef-client. These attributes are taken up as the `normal` attributes and persist, so be very careful if you are treading along that path.

Here is an example of an attribute applied to a node using custom JSON.

Problem: We've a cookbook called `nginx` with an attribute file that takes care of the installation of the Nginx web server. We've a default attribute `default['nginx']` `['workers']` with value `512`. Now, we want to override this value of `512` with `1024` for a particular node.

Solution: Create a JSON file, say `/tmp/chef.json`, on the concerned node:

```
/tmp/chef.json
{
  "nginx": {
      "workers": "1024"
    }
}
```

With the file in place, execute the chef-client as follows:

```
#chef-client -j /tmp/chef.json
```

As you'll see once the chef-client run has completed, you'll have `nginx['workers']` as a `normal` attribute associated with the node object. You can confirm this by issuing the following command:

```
$ knife node show NODENAME -a nginx
NODENAME:
  nginx:
    workers:  1024
```

If you have a mechanism to automate this process of creating custom JSON and you are sure that you won't need to adjust the keys or values specified in it, only then use this way to override attributes; otherwise, things will get really messy once you've scaled out your infrastructure and have multiple cookbooks and types of nodes to manage.

Different sources of attributes

An attribute can be defined at multiple places and it is very important to declare an attribute at the right place with right precedence order. During a chef-client run, attributes are collected from the following different sources:

- Nodes (collected by Ohai at the start of each chef-client run)
- Attribute files (associated with cookbook) are collected during compile time
- Recipes (associated with cookbook. The attributes specified in the recipes might be collected during run time as well
- Environments
- Roles

The life cycle of an attribute can be understood by the following sequence of steps:

1. Developer writes attributes in the attribute file, recipe, role, or environment.
2. The concerned code is pushed to the Chef server.
3. During the chef-client run, Ohai collects all the automatic attributes from the node.
4. The chef-client will pull node object from the chef-server, which will in turn bring in the `normal` attributes that are persistent.
5. The chef-client will update the cookbook (if required). This may change the set of attributes associated with an attribute file or a recipe.
6. The chef-client will update role and environment data (if required).
7. The chef-client will rebuild the attribute list and apply the precedence order to come down to a final list.
8. Finally, the node object will be pushed back to the chef-server at the end of the chef-client run.

Let's look at these sources in more detail,

The attribute file

An attribute file is associated with a cookbook and is placed inside the `attributes` directory in a cookbook. During a chef-client run, all the attributes present in an attribute file are collected and evaluated in the context of a node object. Finally, node methods are used to set an attribute value on a node.

The following is a sample attribute file called `default.rb` for the Nginx web server:

```
default['nginx']['workers'] = "1024"
default['nginx']['user'] = "web-admin"
default['nginx']['ports'] = [ "80", "443" ]
```

The use of node object (`node`) is implicit in this case, and the following example and the previous one are both identical:

```
node.default['nginx']['workers'] = "1024"
node.default['nginx']['user'] = "web-admin"
node.default['nginx']['ports'] = [ "80","443" ]
```

Recipes

We can define attributes within a recipe itself. When the chef-client run is initiated, these attributes are collected along with the attributes from other sources, and eventually precedence order is applied on them to get a final list of attributes to be applied to the node.

There has been a significant change in how the attributes are handled in Chef 11. Earlier you could use something as follows to define an attribute in a recipe:

```
node['attribute'] = 'value'
```

This style of declaration is sometimes referred to as Chef 0.7 style. Since Chef 11, this style of declaring attributes is no longer valid and you have to explicitly specify the precedence in order to declare an attribute. So the following is a valid syntax to declare the default attribute in a recipe:

```
node.default['attribute'] = 'value'
```

You can, however, use `node['attribute']` to reference the merged attribute.

Roles and environments

An attribute can be defined in a role/environment, and then be used to override the default attributes specified in recipes/attribute files. When a role/environment is assigned to a node, the attributes are collected from the concerned role/environment and, finally, precedence order is applied to all the attributes collected from cookbooks, roles, environments, node object, Ohai, and so on, and a final list of attributes is prepared.

A role/environment attribute can only be of a `default` or `override` type.

One of the biggest problem with earlier versions of Chef was that the computation of attribute values using the values overridden in roles or environments was not possible without unexpected results.

For example, say you had an attribute file that was doing something like the following:

```
node.default["server_fqdn"] = node["server_name"] + "." +
  node["domain"]
```

Also, say you were overriding the `server_name` and `domain` attributes in your environment or role. Now, this didn't work as intended because in earlier versions of Chef, role/environment attributes were not evaluated until after attributes in attribute files were evaluated. Hence, the `server_name` and `domain` attributes didn't get the right values, and `server_fqdn` was not populated with the expected values.

In Chef 11, role and environment attributes are managed separately from the attributes in attribute files. So, while the attribute file is being evaluated, the roles and environment attributes are readable.

Ohai

All the automatic attributes associated with a node object are collected from the concerned machine using a tool called Ohai. This is a binary that is installed on the node as part of the chef-client installation. There are a wide variety of attributes that are collected by Ohai:

- Platform details
- Network details
- Kernel info
- CPU info
- Filesystem details
- Memory details
- Hostname
- FQDN
- Other configuration details and data fetched using custom Ohai plugins

The `automatic` attributes are used to identify specific details about a node such as an IP address, hostname, kernel version, and so on. These attributes remain unchanged after the chef-client run is over, and are used by the chef-client in read-only mode.

Extending Ohai itself can extend the information provided to the chef-client by Ohai. This is possible through the concept of Ohai plugins. There are a plenty of Ohai plugins already available in the Chef community; if that's not good enough for you, you can write your own custom Ohai plugin really quickly, using a very simple DSL provided by Chef. We'll look into Ohai plugins a little later.

The following are some of the most commonly used automatic attributes:

Attribute	Description
`node['platform']`	This tells us about the platform on which a node is running. This attribute can be used to decide on package names or the location of config files. For example, CentOS.
`node['platform_family']`	This can be used to determine the family of the operating system associated with a node. For example, both Debian and Ubuntu belong to the same `platform_family`:that is, Debian.
`node['platform_version']`	This can be used to determine the version of the operating system release.
`node['ip_address']`	This tells us the IP address of the concerned node.
`node['macaddress']`	This tells us the MAC address of the concerned node.
`node['hostname']`	This tells us the hostname of the concerned node.
`node['fqdn']`	This tells us the fully qualified domain name of the concerned node.
`node['domain']`	This tells us the domain of the concerned node.
`node['recipes']`	This tells us the recipes associated with a node.
`node['roles']`	This tells us the roles associated with a node.

Generally, Ohai comes with several plugins that you might not require and, unless these plugins are disabled, they will get loaded eventually during the chef-client run. For example, you might not need any Windows-related Ohai collectors; alternatively, if your infrastructure is not on Rackspace, you might not need the Rackspace plugin too. To disable loading of Ohai plugins, you can use the following configuration in your node's `client.rb` file:

```
Ohai::Config[:disabled_plugins] = [:OHAI_7_PLUGIN,
  "ohai_6_plugin"]
```

Remember to use the right notation for Ohai 7 versus Ohai 6 plugins. You'll learn more about the differences in the next chapter.

If you want to know how much time each plugin is taking to load, you can make use of the following custom script:

```
benchmark_plugin.rb
#!/usr/bin/env ruby
require 'benchmark'
require 'ohai'
sys = Ohai::System.new()
runner = Ohai::Runner.new(sys,true)
sys.all_plugins.each do |plugin|
  puts plugin.name
  Benchmark.bm do |res|
    res.report {  runner.run_plugin(plugin) }
  end
end
```

Attribute precedence

Attributes are always applied by the chef-client in the following order:

1. The `default` attribute specified in a cookbook attribute file.
2. The `default` attribute specified in a recipe.
3. The `default` attribute specified in an environment.
4. The `default` attribute specified in a role.
5. The `force_default` attribute specified in a cookbook attribute file.
6. The `force_default` attribute specified in a recipe.
7. The `normal` attribute specified in a cookbook attribute file.
8. The `normal` attribute specified in a recipe.
9. The `override` attribute specified in a cookbook attribute file.
10. The `override` attribute specified in a recipe.
11. The `override` attribute specified in a role.
12. The `override` attribute specified in an environment.
13. The `force_override` attribute specified in a cookbook attribute file.
14. The `force_override` attribute specified in a recipe.
15. The `automatic` attribute collected during the Ohai run.

The last attribute in this list has highest precedence and it's the one that dictates the value associated with an attribute.

Note that the precedence order for roles and environments gets reversed between the default and override attributes. The precedence order for the default attribute is environment followed by role; while, for the override attribute, it's role followed by environment.

The force_override attributes are an addition to the attribute types in Chef 11. These are especially useful for people who rely on specifying attributes in recipes and don't wish them to be overridden by the values specified in roles or environments.

Attribute precedence can also be visualized through the following diagram:

	Attribute Files	Node / Recipe	Environment	Role
default	1	2	3	4
force_default	5	6		
normal	7	8		
override	9	10	12	11
force_override	13	14		
automatic		15		

Attribute whitelisting

So, you've got this whole bunch of attributes that have been collected from all different sources and now a final list of attributes has been prepared by the chef-client after applying the precedence order. However, you might not want each and every attribute to persist on the Chef server and this is where we can make good use of whitelisting capabilities. We can specify a whitelist of a set of attributes that we want to be saved by a node. This whitelist can be specified in client.rb. A whitelist is a hash that specifies attributes that need to be saved.

Each attribute type has to be whitelisted separately. Each attribute type—automatic, default, normal, and override—may define whitelists by using the following settings in the client.rb file:

Setting	Description
automatic_attribute_whitelist	This can be used to specify a hash that whitelists the automatic attributes and prevents non-whitelisted attributes from being saved. If a hash is empty, no attribute is saved.
default_attribute_whitelist	This can be used to specify a hash that whitelists the default attributes.
normal_attribute_whitelist	This can be used to specify a hash that whitelists the normal attributes.
override_attribute_whitelist	This can be used to specify a hash that whitelists the override attributes.

Generally, you'll only want to whitelist the automatic attributes, as those are the ones with too many keys.

For example, we might want to only persist the network attribute and prevent all other attributes in the following list of normal attributes:

```
{
    "filesystems" => {
        "/dev/sda" => {
            "size" => "10240mb"
        }
    },
      "network" => {
          "interfaces" => {
              "/dev/eth0" => { ... },
              "/dev/eth1" => { ... }
          }
      }
}
```

To do this, we can specify a whitelist of normal attributes as follows:

```
normal_attribute_whitelist = ["network/interfaces/"]
```

If the attributes contain slashes within the attribute value, for example, in the filesystem attribute /dev/sda, one should make use of an array as follows:

```
normal_attribute_whitelist = [['filesystem','/dev/sda']]
```

With the knowledge of attributes to hand, let's quickly use it to write a cookbook to set up the Passenger gem. Passenger is a very popular Rails application server and is used by many Rails shops for their web app hosting. Our setup has the production and staging environments, and we would like to install Passenger version 4.0.40 in production environment, while everywhere else we are happy with the 4.0.48 version of Passenger.

The following is the associated directory structure of our Chef repository:

```
code/chef-repo [master] " tree -L 1
.
|-- README.md
|-- cookbooks
|-- data_bags
|-- environments
'-- roles
```

We'll have the following files used in this exercise:

```
environments/production.rb
name "production"
description "Production Environment"
default_attributes (
    "passenger" => {
        "version" => "4.0.40"
    }
}
environments/staging.rb
name "staging"
description "Staging Environment"
cookbooks/passenger/attributes/default.rb
default['passenger']['version'] ="4.0.48"
cookbooks/passenger/recipes/default.rb
gem_package "passenger" do
    version node["passenger"]["version"]
end
```

Update the environments, upload the cookbook, and you should be able to see the right version of Passenger installed on the concerned machines.

Summary

This brings us to the end of our journey in the world of attributes. We've learned about different kinds of attributes and the different sources from which attributes are collected. We've also learned about whitelisting of attributes and touched upon the use of Ohai for collection of automatic attributes. For more details about attributes, refer to `http://docs.getchef.com/essentials_cookbook_attribute_files.html`. In the next chapter, we'll dive deep into Ohai and its plugin ecosystem. We'll also see how to go about writing custom Ohai plugins.

9

Ohai and Its Plugin Ecosystem

As part of chef-client run, one of the concerns is to collect information about the underlying operating system, hardware, and other environment-related details. The chef-client relies on a utility called Ohai for this purpose.

Ohai is a tool that is used to detect attributes on a node and, once it has profiled the concerned node, it can emit a JSON data blob, containing all the attributes collected by it. Ohai can be used as a stand-alone utility. However, generally, a chef-client uses it to collect node attributes. When Ohai is used in stand-alone mode, it emits the data as JSON; however, when used by the chef-client, it reports back the data through node attributes.

Ohai comes with its own set of plugins that can be used to extend its functionality or scope of its data collection capabilities.

Ohai is a mandatory requirement for a successful chef-client run; hence it must be present on a node. Generally, it is distributed as a Ruby gem during installation of Chef. To quickly verify the status of the Ohai installation, run the following command:

```
☒  ~  gem list ohai


*** LOCAL GEMS ***


ohai (7.2.4)
```

Cool! So, we have Ohai version 7.2.4 installed on our machine. Keep a note about the version as things have changed between Ohai 6 and 7. We'll be covering Ohai 7 for most part of this chapter; however, I'll try to explain the difference between the versions where it's most required.

As we saw earlier, Ohai is used to collect various attributes corresponding to a node. The following is a list of few different types of attributes collected by Ohai:

- Platform details
- CPU information
- Memory information
- Disk and filesystem information
- Network information
- Kernel details
- Hostnames
- Fully qualified domain name and so on

Attributes collected by Ohai are automatic attributes and chef-client ensures that these attributes aren't changed after the latter is done with the configuration of a node.

As you can see, most of these details are exposed by operating systems through different mechanisms, and hence Ohai comes with collectors for different platforms including Linux, Windows, FreeBSD, OpenBSD, Solaris, AIX, Darwin, and so on. All of these collectors are available as plugins and form a part of the Ohai plugin ecosystem. Now, if you have a particular kind of system to provision and bootstrap, you would not want to enable collectors for other kinds of system as every plugin that is enabled is loaded into memory and can reduce the overall performance of the chef-client run. We'll see how to go about accomplishing this later in this chapter.

There will be times when you want to expose certain attributes via Ohai. For example, say you are running different kinds of instances on AWS (http://aws.amazon. com/ec2/instance-types/). Now, these instances are called by different names on AWS, for example, m1.xlarge, c1.xlarge, and so on. Say you want to expose this instance type name as a node attribute. Now, since this attribute is associated with a node and is something that is not required to be overridden by environments, roles, or cookbooks, we can expose it through Ohai. In order to do this, we can either make use of community Ohai plugins or, if there are none available, you can write your own and make use of it. Later, during the course of this chapter, we'll see how to go about writing our own custom plugins and understanding Ohai API.

Chef uses all these attributes to incorporate system-specific behavior into cookbooks. For example, Chef utilizes the information provided by Ohai to find out the platform details and thereby decide the package manager to use for installation of different packages. It is also used a lot by developers to write the code that can be used to provision machines across different platforms. For example, you might want to create a config file called `httpd.conf` for operating systems belonging to the RedHat family, while for operating systems of the Debian family you might want to set up a configuration file called `apache2.conf`. All this is made possible through different platform-related attributes provided by Ohai.

Running the Ohai binary

Ohai can be executed in stand-alone mode using the following command:

```
$ ohai
{

   ...

  "kernel": {
    "name": "Linux",
    "release": "2.6.32-220.23.1.el6.x86_64",
    "version": "#1 SMP Mon Jun 18 18:58:52 BST 2012",
    "machine": "x86_64"

    ...

}
```

The command scanned through the system, tried to fetch the required details such as kernel, platform, hostname, and so on, and eventually it emitted the output as JSON.

If you know which attributes to look out for, you can quickly write a wrapper around Ohai and use it to fetch the required details. For example, the following script will help you get the required attribute from Ohai output:

```
#!/usr/bin/env ruby
require 'json'
if ARGV.length != 1
  puts "Usage: cohai attribute . For e.g. - cohai kernel.release"
  exit 1
end
```

```
ohai_output = JSON.parse('ohai')')
ARGV[0].split(".").each do |key|
  ohai_output = ohai_output[key]
end
puts ohai_output
```

The Ohai binary searches for the available plugins in a predefined search path. If you want to keep Ohai plugins in a directory that is not the default search path, then you can specify the directory using the –d option, or you can specify the location of the plugin directory in the client.rb file by modifying the value of the Ohai::Config[:directory] property.

The Ohai binary supports the following options:

Option	Description
ATTRIBUTE_NAME	This sets up Ohai to show only the output for named attributes.
-d PATH or --directory PATH	This is the directory in which Ohai plugins are located.
-h or --help	This shows help for a command.
-l level or --log_level LEVEL	This is the logging level to be used while storing logs in a log file.
-L LOGLOCATION or --logfile c	This is the location for a log file.
-v or --version	This is the version of Ohai.

Ohai can be configured through client.rb as well. The following Ohai configuration settings can be added to the client.rb file on the node:

Configuration	Description
Ohai::Config[:directory]	This is the directory where Ohai plugins are located.
Ohai::Config[:disabled_plugins]	This is an array of Ohai plugins to be disabled.
Ohai::Config[:hints_path]	This is the path where the file containing hints for Ohai can be found.
Ohai::Config[:log_level]	This is the logging level to be used while storing logs in a log file.
Ohai::Config[:logfile]	This is the location for a log file.
Ohai::Config[:version]	This is the version of Ohai.

When Ohai is executed independently of the chef-client, then the settings in `client.rb` have no effect.

The way in which we address plugins in Ohai has changed between version 6 and 7. Hence be careful when using configurations such as the following:

```
Ohai::Config[:disabled_plugins]
```

To disable a Ohai 7 version plugin, use the following syntax:

```
Ohai::Config[:disabled_plugins] = [ :PLUGIN_NAME ]
```

To disable a Ohai 6 version plugin, use the following syntax:

```
Ohai::Config[:disabled_plugins] = [ "PLUGIN_NAME" ]
```

Since Ohai 7, a new DSL has been introduced that is far more modular in nature as compared to the DSL in Ohai 6.

Ohai plugins

Ohai comes with a few plugins by default. These plugins form the ecosystem of Ohai and help collect diverse information about the machine. Some of the plugins provide information specific to an operating system, while some of the plugins are specific to languages, and some are specific to platforms. Let's look at a few of them before we move ahead into writing our own custom plugins.

Take a sneak peek into the `plugins` directory (usually, found in `$GEMS_PATH/gems/ohai-xxx/lib/ohai/plugins`) and you'll find a bunch of Ruby files lying around.

Some of the useful plugins are kernel, hostname, platform, network, ohai, cloud, ec2, azure, virtualization, languages, and more.

All these plugins are meant to perform a certain task and emit attributes that can be useful for the purpose of the chef-client run.

These plugins are loaded by `$GEMS_PATH/gems/ohai-xxx/lib/ohai/system.rb` when we invoke the `ohai` command.

Some of these plugins are meant to perform different actions, depending on the platform on which they are executed. Ohai makes use of `::RbConfig::CONFIG['host_os']` to determine the underlying OS, as can be seen in `$GEMS_PATH/gems/ohai-xxx/lib/ohai/mixin/os.rb`:

```ruby
require 'rbconfig'

module Ohai

  module Mixin
    module OS

      def collect_os
        case ::RbConfig::CONFIG['host_os']
        when /aix(.+)$/
          return "aix"
        when /darwin(.+)$/
          return "darwin"
        when /hpux(.+)$/
          return "hpux"
        when /linux/
          return "linux"
        when /freebsd(.+)$/
          return "freebsd"
        when /openbsd(.+)$/
          return "openbsd"
        when /netbsd(.*)$/
          return "netbsd"
        when /solaris2/
          return "solaris2"
        when /mswin|mingw32|windows/
          return "windows"
        else
          return ::RbConfig::CONFIG['host_os']
        end
      end

      module_function :collect_os
    end
  end
end
```

Each of these plugins has different `collect_data` blocks for different platforms and there is a `collect_data` block, with the default platform, that is applicable to all the platforms that aren't matched to the results found by `$GEMS_PATH/gems/ohai-xxx/lib/ohai/mixin/os.rb`.

The `$GEMS_PATH/gems/ohai-xxx/lib/ohai/dsl/plugins/versionvii.rb` file ensures that the right `collect_data` block is called upon, and hence the right information is provided back to the end user.

For plugins such as ec2, azure, languages, and so on, there is no need for platform specification, and hence they don't have any `collect_data` block specific to any platform.

Custom plugins

For most purpose, the plugins provided by Ohai will be good enough. However, sooner or later, one lands up in a situation where one wants some attributes associated with nodes being provisioned, and these attributes define a system-level property that can be used to make certain decisions during the chef-client run. For such cases, Ohai provides us with the ability to write our own custom plugins. Ohai provides a very simple DSL that can be used for this purpose. For example, we run a large number of machines on AWS and there are different kinds of machines available known by different names such as m1.xlarge, c1.xlarge, and so on. We want to push different configurations on the basis of different types of EC2 instance. So, we go ahead and write our plugin that emits an attribute called `node['machine_type']`. Now, in our cookbooks, we can make use of this attribute to decide which config to push to the node.

A custom plugin describes a set of attributes to be collected by Ohai, and provided to chef-client at start of the chef-client run.

The syntax for an Ohai plugin looks like the following:

```
Ohai.plugin(:Name) do
  include Ohai::Name
  provides "attribute", "attribute/subattribute"
  depends "attribute", "attribute"

  collect_data (:default) do
      # Our code here
      attribute my_data
    end
```

```
        collect_data (:platform) do
          # Our code here
          attribute my_data
        end
    end
```

The plugin syntax has the following options:

- `:Name`: This is the name of the plugin used to identify the plugin. If two plugins have the same name, they are joined together and executed as a single plugin. The name of a plugin must be a valid Ruby class name and should start with an upper case and contain only alphanumeric characters.

- `include`: This is a standard Ruby method to include a class.

- `provides`: This is a comma-separated list of attributes that are exposed by a plugin. All these attributes will be the `automatic` attributes. These attributes can also be defined using an attribute/subattribute pattern.

- `depends`: This is a comma-separated list of attributes collected by other Ohai plugins.

- `collect_data`: This is a block of a Ruby code that is called when a plugin is executed. There can be more than one `collect_data` block in a plugin definition; however, only one block is executed.

  There can be different `collect_data` blocks for each platform and Ohai selects the right `collect_data` block by determining the platform of a node. If no platform is defined or matched, the `collect_data(:default)` code block is executed.

- `collect_data(:platform)`: This is a platform-specific code block. When a code block with platform is matched, it's picked up for execution. The values of platform can be `linux`, `darwin`, `aix`, `windows`, and so on. For the entire list of acceptable values, check the values from `RbConfig::CONFIG['host_os']`.

- `my_data`: This is a string or an empty mash (`{ :key_a => 'value_a', :key_b => 'value_b' }`). This is used to define the data to be collected by the plugin.

Ohai uses a mash to store data. This is done by creating a new mash and setting attributes on it. For example:

```
provides "some_name"
some_name Mash.new
some_name[:some_attribute] = "some_value"
```

Here is an example of using the `collect_data` block:

```
Ohai.plugin(:EC2) do
  provides "ec2"
  collect_data do
      ec2 Mash.new
      require 'open-uri'
      ec2[:instance_type] = open("http://169.254.169.254/
        latest/meta-data/instance-type").read
    end
end
```

This is where a major difference has come up between Ohai 6 and Ohai 7. In Ohai 6, the `plugin` class was a single monolithic Ruby file with no method definitions, and extending the plugins then was hard at times. To extend a plugin in Ohai 6, one had to "require" the `plugin` class that defines the attribute. This necessitated locating the filename of the class that implemented the plugin we wanted to extend and "requiring" that plugin. With Ohai 7, things are a lot more modular.

Say we wanted to extend an attribute, say `ec2` in our last example. Doing so in Ohai 6 would have necessitated us to require our `ec2.rb` file as follows:

```
require '/etc/chef/ohai/custom_plugins/ec2.rb'
```

In Ohai 7, we just need to specify the name of an attribute we wish to extend by using the `depends` statement as follows:

```
depends 'ec2'
```

With this new DSL, it has become a lot easier to develop new plugins given the rapid pace of technology changes and heterogeneous nature of platforms.

As we discussed earlier, we can make use of the `require` method to load any class. Ohai, by default, will attempt to fully qualify the name of any class by prepending `Ohai::` to the loaded class.

Consider this as an example:

```
require Mixin::OS
```

Now consider this example as well:

```
require Ohai::Mixin::OS
```

Both these examples are understood by Ohai as the same.

When a class is an external class, one should use `::` to let Ohai know. For example:

```
require ::External::Class::Library
```

Logging in Ohai plugins

Like any other application, Ohai plugins can also log output to some log files. This is especially useful in troubleshooting issues with plugins.

One can make use of the `Chef::Log` class in Ohai plugins to define log entries that are created when the chef-client run is invoked. The syntax for a log message is as follows:

```
Ohai::Log.log_type("message")
```

Here, `log_type` can be `.debug`, `.info`, `.warn`, `.error`, or `.fatal`; `message` is the message to be logged.

One should make use of the `rescue` clause to ensure that log messages are always provided in the event of an issue. For example:

```
rescue LoadError => e
   Ohai::Log.error("Error loading the plugin")
end
```

Hints are another concept that are very useful when working with a cloud-based heterogeneous infrastructure. Ohai's hint system allows a plugin to receive a hint by the existence of a file. These are JSON files that help the plugin determine which cloud service provider we are making use of, and it also allows passing additional information about the environment such as region and so on. When a hint file is found, Ohai assumes it is running in one of the concerned environments. The files are named `ec2.json`, `rackspace.json`, and so on.

Here is our ec2 plugin with a more robust logging mechanism in place:

```
Ohai.plugin(:EC2) do
   provides "ec2"
   collect_data do
     if hint?('ec2')
        ec2 Mash.new
         require 'open-uri'
        ec2[:instance_type] = open("http://169.254.169.254/
          latest/meta-data/instance-type").read
     else
        Ohai::Log.debug("Doesn't look like a EC2 instance")
      end
    end
end
```

Summary

This brings us to the end of our journey to understanding Ohai and its plugin ecosystem. We learned about Ohai and its associated plugins and went on to develop our own custom plugin. We learned about how to make use of the Ohai DSL and how Ohai is used by chef-client to fetch information about the concerned node. In the next chapter, we are going to learn about data bags and templates in detail and how they can make your life easier.

10
Data Bags and Templates

So we have decided to push the required configuration through Chef into our infrastructure. However, any configuration management system gets true power once it allows us to provision different kinds of machines using a minimal piece of code. Imagine having different types of systems in your infrastructure such as dev machines running over laptops, staging environments that are set up on virtual machines, and production environments running on a beefy hardware. It's quite likely that for one class of application, the configuration for these three different sets of machines might be different. However, in most cases, the amount of difference between these configurations is minimal. For example, let's say you are managing infrastructure, running Hadoop. It's pretty obvious that the amount of data that you'll be working with in a staging environment would be substantially less than in a production environment. This would lead to a difference in the configuration of Hadoop in both these environments. However, usually, the configuration keys are the same and only the values vary. Now, one way to handle the configuration of systems in different environments would have been to set up multiple files for each environment. However, as the number of configuration files increases, or if the number of environments increase, the complexity of this approach begins to unfold and this leads to a lot of duplicate information residing in the Chef repository's code base. As developers, we are always told to reduce the amount of duplicate information in code bases and there is a good reason for it. The more the duplicity, the higher are the chances of errors popping out in places you wouldn't have imagined.

Templates are just meant to address these issues and they are a must-know for any Chef developer. Templates are nothing fancy, but embedded Ruby code, which is used to create files based on the variables and logic described within the template. Templates may contain Ruby expressions and statements and are one of the best ways to manage configurations through Chef.

The chef-client makes use of Erubis to manage templates. You can find more information about Erubis at `http://www.kuwata-lab.com/erubis`.

A data bag, on the other hand, is a global variable stored as JSON data and is accessible from a Chef server. A data bag is indexed by the Chef server and is searchable. So you can just search for elements in a data bag by invoking search in a recipe, or just query for items using the `knife` command.

Let's say you want to manage users on a set of machines being managed by Chef. One way to do this would be to create each user individually using a *user* resource. A better way would be to store information about each user such as the SSH key, name, home directory, and so on, in a data bag called users and eventually iterate over this data bag and set up users.

Data bags, thereby, allow us to store structured data as a JSON file and manage them using some version control system such as Git. One of the other uses of data bags is being used as databases. We can also encrypt the data bag's contents, and hence you can make use of a data bag to store credentials or any other sensitive data.

In this chapter, we'll see how to go about making use of the templates and data bags in our Chef code to write neat and concise code to manage our infrastructure. We'll cover data bags first, followed by templates, as we'll try to incorporate the use of the data bags in the templates.

Data bags

A data bag is a global variable that's stored as JSON data and is accessible from a Chef server or chef-solo. A Chef server indexes a data bag, and hence it can be searched using Chef API. Recipes can also search a data bag and access its items.

A data bag has the following structure:

```
{
    "id": "item_name",
     "key_1": "value_1",
        . . .
        "key_n": "value_n"
}
```

Before an item can be uploaded to a data bag, a directory structure needs to be put in place to store the JSON files. In `chef-repo`, create a directory structure as follows:

chef-repo

|-- cookbooks

|-- data_bags

|-- environments

'-- roles

All the data bags will get stored in the `data_bags` directory. Let's say we've a data bag called `users` that will be used to store information such as the name, SSH key, and home directory of different users. This will require us to create a directory structure as follows:

```
chef-repo/data_bags
|-- users
```

All the JSON files corresponding to different users will go inside this directory.

Management of a data bag

A data bag can be managed either through the use of Knife or manually. Generally, Knife is used for this purpose, however, either method is equally safe and effective to use.

Creating a data bag

Knife can be used to create a data bag and data bag items using the `knife data bag` command. This command will need to make use of the `create` argument to create the data bag on the Chef server.

For example:

```
$ knife data bag create users
```

With a data bag in place, we can go about populating it with items. To do so, we'll use the same command, however, we'll also pass item name as an argument.

```
$ knife data bag create users user1
```

This will open up your default text editor with the following template:

```
{
  "id": "user1"
}
```

You can now edit this file and add stuff such as the SSH key, home directory, shell details, and so on:

```
{
  "id": "user1",
  "home": "/home/user1",
  "ssh_keys": [ "ssh-rsa XXXXXX", "ssh-rsa YYYYYYY" ]
}
```

Save and quit your editor and you'll see that Knife will report the data bag item as created:

```
✓  chef-repo git:(master) × knife data bag create user user1
Data bag user already exists
Created data_bag_item[user1]
```

If you look closely at the output, you'll see that Knife tried to create the data bag named user before creating the item user1. So you don't really need to bother about the creation of the data bag before populating it with items, and Knife will gladly do it for you. However, it's a good practice to create a data bag before pushing items into it.

We could've also accomplished the same by manually creating the required directory structure and the JSON files.

To do so, create a user1.json file in the chef-repo/data_bags/users directory:

```
{
    "id": "user1",
    "home": "/home/user1",
    "ssh_keys": [ "ssh-rsa XXXXXX", "ssh-rsa YYYYYYY" ]
}
```

In order to populate the data bag with all the required user details, we'll use the knife data bag command with the from file argument. This command takes the data bag name and item_name.json as arguments. As long as the file is in the correct directory, Knife will be able to find the data bag and corresponding item from the JSON document.

For example:

```
$ knife data bag from file users user1.json
```

This will load the contents of user1.json from data_bags/users/user1.json to the data bag.

In some cases where knife is not being executed from the root of the Chef repository, you might need to provide the full path to ITEM_NAME.json, as follows:

```
$ knife data bag from file DATA_BAG_NAME /path/to/file/ITEM_NAME.json
```

Now, to add more users, just add more JSON files and populate the data bag using the knife data bag from file command.

It's beneficial to store the JSON files manually, instead of just using the Knife data bag to create the DATA_BAG_NAME ITEM_NAME command because we can store the JSON files in a version control system and track the changes. This is crucial in order to maintain different versions; because, unlike cookbooks, you cannot maintain different versions of data bags on the Chef server.

Editing a data bag item

There will be a time when you might want to edit the contents of a data bag item. To do so, you can either use the knife data bag edit BAG ITEM command, or you can modify the data bag item in a locally-stored JSON file and update the data bag using the knife data bag from file command.

Let's say you want to add another SSH key for the user named user1. To do so, run the following command:

```
$ knife data bag users user1
```

This will open up your configured text editor with JSON associated with user1. Edit the JSON file and new SSH key:

```
{
    "id": "user1",
    "home": "/home/user1",
    "ssh_keys": [ "ssh-rsa XXXXXX", "ssh-rsa YYYYYY",
"ssh-rsa ZZZZZZ" ]
}
```

Save the file and quit the editor and you are done.

Another way to go about doing this is to edit the chef-repo/data_bags/users/user1.json file and once you've made the required changes, use the following command to update the data bag item:

```
$ knife data bag from file users user1
```

Deleting a data bag item or a data bag

You can use the knife data bag delete BAG [ITEM] command to delete a specific data bag item or a data bag all together.

The following command will delete an item called user1 from a data bag called users:

```
$ knife data bag delete users user1
```

The following command, on the other hand, will delete the `users` data bag itself:

```
$ knife data bag delete users
```

Getting a list of all the data bags set up on the Chef server

You can use the `knife data bag list` command to get a list of all the data bags configured on the Chef server, as follows:

```
$ knife data bag list
users
```

As you can see, we got `users` as one of the data bags set up on the Chef server.

Getting a list of items and their properties

The `knife data bag show` command can be used to get a list of items in a data bag and the same command can be used to get all the properties associated with an item:

```
$ knife data bag show users
user1
```

When only a data bag name is passed as an argument, we get a list of items associated with the data bag:

```
$ knife data bag show users user1
home: /home/user1
id: user1
ssh_keys:
    ssh-rsa XXXXXX
    ssh-rsa YYYYYY
    ssh-rsa ZZZZZZ
```

When an item's name is also passed to the command along with the data bag name, the properties associated with the item are displayed.

If you look closely, the output of the last command wasn't really a JSON and that's because the default format for output is text. If you want, you can change the format to JSON; try the following command:

```
$ knife data bag show users user1 -F json
```

Then, you'll get a JSON output:

```
{
    "home": "/home/user1",
    "id": "user1",
    "ssh_keys": [
        "ssh-rsa XXXXXX",
        "ssh-rsa YYYYYY",
        "ssh-rsa ZZZZZZ"
    ]
}
```

Using the data bags in recipes

Now, with a data bag created and populated with the necessary items, it's time to make use of it in our recipes. As we saw earlier, data bags are indexed, and hence can be searched. We'll be leveraging on this fact to set up a data bag containing the details of multiple users and we'll use it in a cookbook called *base* to set up user accounts.

Let's first create a few data bag items:

```
data_bag/users/user1.json
{
    "id": "user1",
    "home": "/home/user1",
    "ssh_keys": [ "ssh-rsa XXXXXX", "ssh-rsa YYYYYYY" ]
}
data_bag/users/user2.json
{
    "id": "user2",
    "home": "/home/user2",
    "ssh_keys": [ "ssh-rsa XXXXXX", "ssh-rsa YYYYYYY" ]
}
data_bag/users/user3.json
{
    "id": "user3",
    "home": "/home/user3",
    "ssh_keys": [ "ssh-rsa XXXXXX", "ssh-rsa YYYYYYY" ]
}
```

We'll now go ahead and upload these items to a Chef server. From the root of the Chef repository, execute this command:

```
$ for i in {1...3};do knife data bag from file users user$i;done
```

The last command presumes that you are making use of a bash shell. If you are using any other shell, please set up the iterator accordingly or upload each item individually.

Let's quickly check the status of our data bag:

```
$ knife data bag show users
user1
user2
user3
```

Cool! So, now the `users` data bag has all the information about all the different users.

Now, let's move on to our cookbook setup. As I mentioned earlier, we'll be setting up user accounts using a cookbook called *base*. Now, I've this habit of having a cookbook that does the basic system setup, such as the setting up of user accounts, the fine-tuning of sudoer's file, the fine-tuning of `limits.conf`, the fine-tuning of sysctl, and so on, and I call this cookbook `base`. Every machine that is managed by Chef in my infrastructure has to have this cookbook in its run-list. This is not mandatory, but I've found it to be a useful practice.

Let's create a new cookbook called `base` if it's not already present:

```
$ knife cookbook create base
```

In your `chef-repo/cookbooks` directory, you'll now see a directory called `base`. Fire up your favorite editor and open `chef-repo/cookbooks/base/recipes/default.rb` and add the following content to the file (don't worry, we'll look at each line in detail in the next few minutes):

```
include_recipe 'user'
users = data_bag('users')
users.each do |user_name|
    user_details = data_bag_item("users",user_name)
    user_account user_name do
        home     user_details['home']
        ssh_keys user_details['ssh_keys']
    end
end
```

Also, edit `chef-repo/cookbooks/base/metadata.rb` and add the following to it:

```
depends "user"
```

 Ensure that you've a user cookbook available on the Chef server. If not, download it from `https://supermarket.chef.io/cookbooks/user` and upload it to your private Chef repository. To get this cookbook, either use Knife (`knife cookbook site install user`), or get the code from a remote repository and publish it into your Chef repository.

With this, we are ready to upload our new cookbook to the Chef server:

```
$ knife cookbook upload base
```

Next time, whenever a chef-client will run on any machine that has the base cookbook in its run list, all the user accounts managed by a data bag called `users` will be set up on the machine.

Let's now go on to see what's really happening in our cookbook code. We are using a community cookbook called `user` by fnichol (alias Github). The code from this cookbook can be found at `https://github.com/fnichol/chef-user`. What this cookbook does is it provides us with a resource called `user_account`. This is a more powerful resource in comparison to a standard user resource provided by Chef as it allows the management of SSH keys for every user.

To make use of this cookbook, we mention in `cookbooks/base/metadata.rb` that our `base` cookbook depends upon `user` cookbook, and finally in our base cookbook recipe, we include this cookbook.

Next, we search for a data bag called `users` in the Chef server. Chef provides a DSL. Using this, we can search the data bags and this method is called `data_bag`. This takes the name of the data bag to search as an argument and returns an array with the key for each data bag item found in the data bag. So, in effect, this piece of code:

```
users = data_bag('users')
```

This code would've resulted in this:

```
users = ['user1','user2','user3']
```

Now, we just iterate over this array and for each element of this array, we call a method called `data_bag_item`. This method is again provided as part of the recipe DSL and it takes two arguments: the name of the data bag and item. It eventually returns a Ruby hash with each property of the item as a key and a value for each property of the item as the value for the key.

So, consider the following code:

```
user_details = data_bag_item("users",user)
```

Here, user is coming through iteration, which will result in something like this for the first iteration:

```
user_details = {"home" => "/home/user1", "id" => "user1",
"ssh_key" => ["ssh-rsa XXXXXX","ssh-rsa YYYYYY",
"ssh-rsa ZZZZZZ"] }
```

Next, we use this information to set up our user account using the user_account resource.

 The user_account resource requires each user's information to be stored in a data bag called users.

Apart from using the recipe DSL, Chef also provides a facility called search. This can be used with Knife or in a recipe.

Any search for a data bag (or item) should specify the name of the data bag and search a query string, which will be used during a search.

 The search query happens against a *solr* index and this index is built asynchronously, so you might not find something you have just updated.

For example, to search for the users in a data bag called users, we can use the following knife command:

```
$ knife search users "(id:*)" -F json
```

Here, we are asking Chef to search a data bag called users and report back with results for items where the ID can be anything.

This will result in the following output:

```
{
  "results": 3,
  "rows": [
  {
    "name": "data_bag_item_users_user1",
    "json_class": "Chef::DataBagItem",
```

```
      "chef_type": "data_bag_item",
      "data_bag": "users",
      "raw_data": {
        "home": "/home/user1",
        "id": "user1",
        "ssh_keys": [
          "ssh-rsa XXXXXX",
          "ssh-rsa YYYYYY",
          "ssh-rsa ZZZZZZ"
        ]
      }
    },
    {
      "name": "data_bag_item_users_user2",
      "json_class": "Chef::DataBagItem",
      "chef_type": "data_bag_item",
      "data_bag": "users",
      "raw_data": {
        "home": "/home/user2",
        "id": "user2",
        "ssh_keys": [
          "ssh-rsa XXXXXX",
          "ssh-rsa YYYYYY",
          "ssh-rsa ZZZZZZ"
        ]
      }
    },
    {
      "name": "data_bag_item_users_user3",
      "json_class": "Chef::DataBagItem",
      "chef_type": "data_bag_item",
      "data_bag": "users",
      "raw_data": {
        "home": "/home/user3",
        "id": "user3",
```

```
   "ssh_keys": [
     "ssh-rsa XXXXXX",
     "ssh-rsa YYYYYY",
     "ssh-rsa ZZZZZZ"
   ]
 }
}
]
}
```

As you can see, the Chef server reported back three users for this search query, which is consistent with what we had set up.

You can also make use of the search method in the recipe. Let's modify our base recipe to make use of the search method instead of the data_bag and data_bag_item DSL methods:

```
include_recipe 'users'
search(:users, "*:*").each do |user_item|
    user_name = user_item["id"]
    user_account user_name do
        home user_item["home"]
        ssh_keys user_item["ssh_keys"]
    end
end
```

As you can see, we've have used *:* as a query string in our recipe. This will search for all the items in our data bag. However, if you want to be specific, say you wanted to set up just an account for a user called user1, the above code would've looked like this:

```
include_recipe 'users'
user_item = search(:users, "id:user1")
user_name = user_item["id"]
user_account user_name do
    home user_item["home"]
    ssh_keys user_item["ssh_keys"]
end
```

Encrypted data bags

An item in a data bag can be encrypted using a shared secret encryption. This allows each data bag item to store confidential information. Each data bag item may be encrypted individually.

An encrypted data bag item is written using JSON and Base64 encoding is used to preserve special characters in encrypted contents. The data is encrypted using AES-256-CBC. A data bag item is encrypted using a random initialization vector each time a value is encrypted. The encrypted content can be decrypted on the node, only if a matching shared key is present on the node. The matching shared key can be set up on the node through various mechanisms. For example, on AWS, user data can be used to set up the shared key, or the machine image itself can contain the shared key. In other environments, some pre-bootstrap script can be used to set up this shared key.

The /etc/chef/client.rb eventually looks for a secret at the path specified by encrypted_data_bag_secret, setting in client.rb.

Knife can be used to encrypt or decrypt a data bag item when the knife data bag command is executed with the create, edit, from file, or show arguments, along with either of the following options:

- --secret SECRET: This is the encryption key that is used for the values contained within a data bag item.

- --secret-file FILE: This is the path to the file that contains the encryption key.

You can make use of openssl to generate a secret key as follows:

```
$ openssl rand -base64 512 | tr -d '\r\n' > my_secret_key
```

This will generate a file called my_secret_key, which can be used to encrypt a data bag item.

The following command shows how we can use Knife to encrypt a data bag item:

```
$ knife data bag create passwords db -secret-file my_secret_key
```

This will open your text editor, and as with the other data bags that we created earlier, we'll create a property called password along with a valid password:

```
{
    "id": "db",
    "password": "123456"
}
```

Save the file and exit the editor and you'll see that the item in question has been set up on the Chef server.

Now, to verify that the password is indeed stored in an encrypted form, let's quickly try and see the contents of an item, the db inside a data bag, and passwords:

```
$ knife data bag show passwords db -F json
{
  "id": "db",
  "password": {
    "version": 1,
    "cipher": "aes-256-cbc",
    "encrypted_data": "CJl6quHZQyr...j8=\n",
    "iv": "R5ZuEapsXm1g7nFO2CvmJA==\n"
  }
}
```

As you can see, the property password has an encrypted value instead of a default value, 123456.

In order to see the real content of the data bag item, we'll need to pass our secret key to the `knife` command as follows:

```
$ knife data bag show passwords db -secret-file my_secret_key -F json
```

Also, now we'll get the decrypted version as follows:

```
{
  "id": "db",
  "password": "123456"
}
```

In the case of recipes, you can use the `EncryptedDataBagItem.load` method, which takes the data bag name, item name, and shared secret as arguments. However, most likely, you'll have a secret stored as a file somewhere on the node. Thus, you can make use of the `EncryptedDataBagItem.load_secret` method to first load the secret from the file into some variable, and then use that variable as an argument to the `EncryptedDataBagItem.load` method.

Let's say you've kept the shared secret in /etc/chef/shared_secret on the node. Now, you can use the following code in your recipe to get the desired password for an item, the db in a data bag, and passwords:

```
secret = Chef::EncryptedDataBagItem.load_secret("/etc/chef/shared_
secret")
creds = Chef::EncryptedDataBagItem.load("passwords","db", secret)
password = creds["password"]
```

Templates

As we mentioned earlier, templates are **Embedded Ruby** (**ERB**) templates, which can be used to generate configuration files based upon some variables and logic. These files may contain Ruby statements and expressions. To make use of templates, one has to use the template resource in a cookbook and specify in the source the path to the template itself. The template file is placed in the templates directory of a cookbook.

Unless you are creating your cookbooks manually, Knife will automatically take care of creating the templates directory structure. A template is stored in the cookbook_name/templates directory and is referenced by the template resource in the cookbook recipe. Generally, cookbooks are developed, keeping different platforms in mind, and hence one can keep different files per platform type using the concept of file specificity. The template directory can have the following structure on Chef repo:

```
templates
|-- host-node[:fqdn]
|-- node[:platform]-node[:platform_version]
|-- node[:platform_version_components]
|-- node[:platform]
'-- default
```

During the chef-client, the template source is fetched from the Chef server for the first time and cached (generally, in the /var/chef/cache directory of a node). However, during all subsequent runs, the template is not fetched unless there is a change.

Template resources and a template in action

In our discussion about data bags, we went on to create a data bag containing users' details and we used that data bag in a cookbook called `base` to manage user accounts.

Now, say you wanted to ensure that all these users in the data bag are able to run `commands/scripts` as a super user. To do this, we'll need to modify the `sudoers` file on the node. One way to accomplish this would be to use the `cookbook_file` resource and push a custom `sudoers` file on to the node during the chef-client run. However, this will require us to modify the sudoer source file in the chef-repo, every time we go about adding a new user to the data bag. This is one such case where we can make use of templates.

Let's modify our `base` cookbook to use template resource to manage the `/etc/sudoers` file:

```
include_recipe 'user'
users = data_bag('users')

users.each do |user_name|
    user_details = data_bag_item("users",user_name)
    user_account user_name do
        home     user_details['home']
        ssh_keys user_details['ssh_keys']
    end
end

template '/etc/sudoers' do
  source 'sudoers.erb'
  owner 'root'
  group 'root'
  mode '0440'
  variables({
    :sudoers_user => users
  }
end
```

Next, let's add an ERB template named `sudoers.erb` to `base/templates/default`:

```
#/etc/sudoers
#Generated by Chef for <%= node[:fqdn] %>
Defaults     requiretty
Defaults     !visiblepw
```

```
Defaults    always_set_home
Defaults     secure_path = /sbin:/bin:/usr/sbin:/usr/bin
root  ALL=(ALL)    ALL
<% @sudoers_user.each do |user| %>
<%= user %> ALL=NOPASSWD: ALL
<% end %>
```

Let's dissect this piece of code and see what's happening here.

In our template resource, we asked Chef to set up a configuration file called /etc/sudoers. This file will be set up according to a ERB template called sudoers, which can be found in the templates/default directory. Next, we went on to set the ownership and permission of the file in question. Finally, we decided to pass some variables to the ERB template. When a template is rendered, Ruby expressions and statements are evaluated by the chef-client. The variables listed in a resource's variables parameter and node object are evaluated. The chef-client then goes on to pass these variables to the template, where they are accessible as instance variables within the template; the node objects can be accessed in the same fashion as they are accessed in recipes.

In our cookbook recipe, we searched for a data bag called users and got an array containing a list of all users. Next, we iterated over this array to set up user accounts. Finally, we went on to pass this array as a variable named sudoers_user to the template resource.

In our sudoers.erb template, we created a skeleton of the desired sudoers file. Finally, in the end, we iterated over the @sudoers_user array (as you can see, this is an instance variable, prefixed by a @ sign) and populated the template.

Templates and data bags together are a very powerful combination. For example, you might have split your infrastructure into different environments. Now, we can set up a data bag for different applications and have the environment name as the item name and use this data bag to fetch the desired properties for applications per environment.

For example, let's say we want to set up Hadoop in different environments. I, generally, go about setting a default attribute called device_class in my custom JSON file on the node. This attribute is used to describe the applications that are running on the node. For a Hadoop name node, I set this attribute as namenode, while for data nodes, it's set as datanode.

Next, in my chef-repo, I create data bags called `namenode` and `datanode` and for each of these data bags, I go about adding items as follows:

`coresite.json` (used to manage `core-site.xml`)

```
{
    "id": "coresite",
    "production": {
          "hadoop.tmp.dir": "/data/hadoops",
          "io.compression.codecs":
    "com.hadoop.compression.lzo.LzoCodec",

                     . . .

    },
    "staging": {
          "hadoop.tmp.dir": "/data/hadoops",
          "io.compression.codecs":
    "com.hadoop.compression.lzo.LzoCodec",
    }
}
```

In my cookbook, I go about searching the data bag as follows:

```
config_coresite =
data_bag_item("#{node[:device_class]}","coresite")["#{node.chef_
environment}"]
```

Finally, in my template resource, I say something like this:

```
template "/apps/hadoop/conf/core-site.xml" do
  source "/apps/hadoop/conf/core-site.xml.erb"
  owner "#{node["app"]["user"]}"
  group "#{node["app"]["user"]}"
  mode "0644"
  variables ({
      :hadoop_tmp_dir => config_coresite["hadoop.tmp.dir"],
      :io_compression_codecs =>
config_coresite["io.compression.codecs"],
      :io_compression_codec_lzo_class =>
config_coresite["io.compression.codec.lzo.class"],
      :fs_default_name => config_coresite["fs.default.name"],
      :hadoop_security_authorization =>
config_coresite["hadoop.security.authorization"],
      :io_serialization => config_coresite["io.serializations"]
  })
end
```

The template itself looks something like this:

```
<?xml version="1.0"?>
<?xml-stylesheet type="text/xsl" href="configuration.xsl"?>

<configuration>
<property>
    <name>hadoop.tmp.dir</name>
    <value><%= @hadoop_tmp_dir %></value>
    <description>A base for other temporary
                 directories.</description>
</property>

<property>
    <name>io.compression.codecs</name>
    <value><%= @io_compression_codecs %></value>
</property>

<property>
    <name>io.compression.codec.lzo.class</name>
    <value><%= @io_compression_codec_lzo_class %></value>
</property>

<property>
    <name>fs.default.name</name>
    <value><%= @fs_default_name %></value>
    <description>The name of the default file system.
A URI which determines the FileSystem implementation.</description>
</property>

<property>
    <name>hadoop.security.authorization</name>
    <value><%= @hadoop_security_authorization %></value>
</property>
</configuration>
```

Partial templates

Often, you'll come across large configuration files and you'll be sweating, considering the fact that you'll need to tune all those different parameters in the configuration. Fortunately, Chef allows us to break apart these configurations into small chunks, known as partial templates. This way, we can only process a part of the configuration, which we actually need to configure.

Let's split our template in the previous example into multiple partial templates, and finally use them to build our final template.

We'll have five different ERB templates for each configuration property, and we'll use the `render` method to render these partial templates inside the final template.

Here are few of those partial templates:

- `hadoop_tmp_dir.erb`

```
<property>
    <name>hadoop.tmp.dir</name>
    <value><%= @hadoop_tmp_dir %></value>
    <description>A base for other temporary
                directories.</description>
</property>
```

- `final_template.erb`

```
<?xml version="1.0"?>
<?xml-stylesheet type="text/xsl" href="configuration.xsl"?>

<configuration>
<%= render "hadoop_tmp_dir.erb", :variables =>
{:hadoop_tmp_dir => @hadoop_tmp_dir } %>
<%= render "io_compression_codecs.erb", :variables => {:
io_compression_codecs => @io_compression_codecs}  %>
<%= render "io_compression_codecs_lzo_class.erb",
:variables => {: io_compression_codecs_lzo_class =>
@io_compression_codecs_lzo_class} %>
<%= render "fs_default_name.erb", :variables =>
{:fs_default_name => @fs_default_name } %>
<%= render "hadoop_security_authorization.erb", :variables
=> {:hadoop_security_authorization =>
@hadoop_security_authorization} %>
</configuration>
```

Try to avoid using partials inside partial templates, as they can lead to unexpected results and often, they just fail.

Summary

This brings us to the end of our journey in to the world of data bags and templates. We've seen how to manage data bags, and use data bags to store sensitive data by encrypting the content. We have, finally, learnt about using templates and also touched upon the use of partial templates. By now, you would've realized how useful these two features of Chef are. With the proper use of data bags and templates, you can write really efficient Chef code, which is more robust and clean. In the next chapter, we will look into one of the very powerful features of Chef, called search, and along the way we will also explore its API.

11
Chef API and Search

Chef provides a simple and wonderful API to interact with it and get information about different objects that are stored within it. The API provided by Chef is the REST API, and hence it can be used with any programming language that provides support to make HTTP calls. However, one of the more fundamental questions is: why would we even want to learn about API interfaces provided by Chef?

Well, most of the time, we will be writing cookbooks for handling the installation and configuration of different aspects of our infrastructure. At other times, we'll be managing information stored in data bags, or defining environments and roles. However, there will be a time when configuration of a machine or service won't be enough and you'll want to rely on information about the nodes stored in the Chef server for the purpose of configuration. These are times when we'll need to rely on Chef API and the search capabilities provided by Chef. Then, there is another case where you are entitled to the responsibility of integrating a third party application with Chef, and this is when you'll want to make use of your understanding of Chef API to handle the integration effectively.

Through Chef API, you can get access to objects such as nodes, environments, roles, cookbooks, client lists, and so on. You can make use of the API to either query a Chef server for information about different objects, or it can even be used to edit the objects.

In this chapter, we'll see some use cases where we'll make use of Chef API to perform some tasks that would otherwise seem very complex to perform. We will also look at ridley, which is a Chef API client written in Ruby.

Prerequisites for using Chef API

Before we start using Chef API, we need to follow a few rules:

1. Use a Chef server running the version 11.X.

2. The Accept header must be set to `application/JSON`.

3. For the `PUT` and `POST` requests, the Content-Type header must be an application/JSON.

4. The X-Chef-Version header should be set to the version of Chef that we are using.

5. The request must be signed using `Mixlib::Authentication`. We'll see more about this later in this chapter.

6. The request must be well formatted. You can use the `Chef::REST` library to ensure this or use ridley.

Authentication of requests

As is the case with most APIs, Chef API is authenticated before the request is processed, and the result is transmitted back to the client. The authorization of the request is done by the Chef server. A few HTTP headers are signed by the private key on the client machine, and the Chef server verifies the signature by using the public key. Only once the request has been authorized, can processing take place.

Generally, when using utilities such as Knife and so on, we don't have to be really concerned about handling authorization, as this is something that is automatically taken care of by the tool. However, when using libraries such as cURL or any arbitrary Ruby code, it is necessary to include a full authentication header as part of a request to the Chef server.

All of the hashing is done using the SHA1 algorithm and encoding in Base64. Each header should be encoded in the following format:

```
Method: HTTP_METHOD
Hashed Path: HASHED_PATH
X-Ops-Content-Hash: HASHED_BODY
X-Ops-Timestamp: TIME
X-Ops-UserId: USERID
```

The `HTTP_METHOD` refers to the method used in the API request (`GET`, `POST`, and so on.).

The `HASHED_PATH` is the path of the request: `/organizations/organization_name/name_of_endpoint`.

The hashed path should not include a query string.

The private key must be an RSA key in the SSL `.pem` file format.

Once the request is received by the Chef server, along with these headers, the Chef server decrypts this header and ensures that the content of the nonencrypted headers matches with what it has. The request also has a timestamp, and it's checked if the request was received in time by evaluating the timestamp.

The following are the headers that are required to carry out the authentication of every request:

Header	Description
Accept	This header is to used to define the format in which the response data will be provided by the Chef server. For Chef's use, this header should always have a value: application/json.
Content-Type	This header describes the format in which the data is sent to the Chef server. This header should always have a value: application/json.
Host	This is the hostname and port to which the request is sent.
X-Chef-Version	This header describes the version used by the chef-client executable.
X-Ops-Authorization-N	One (or more) 60 character segments that comprise the canonical header. N here represents the integer used by the last header as part of the request.
X-Ops-Content-Hash	This is the body of the request. The body is hashed using SHA1 and is encoded using Base64. The Base64 encoding should have line breaks every 60 characters.
X-Ops-Sign	This header should be set to a value: version=1.0.
X-Ops-Timestamp	This is the timestamp in the ISO-8601 format and the time zone is in UTC. For example, 2014-09-28T11:10:43Z.
X-Ops-UserId	This is the name of the API client whose private key is going to be used for the purpose of signing the headers.

Let's try to make use of this knowledge to get a list of nodes set up on our Chef server. We'll make use of cURL for the purpose of connecting to our Chef server:

```
#!/usr/bin/env bash

_chomp () {
```

```
    awk '{printf "%s", $0}'
}

chef_api_request() {
  local method path body timestamp chef_server_url client_name hashed_
body hashed_path
  local canonical_request headers auth_headers

  chef_server_url="https://chef.indix.tv"
  endpoint=${2%%\?*}
  path=${chef_server_url}$2
  client_name="mayank"
  method=$1
  body=$3

  hashed_path=$(echo -n "$endpoint" | openssl dgst -sha1 -binary |
openssl enc -base64)
  hashed_body=$(echo -n "$body" | openssl dgst -sha1 -binary | openssl
enc -base64)
  timestamp=$(date -u "+%Y-%m-%dT%H:%M:%SZ")

  canonical_request="Method:$method\nHashed Path:$hashed_path\nX-
Ops-Content-Hash:$hashed_body\nX-Ops-Timestamp:$timestamp\nX-Ops-
UserId:$client_name"
  headers="-H X-Ops-Timestamp:$timestamp \
    -H X-Ops-Userid:$client_name \
    -H X-Chef-Version:0.10.4 \
    -H Accept:application/json \
    -H X-Ops-Content-Hash:$hashed_body \
    -H X-Ops-Sign:version=1.0"

  auth_headers=$(printf "$canonical_request" | openssl rsautl -sign
-inkey \
    "/Users/mayank/.chef/${client_name}.pem" | openssl enc -base64 |
_chomp |  awk '{ll=int(length/60);i=0; \
    while (i<=ll) {printf " -H X-Ops-Authorization-%s:%s", i+1,
substr($0,i*60+1,60);i=i+1}}')

  case $method in
    GET)
      curl_command="curl -k $headers $auth_headers $path"
      $curl_command
      ;;
    *)
```

```
        echo "Unknown Method. I only know: GET" >&2
        return 1
        ;;
    esac
}
```

```
    chef_api_request "$@"
```

This script can now be executed as follows:

```
⊠  ~  bash curl_chef.sh GET "/users"
{"admin":"https:\/\/chef.sychonet.com:443\/users\/
admin","user":"https:\/\/chef.sychonet.com:443\/users\/
user,"mayank":"https:\/\/chef.sychonet.com:443\/users\/mayank"}
```

Here, we are hitting the endpoint /users using the GET method. There are plenty of other endpoints provided to us by the Chef server and some of them accept methods other than GET, such as POST, DELETE, and so on.

You can also use Knife's subcommand raw to send a REST request to the Chef server API. The syntax of the command is as follows:

```
knife raw REQUEST_PATH [options]
```

The command accepts the following options:

Option	Description
`-i FILE, --input FILE`	The request body should be defined in this file and used with a PUT or POST request.
`--[no-]pretty`	This can be used to disable pretty-print output of JSON.
`-m METHOD, --method METHOD`	This option can be used to specify a request method. The values allowed are DELETE, GET, POST, and PUT. The default value for this method is GET.

For example, the following command will help us get a list of all the users on the Chef server:

```
knife raw -m GET /users
```

Alternatively, we can use this command:

```
knife raw /users
```

Endpoints

With our understanding of authorization, we can now go ahead and start playing with the Chef server API; however, before we jump ahead and get our hands dirty, lets quickly check what endpoints are provided to us by the Chef server and also see what to expect from them.

/users

The users endpoint has two methods:

- The GET method
- The POST method

GET

The GET method is used to get a list of users set up on the Chef server. This method has no parameters. We had used this method to get a list of users configured on our Chef server in the example earlier.

For a request, we can use the following code:

```
GET /users
```

Response:

The response will return a JSON, containing a username and URI corresponding to users on the Chef server:

```
{
    "mayank"=>"https://chef.sychonet.com:443/users/mayank"
}
```

POST

The POST method is used to create a user on the Chef server.

For a request, we can use the following code:

```
POST /users
```

For a response, we can use the following code:

```
{
    "user_name": "https://chef.sychonet.com:443/users/user_name"
}
```

/users/NAME

The /users/NAME endpoint has the following methods:

- The DELETE method
- The GET method
- The POST method
- The PUT method

DELETE

The DELETE method is used to delete a user.

For a request, we can use the following code:

```
DELETE /users/USER_NAME
```

Response:

This will return a JSON as follows:

```
{
    "name": "USER_NAME"
}
```

GET

The GET method is used to get details about a user.

For a request, we can use the following code:

```
GET /users/USER_NAME
```

For a response, we can use the following code:

```
{
  "name": "USER_NAME"
}
```

POST

The POST method is used to create a new user on the Chef server.

For a request, we can use the following code:

```
POST /users/USER_NAME
```

This method accepts a request body that looks something like this:

```
{
  "name": "User Name"
}
```

Response:

The Chef server will respond with a private key corresponding to this user, as follows:

```
{
  "name": "User Name",
  "private_key": "-----BEGIN PRIVATE KEY-----\n
      MIGfNA0XXXXXXXXXXXXXXXXXXXXXXXXXXXX\n
      -----END PRIVATE KEY-----"
  "admin": false
}
```

PUT

The PUT method is used to update a specific user on the Chef server. This method accepts a Boolean:

```
{"private_key": "true"}.
```

If this is specified, a new private key is generated.

For a request, we can use the following code:

```
PUT /users/USER_NAME
```

This method accepts a request body that looks something like this:

```
POST /users { "name": "User Name" }
```

Response:

The response will return something like this:

```
{
  "name": "User Name",
   "private_key": "-----BEGIN PRIVATE KEY-----\n
   MIGfNA0XXXXXXXXXXXXXXXXXXXXXXXXXXXX\n
   -----END PRIVATE KEY-----",
   "admin": false
}
```

If a new private key is generated, then both the public and private keys are returned in response.

/clients

The /clients endpoint is used to manage an API client list and their associated public-private key pairs.

The /clients endpoint has two methods: GET and POST.

GET

The GET method is used to return a list of clients registered with the Chef server, including nodes such as the chef-validator and chef-server-webui clients.

For a request, we can use the following code:

```
GET /clients
```

Response:

The response for this request will look something like this:

```
{
    "chef-validator": "https://chef.sychonet.com:443/clients/chef-
validator",
    "chef-webui": "https://chef.sychonet.com:443/clients/chef-webui",
    "client01": "https://chef.sychonet.com:443/clients/client01"
}
```

POST

The POST method is used to create a new API client on the Chef server.

For request we can use the following code:

```
POST /clients
```

with a request body like this:

```
{
  "name": "Name_of_new_API_client",
  "admin": false
}
```

Here, `name` refers to the name of the new API client, and admin indicates if the new API client will be an admin API client or not.

Response:

The response for this request will look something like this:

```
{
    "uri": "https://chef.indix.tv:443/clients/Name_of_new_API_client",
    "private_key": "-----BEGIN PRIVATE KEY-----\n
                    MIGfNA0XXXXXXXXXXXXXXXXXXXXXXXXXXX\n
                    -----END PRIVATE KEY-----"
}
```

The private key returned by the Chef server should be saved in a safe place as this will be used to communicate with the Chef server later on.

/clients/NAME

The `/clients/NAME` endpoint is used to manage a particular Chef API client. This endpoint has the following methods:

- The `DELETE` method
- The `GET` method
- The `PUT` method

DELETE

The `DELETE` method is used to remove a specific API client.

For a request, we can use the following code:

```
DELETE /clients/NAME
```

Response:

This method has no response body.

GET

The `GET` method is used to get details about a specific client.

For a request, we can use the following code:

```
GET /clients/NAME
```

Response:

The response will look something like this:

```
{
    "clientname": "client_name",
    "validator": false,
    "certificate": "------BEGIN CERTIFICATE ------\n
                        MIID0jCAE45XXXXXXXXXXXXX
                        -------END CERTIFICATE -------",
    "name": "node_name"
}
```

PUT

The PUT method is used to update a specific API client. This method has no parameters.

For a request, we can use the following code:

```
PUT /clients/NAME
```

This has a request body like this:

```
{
    "name": "client_name",
    "private_key": true,
    "admin": false
}
```

If private_key is set to true, a new RSA private key will be generated, and if admin is set to true, the API client will be configured as an admin API client.

Response:

The response will return something like this:

```
{
    "name": "client_name",
    "private_key": "-----BEGIN PRIVATE KEY-----\n
                MIGfNA0XXXXXXXXXXXXXXXXXXXXXXXXXXXXX\n
                -----END PRIVATE KEY-----",
    "admin": false
}
```

/roles

The `/roles` endpoint can be used to manage roles on the Chef server. This endpoint has two methods: `GET` and `POST`.

GET

The `GET` method can be used to get a list of roles along with their associated URIs. This method has no parameters.

For a request, we can use the following code:

```
GET /roles
```

Response:

The response will return something like this:

```
{
  "cannonball-turbo":"https://chef.sychonet.com:443/roles/cannonball-turbo",
  "datanode":"https://chef. sychonet.com:443/roles/datanode",
  "namenode":"https://chef. sychonet.com:443/roles/namenode",
  "services":"https://chef. sychonet.com:443/roles/services",
  "solr":"https://chef. sychonet.com:443/roles/solr",
  "webapp":"https://chef. sychonet.com:443/roles/webapp"
}
```

POST

The `POST` method can be used to create a new role on the Chef server. Again, this method accepts no parameters.

For a request, we can use the following code:

```
POST /roles
```

Which has a request body like this:

```
{
  "name": "webserver",
  "chef_type": "role",
  "json_class": "Chef::Role",
  "default_attributes": {},
  "description": "A webserver",
  "run_list": [
    "recipe[passenger]",
```

```
      "recipe[nginx]"
    ],
    "override_attributes": {}
}
```

Response:

The response will return something like this:

```
{
    "uri": "https://chef.sychonet.com:443/roles/webserver"
}
```

/roles/NAME

The `/roles/NAME` endpoint can be used to manage an individual role. This endpoint has the following methods:

- The GET method
- The DELETE method
- The PUT method

DELETE

The DELETE method can be used to delete an existing role from the Chef server.

For a request, we can use the following code:

```
DELETE /roles/webserver
```

Response:

The response will return something like this:

```
{
  "name": "webserver",
  "chef_type": "role",
  "json_class": "Chef::Role",
  "default_attributes": {},
  "description": "A webserver",
  "run_list": [
    "recipe[passenger]",
    "recipe[nginx]"
  ],
  "override_attributes": {}
}
```

GET

The GET method can be used to get the details about a particular role.

For a request, we can use the following code:

```
GET /roles/webserver
```

Response:

The response will return something like this:

```
{
  "name": "webserver",
  "chef_type": "role",
  "json_class": "Chef::Role",
  "default_attributes": {},
  "description": "A webserver",
  "run_list": [
    "recipe[passenger]",
    "recipe[nginx]"
  ],
  "override_attributes": {}
}
```

PUT

The PUT method can be used to edit an individual role. Let's say we had a role called the webserver already set up, and now we want to override an attribute ["nginx"] ["port"] with a value 8080.

For a request, we can use the following code:

```
PUT /roles/webserver
```

Which has a request body like this:

```
{
  "name": "webserver",
  "chef_type": "role",
  "json_class": "Chef::Role",
  "default_attributes": {},
  "description": "A webserver",
  "run_list": [
    "recipe[passenger]",
```

```
      "recipe[nginx]"
    ],
    "override_attributes": {
      "nginx" { "port": 8080 }
    }
  }
```

Response:

The response will look something like this:

```
{
  "name": "webserver",
  "chef_type": "role",
  "json_class": "Chef::Role",
  "default_attributes": {},
  "description": "A webserver",
  "run_list": [
    "recipe[passenger]",
    "recipe[nginx]"
  ],
  "override_attributes": {
    "nginx" { "port": 8080 }
  }
}
```

/roles/NAME/environments

Let's say we had a role called `webserver` with the following definition:

```
# Role Name:: webapp
# Copyright 2014, Sychonet
name "webapp"
description "Web Role"

env_run_lists "production"   =>
["recipe[ohai]","recipe[base]","recipe[passenger-nginx]","recipe[nodej
s]","recipe[nodejs::nodepkgs]","recipe[memcached]","recipe[crons::weba
pp]","recipe[monit]","recipe[splunk::forwarder]","recipe[monitoring::s
ensu]","recipe[monitoring::ganglia]"],
  "staging"         =>
["recipe[ohai]","recipe[base]","recipe[passenger-nginx]","recipe[nodej
s]","recipe[nodejs::nodepkgs]","recipe[memcached]","recipe[crons::weba
pp]","recipe[monit]"],
```

```
    "perf"            =>
    ["recipe[ohai]","recipe[base]","recipe[passenger-nginx]","recipe[nodej
    s]","recipe[nodejs::nodepkgs]","recipe[memcached]","recipe[crons::weba
    pp]","recipe[monit]"],
              "_default"       =>
    ["recipe[ohai]","recipe[base]","recipe[passenger-nginx]","recipe[nodej
    s]","recipe[nodejs::nodepkgs]","recipe[memcached]"]
    run_list   "recipe[ohai]","recipe[base]","recipe[passenger-nginx]","rec
    ipe[nodejs]","recipe[nodejs::nodepkgs]","recipe[memcached]"
```

As you can see, we've created environment-specific run-lists and we can make use
of the /roles/webapp/environments to get a list of environments for which the
environment specific run-lists have been defined in our role.

This endpoint has just one method called GET.

GET

This method has no parameters and it just returns a list of environments that have
environment-specific run-lists in a given role.

For a request, we can use the following code:

```
/roles/webapp/environments
```

For a response, we can use the following code:

```
["_default","perf","production","staging"]
```

/roles/NAME/environments/NAME

This endpoint takes the name of the role and the name of the environment as an
argument and returns the run-list corresponding to the concerned environment.

This method just has the GET method.

GET

For a request, we can use the following code:

```
/roles/webapp/environment/production
```

This will return run_list corresponding to environment production for the
webapp role.

Response:

The response will look something like this:

```
{
    "run_list":["recipe[ohai]","recipe[base]","recipe[passenger-nginx]",
    "recipe[nodejs]","recipe[nodejs::nodepkgs]","recipe[memcached]","recip
    e[crons::webapp]","recipe[monit]","recipe[splunk::forwarder]","recipe[
    monitoring::sensu]","recipe[monitoring::ganglia]"]
}
```

/cookbooks

The /cookbooks endpoint is used to return hash of all the cookbooks and cookbook versions. This endpoint has the GET method.

GET

This method has the num_versions=n parameters where n is the number of versions to return in the response.

For a request, we can use the following code:

```
GET /cookbooks
```

For a response, we can use the following code:

```
{
    "passenger-nginx":{
        "url":"https://chef.sychonet.com:443/cookbooks/passenger-nginx",
        "versions":[{"version":"0.1.1","url":"https://chef.sychonet.
    com:443/cookbooks/passenger-nginx/0.1.1"}]
    }
}
```

As you can see, we got a response with the latest version of cookbook named passenger-nginx. However, I know that we have two versions of passenger-nginx and the following request will help us get both versions in our response.

For a request, we can use the following code:

```
GET /cookbooks?num_versions=2
```

For a response, we can use the following code:

```json
{
  "passenger-nginx":{
    "url":"https://chef.sychonet.com:443/cookbooks/passenger-nginx",
    "versions":[
      {"version":"0.1.1","url":"https://chef.sychonet.com:443/
cookbooks/passenger-nginx/0.1.1"},
      {"version":"0.1.0","url":"https://chef.sychonet.com:443/
cookbooks/passenger-nginx/0.1.0"}
    ]
  }
}
```

To get a list of all the versions, replace N in `num_versions=N` with `all`.

/cookbooks/NAME

The `/cookbooks/NAME` endpoint can be used to get information about a particular cookbook. This endpoint has just one method GET.

GET

The GET method can be used to get information about a particular cookbook.

Let's use it to get details of our cookbook called `passenger-nginx`.

For a request, we can use the following code:

```
GET /cookbooks/passenger-nginx
```

Response:

The response will look something like this:

```json
{
  "passenger-nginx":{
    "url":"https://chef.sychonet.com:443/cookbooks/passenger-nginx",
    "versions":[
      {"version":"0.1.1","url":"https://chef.sychonet.com:443/
cookbooks/passenger-nginx/0.1.1"},
      {"version":"0.1.0","url":"https://chef.sychonet.com:443/
cookbooks/passenger-nginx/0.1.0"}
    ]
  }
}
```

/cookbooks/NAME/VERSION

The `/cookbooks/NAME/version` endpoint can be used to get information about a particular version of a cookbook. This endpoint has the following methods:

- The `DELETE` method
- The `GET` method
- The `PUT` method

DELETE

This method can be used to delete a particular version of a cookbook called `NAME` from the Chef server.

For a request, we can use the following code:

```
DELETE /cookbooks/NAME/VERSION
```

Or, we can use the following code:

```
DELETE /cookbooks/passenger-nginx/0.1.0
```

This request can be used to delete version 0.1.0 of the `passenger-nginx` cookbook.

Response:

This method has no response body. Unused checksum values will be garbage collected.

GET

The `GET` method is used to get the description of a cookbook, including all of its metadata and links to component files. This method has no parameters.

For a request, we can use the following code:

```
GET /cookbooks/NAME/VERSION
```

Or, we can use the following code:

```
GET /cookbooks/passenger-nginx/0.1.0
```

Here, version can be `_latest` in order to get the latest version.

Response:

The response will return something like this:

```
{
  "cookbook_name": "passenger-nginx",
  "files": [
  ],
  "chef_type": "cookbook_version",
  "definitions": [
  ],
  "libraries": [
  ],
  "attributes": [
      {
        "name": "default.rb",
        "path": "attributes/default.rb",
        "checksum": "XXX",
        "specificity": "default",
        "url": "https://chef.sychonet.com:443/bookshelf/
organization-0000/checksum-XXX"
      }
  ]
  "files": [
      {
        "name": "nginx.conf
      }
  ]
  ...
}
```

PUT

The PUT method is used to create or update a cookbook version. This method has no parameters.

For a request, we can use the following code:

```
PUT /cookbooks/NAME/VERSION
```

It has a request body that looks like this:

```
{
  "cookbook_name": "passenger-nginx",
```

```
    "files": [
    ],
    "chef_type": "cookbook_version",
    "definitions": [
    ],
    "libraries": [
    ],
    "attributes": [
        {
            "name": "default.rb",
            "path": "attributes/default.rb",
            "checksum": "XXX",
            "specificity": "default",
            "url": "https://chef.sychonet.com:443/bookshelf/
organization-0000/checksum-XXX"
        }
    ]
    "files": [
        {
            "name": "nginx.conf
        }
    ]
    ...
}
```

Here, the checksum values must have already been uploaded to the Chef server, using the sandbox endpoint. Once a file with a particular checksum has been uploaded by a user, redundant updates are not necessary. Unused checksums are garbage collected.

Response:

This method has no response body.

/data

The /data endpoint is used to manage the data bags stored on the Chef server. The /data endpoint has two methods:

- The GET method
- The POST method

GET

The GET method is used to return a list of all the data bags on the Chef server. This method has no parameters.

For a request, we can use the following code:

```
GET /data
```

Response:

The response will return something like this:

```
{
  "hdfs":"https://chef.sychonet.com:443/data/hdfs",
  "ganglia":"https://chef.sychonet.com:443/data/ganglia",
  "sensu":"https://chef.sychonet.com:443/data/sensu",
  "users":"https://chef.sychonet.com:443/data/users"
}
```

POST

The POST method can be used to create a new data bag on the Chef server. This method has no parameters.

For a request, we can use the following code:

```
POST /data
```

Which has a request body that looks something like this:

```
{
    "name": "data_bag_name"
}
```

Here data_bag_name holds the name of the data bag to create.

Response:

The response will return something like this:

```
{
    "chef_type": "data_bag",
    "data_bag": "data_bag_name",
    "id": "123456"
}
```

/data/NAME

The /data/NAME endpoint is used to view and update a specific data bag. This endpoint has the following methods:

- The DELETE method
- The GET method
- The PUT method

DELETE

The DELETE method can be used to delete the data bag specified in the request.

For a request, we can use the following code:

```
DELETE /data/NAME
```

For example, DELETE /data/sensu will delete the data bag named sensu from the Chef server.

Response:

The response will look something like this:

```
{
    "id": "sensu",
    "real_name": "sensu"
}
```

GET

The GET method can be used to return a hash of all the entries in the specified data bag.

For a request, we can use the following code:

```
GET /data/NAME
```

Or, we can use the following code:

```
GET /data/users.
```

Response:

The response will return something like this:

```
{
"application":"https://chef.sychonet.com:443/data/users/application",
  "hadoop":"https://chef.sychonet.com:443/data/users/hadoop",
  "sychonet"" "https://chef.sychonet.com:443/data/users/sychonet"
}
```

POST

The POST method can be used to create a new data bag item. This method has no parameters.

For a request, we can use the following code:

```
POST /data/NAME
```

It has a request body that looks something like this:

```
{
    "id": "data_bag_name",
    "real_name": "data bag name"
}
```

For example, the following request can be used to create a new user called mayank.

```
POST /data/mayank
```

It has a request body that looks something like this:

```
{
    "id": "mayank",
    "real_name": "Mayank"
}
```

Response:

This method has no response body.

/data/NAME/ITEM

The /data/NAME/ITEM endpoint allows the key-value pairs within a data bag to be viewed or managed. The endpoint has the following methods:

- The DELETE method

- The GET method
- The PUT method

DELETE

The DELETE method is used to delete the key-value pair in the data bag.

For a request, we can use the following code:

```
DELETE /data/NAME/ITEM
```

For example, we might have a user called mayank and we might want to delete this user. The following request can be used to accomplish this:

```
DELETE /data/users/mayank
```

Response:

The response will return something like this:

```
{
  "name": "data_bag_item_users_mayank",
  "json_class": "Chef::DataBagItem",
  "chef_type": "data_bag_item",
  "data_bag": "users",
  "raw_data": {
    "id": "mayank",
    "ssh_keys": [
      "ssh-rsa XXXXXXXXXXX mayank@sychonet.com"
    ],
    "home": "/home/mayank",
    "comment": "Mayank"
  }
}
```

GET

The GET method can be used to get all the key-value pairs in a data bag item.

For a request, we can use the following code:

```
GET /data/NAME/ITEM
```

For example, we can use the following request to get details about the data bag item called mayank in a data bag called users:

```
GET /data/users/mayank
```

Response:

The response will be something like this:

```
{
  "id":"mayank",
  "ssh_keys":["ssh-rsa XXXXX mayank@sychonet.com"],
  "home":"/home/mayank",
  "comment":"Mayank"
}
```

PUT

The PUT method can be used to replace the contents of a data bag item with those from the request.

For a request, we can use the following code along with a request body:

```
PUT /data/NAME/ITEM
```

For example, we might want to replace the SSH key for the user mayank, and this can be accomplished as follows:

```
PUT /data/users/mayank
```

It has a request body as follows:

```
{
    "ssh_keys": ["ssh-rsa YYYYYYY mayank@sychonet.com"]
    "home": "/home/mayank",
    "comment": "Mayank"
}
```

Response:

The response will return something like this:

```
{
    "id": "mayank",
    "ssh_keys": [
      "ssh-rsa YYYYYY mayank@sychonet.com"
    ],
    "home": "/home/mayank",
    "comment": "Mayank",
    "chef_type": "data_bag_item",
    "data_bag": "users"
}
```

/environments

The /environments endpoint can be used to view or edit environments. This endpoint has two methods:

- The GET method
- The POST method

GET

The GET method returns a JSON containing a link to each available environment on the Chef server.

For a request, we can use the following code:

```
GET /environments
```

Response:

The response will return something like this:

```
{
  "_default": "https://chef.sychonet.com:443/environments/_default",
  "staging": "https://chef.sychonet.com:443/environments/staging",
  "perf": "https://chef.sychonet.com:443/environments/perf",
  "prod": "https://chef.sychonet.com:443/environments/prod"
}
```

POST

The POST method is used to create a new environment.

For a request, we can use the following code with a request body:

```
POST /environments
```

For example, we might want to create a new environment called qa. This can be accomplished with the following request:

```
POST /environments
```

It has the following request body:

```
{
  "name": "qa",
  "override_attributes": {},
```

```
    "json_class": "Chef::Environment",
    "description": "",
    "cookbook_versions": {},
    "chef_type": "environment"
}
```

Response:

The response will return something like this:

```
{
    "uri": "https://chef.sychonet.com:443/environments/qa"
}
```

/environments/NAME

The `/environments/NAME` endpoint can be used to manage an individual environment. This endpoint supports the following methods:

- The DELETE method
- The GET method
- The PUT method

DELETE

The DELETE method can be used to delete an environment.

For a request, we can use the following code:

```
DELETE /environments/NAME
```

For example, the following request will delete the environment called qa, which we created in the last example:

```
DELETE /environments/qa
```

Response:

The response will return something like this:

```
{
    "name": "qa",
    "override_attributes": {},
    "json_class": "Chef::Environment",
    "description": "",
```

```
    "cookbook_versions": {},
    "chef_type": "environment",
    "default_attributes": {}
}
```

GET

The GET method can be used to get the details of an environment.

For a request, we can use the following code:

```
GET /environments/NAME
```

For example, the following request will help us get details of an environment called prod:

```
GET /environments/prod
```

Response:

The response will return something like this:

```
{
    "name": "prod",
    "description": "Production Environment",
    "cookbook_versions": {},
    "json_class": "Chef::Environment",
    "chef_type": "environment",
    "default_attributes": {},
    "override_attributes": {}
}
```

PUT

The PUT method can be used to edit an existing environment.

For a request, we can use the following code along with its request body:

```
PUT /environments/NAME
```

For example, we might want to set a default attribute called ldap_server with a value, ldaps://ldap.sychonet.com, for an environment called prod. This task can be accomplished using the following request:

```
PUT /environments/prod
```

It has the following request body:

```
{
  "name": "qa",
  "default_attributes": { "ldap_server": "ldap.sychonet.com" },
  "override_attributes": {},
  "json_class": "Chef::Environment",
  "description": "",
  "cookbook_versions": {},
  "chef_type": "environment"
}
```

Response:

The response will return something like this:

```
{
  "name": "qa",
  "default_attributes": {
    "ldap_server": "ldap.sychonet.com"
  },
  "override_attributes": {},
  "json_class": "Chef::Environment",
  "description": "",
  "cookbook_versions": {},
  "chef_type": "environment"
}
```

/environments/NAME/cookbooks

The `/environments/NAME/cookbooks` endpoint can be used to get a list of cookbooks and cookbook versions that are available to the specified environment.

This method accepts `num_versions=n` as a parameter. This parameter determines how many versions of cookbooks to include in the response.

This endpoint accepts the `GET` method.

GET

For a request, we can use the following:

```
GET /environments/NAME/cookbooks
```

For example, the following request will list all the cookbooks associated with a production environment:

```
GET /environments/prod/cookbooks
```

Response:

The response will return something like this:

```
{
  "passenger-nginx": {
    "url": "https://chef.sychonet.com:443/cookbooks/passenger-nginx",
    "versions": [
      {
        "url": "https://chef.sychonet.com:443/cookbooks/passenger-
nginx/0.1.1",
        "version": "0.1.1"
      }
    ]
  }
}
```

/environments/NAME/nodes

The `/environments/NAME/nodes` endpoint can be used to get a list of all the nodes in a particular environment. This endpoint has the GET method.

GET

The GET method will return a list of nodes in a given environment.

For a request, we can use the following code:

```
GET /environments/NAME/nodes
```

For example, the following request will give a list of all the nodes in a production environment.

```
GET /environments/prod/nodes
```

Response:

The response will return something like this:

```
{
  "web01.production.sychonet.com": "https://chef.sychonet.com:443/
nodes/web01.production.sychonet.com",
```

```
    "web02.production.sychonet.com": "https://chef.sychonet.com:443/
    nodes/web02.production.sychonet.com"
    }
```

/environments/NAME/recipes

The endpoint /environments/NAME/recipes can be used to get a list of recipes available to a particular environment. This endpoint has the GET method.

GET

The GET method will return a list of recipes available to a given environment:

For a request, we can use the following code:

```
GET /environments/NAME/recipes
```

For example, the following request will give a list of recipes available to the production environment:

```
GET /environments/prod/recipes
```

Response:

The response will return something like this:

```
[
    "passenger-nginx"
]
```

/environments/NAME/roles/NAME

This endpoint can be used to return the run_list attribute of the role, when the environment is _default, or to return env_run_lists[environment_name] for non-default environments.

This endpoint only has the GET method.

For a request, we can use the following code:

```
GET /environments/NAME/roles/NAME
```

For example, we might want to get the run-list associated with a role called webserver in the prod environment. To accomplish this, we'll need to make the following request:

```
GET /environments/prod/roles/webserver
```

Response:

The response will return something like this:

```
{
  "run_list": [
    "recipe[ohai]",
    "recipe[base]",
    "recipe[passenger-nginx]",
    ...
  ]
}
```

Search

Apart from these endpoints, the Chef server API provides us with an endpoint to query data indexed by the Chef server. This includes data bags, environments, roles, and nodes. The Chef server API provides two endpoints for the purposes of search: /search and /search/INDEX. The search engine used by Chef is based on Apache Solr. You can do a full-text query using a defined query syntax. Chef provides support for search, using different patterns such as exact, wildcard, range, and fuzzy.

/search

The /search endpoint allows you to search for data bags, roles, nodes, and environments. It has support for the GET method.

GET

The GET method returns a JSON with links to each available search index.

For a request, we can use the following code:

```
GET /search
```

Response:

The response will return something like this:

```
{
  "client": "https://chef.indix.tv:443/search/client",
  "environment": "https://chef.indix.tv:443/search/environment",
  "node": "https://chef.indix.tv:443/search/node",
  "role": "https://chef.indix.tv:443/search/role",
  "hdfs": "https://chef.indix.tv:443/search/hdfs",
```

```
    "ganglia": "https://chef.indix.tv:443/search/ganglia",
    "sensu": "https://chef.indix.tv:443/search/sensu",
    "users": "https://chef.indix.tv:443/search/users"
}
```

As you can see, the request has returned a client, environment, node, role, and different data bags (hdfs, ganglia, sensu, and users) configured on the Chef server.

/search/INDEX

The /search/INDEX endpoint can be used to access the search indexes on the Chef server. This endpoint has the following methods:

- The GET method
- The POST method

A search query comprises of two parts: the key and search pattern with the following format:

```
key:search_pattern
```

Both key and search_pattern are case sensitive. The key has very limited support for multiple characters' wildcard matching using *.

GET

The GET method is used to return data matching the query in the GET request.

This method accepts the following parameters:

Parameter	Description
q	The search query used to identify a list of items on a Chef server
rows	This parameter can be used to limit the number of rows returned
sort	This parameter determines the order in which results are sorted
start	This parameter determines the row in which results will start

For a request, we can use the following code:

```
GET /search/INDEX
```

For example, the following request will help us get a list of all clients with their details:

```
GET /search/clients
```

Response:

The response from the last request will return something like this:

```
{
  "total": 2,
  "start": 0,
  "rows": [
    {
      "public_key": "XXXXXX",
      "name": "chef-webui",
      "admin": true,
      "validator": false,
      "json_class": "Chef::ApiClient",
      "chef_type": "client"
    },
    {
      "public_key": "YYYYYY",
      "name": "chef-validator",
      "admin": false,
      "validator": true,
      "json_class": "Chef::ApiClient",
      "chef_type": "client"
    }
  ]
}
```

POST

However, there will be times when we'll only want a partial search query to be made. A partial search query allows a search query to be made against specific attribute keys that are stored on the Chef server. It can specify an object index and provide a query that can be matched to the relevant index. You must use a partial query instead of a full-text query most of the times as it requires less memory and network bandwidth.

The POST method is used to return partial search results. For example, perhaps we only want the name, IP address, and run-list associated with nodes. For such a use case, we'll need to make a POST request as follows:

For a request, we can use the following code:

```
POST /search/nodes
```

It has the following request body:

```
{
 "name":   ["name"],
 "ip": ["ipaddress"],
 "run-list": ["run_list"]
}
```

Response:

The response will return something like this:

```
{
   "total": 2,
   "start": 0,
   "rows": [
      {
        "url": "https://chef.sychonet.com:443/nodes/webserver01.
production.sychonet.com",
         "data": {
           "name": "webserver01.production.sychonet.com",
           "ip": "10.181.1.219",
           "run-list": [
             "role[webserver]"
           ]
         }
      },
      {
        "url":
"https://chef.sychonet.com:443/nodes/webserver02.production.sychonet.
com",
         "data": {
           "name": "webserver02.production.sychonet.com",
           "ip": "10.181.1.189",
           "run-list": [
             "role[webserver]"
           ]
         }
      }
   ]
}
```

The search till now has been made against indexes such as nodes, data bags, clients, and so on, using the keys. However, there might be a case where you wanted to search for an index by virtue of its value. For example, you might want to search for an IP address and a run-list for a node with FQDN, starting with the string `webserver01`. For such cases, you can use the following request.

For a request, we can use the following code:

```
POST /search/node?q=fqdn:webserver01*
```

Along with the following request body:

```
{
    "name": ["name"],
    "ip": ["ipaddress"],
    "run_list": ["run_list"]
}
```

Response:

This request will result in a response like this:

```
{
   "total": 1,
   "start": 0,
   "rows": [
      {
         "url": "https://chef.sychonet.com:443/nodes/webserver01.
production.sychonet.com",
         "data": {
            "name": "webserver01.production.sychonet.com",
            "ip": "10.181.1.219",
            "run_list": [
               "role[webserver]"
            ]
         }
      }
   ]
}
```

If you want to try out this request, create a JSON file (say `request_body.json`) with content similar to that found in the request body and use the following command:

```
$ knife raw -m POST \
-i request_body.json \
'/search/node?q=fqdn=webserver01*'
```

Patterns

As we mentioned earlier, we can make use of search patterns to fine-tune search results by returning anything that matches some type of incomplete search query. Chef provides us with four types of search patterns, namely: exact, wildcard, range, and fuzzy.

Let's see how we can make use of each of them for the purpose of search.

We'll make use of the `knife` subcommand called `search` for the purpose of examples in the following sections.

Syntax

The syntax for the `knife search` subcommand is as follows:

```
knife search INDEX QUERY [options]
```

One of the most used options with this subcommand is `-a`, which is used to filter attributes returned in the search result.

For example, the following command will display an IP address and a run-list associated with a node with FQDN, starting with the `webserver01` string:

```
knife search node "fqdn:webserver01*" -a "name" -a "ipaddress" -a "run_
list"
```

```
1 items found
webserver01.production.sychonet.com:
   ipaddress: 10.181.1.219
   name:       webserver01.production.sychonet.com
   run_list:   role[webserver]
```

Exact matching

An exact pattern is used to search for a key with a name that exactly matches a search query. If the name of the key contains spaces, quotes must be used to ensure that the search query finds the key. You should quote the entire search query in single quotes and the search pattern should be quoted in double quotes.

For example, the following query will try to find a node with FQDN equal to `webserver01.production.sychonet.com` and will display an IP address and a run-list associated with the node.

```
knife search node "fqdn:webserver01.production.sychonet.com" -a "name" -a
"ipaddress" -a "run_list"
```

This will result in the following output:

```
1 items found
webserver01.production.sychonet.com:
  ipaddress: 10.181.1.219
  name:       webserver01.production.sychonet.com
  run_list:   role[webserver]
```

Wildcard matching

Sometimes, instead of an exact match you might want to get a list of search results matching some criteria. For example, you might be interested in knowing the IP addresses and run-lists of all the nodes whose FQDN begins with the webserver string. A wildcard match can be of a great help in these cases. You can use the following two types of wildcard searches:

- Use * to replace zero or more characters
- Use ? to replace exactly one character.

For example, the following query will help us achieve our goal to find nodes with FQDN beginning with the webserver string:

```
knife search node "fqdn:webserver*" -a "name" -a "ipaddress" -a "run_
list"
```

This will result in the following output:

```
2 items found
webserver01.production.sychonet.com:
  ipaddress: 10.181.1.219
  name:       webserver01.production.sychonet.com
  run_list:   role[webserver]


webserver02.production.sychonet.com:
  ipaddress: 10.181.1.189
  name:       webserver02.production.sychonet.com
  run_list:   role[webserver]
```

Range matching

If there is any key with values limited between an upper and lower boundary, then you can make use of range matching to limit the search within a range. The range can be inclusive or exclusive. We can use `[]` to specify a range that denotes inclusive boundaries and `{}` to specify a range that denotes exclusive boundaries.

Let's say, we've a bunch of data bag items called `bag01`, `bag02`, ..., and `bag10` in a data bag called `bag`, and we only want to see details of the bags between `bag03` to `bag 07`.

The following query will help us get this done:

```
knife search bag "id:[bag03 TO bag07]"
```

If we don't want `bag03` and `bag07` in the result, the query would look something like this:

```
knife search bag "id:{bag03 TO bag07}"
```

Fuzzy matching

This pattern is used to search based on the proximity of two strings of characters. A fuzzy matching search pattern has the following syntax:

```
"search_query"~edit_distance
```

While `search_query` is the string to be used during the search, `edit_distance` determines the proximity. A tilde ~ is used to separate a search string from `edit_distance`.

The edit distance is actually the Levenshtein distance and the algorithm for this kind of search is known as the Levenshtein distance algorithm. The edit distance can have values between 0 and 1, with a value closer to 1, and only terms with higher similarity are matched.

You can find more details about this algorithm at: `http://en.wikipedia.org/wiki/Levenshtein_distance`.

Operators

We can use operators to build complex search queries by combining search results or negating the effects of search. Chef provides the following operators for this purpose:

Operator	Description
AND	Finds a match when both terms exist
OR	Finds a match when either of the terms exist
NOT	Excludes the term after NOT from the search results

For example, we might want to find a list of machines belonging to a production environment, which has `webserver` as a role. This can be accomplished using the following search query:

```
$ knife search node 'chef_environment:production AND roles:webserver'
```

Using search in recipes

Till now, we've seen the use of search via the API or through Knife. Chef also provides a DSL that allows you to query from within recipes.

If you are doing a full-text query, all you need to do is to make a call to a `search` method. The syntax of the search method is as follows:

```
search(:INDEX, "QUERY")
```

Or it can also be used with the following syntax:

```
search(:node, "hostname:webserver01")
```

This method will return a JSON with all the important information about a node with a hostname equal to `webserver01`, which is indexed by the Chef server.

In the case of partial search queries, you need to ensure that the recipe contains a dependency on the `partial_search` cookbook.

The syntax for a partial search query is as follows:

```
partial_search(:INDEX, "QUERY", :keys => { 'attr1' => [ 'key1' ],
'attr2' => ['key2'] ... })
```

For example:

```
partial_search(:node, 'role:webserver',
  :keys => { 'name' => [ 'name' ],
             'ip'   => [ 'ipaddress' ],
             'kernel_version' => [ 'kernel', 'version' ]
           }
).each do |result|
```

```
    puts result['name']
    puts result['ip']
    puts result['kernel_version']
end
```

This will search for nodes with `webserver` as the role in the top-level `run_list`, and finally prints `name`, `ipaddress`, and `kernel_version` for the nodes.

Ridley

Ridley is a Chef API client written in Ruby, which can be used to perform all the operations we looked at earlier, in a very elegant way.

Ridley is available as a gem and can be installed using the following command:

```
gem install ridley
```

Before we can use Ridley in our application, we need to require the library. This can be done using the standard Ruby `require`:

```
require 'ridley'
```

Once the library has been required, we just need to create our `ridley` client and use it to perform all the actions:

```
ridley = Ridley.new(
    server_url: "CHEF_SERVER_URL",
    client_name: "CLIENT_NAME",
    client_key: "PATH_TO_CLIENT_KEY"
)
```

You can also provide `encrypted_data_bag_secret` as a key, which can be used to provide a secret that can be used to decrypt the encrypted data bags.

You can use different functions exposed by Ridley to either retrieve or create objects on the Chef server. For example, the following example will help us get a list of all the users configured on the Chef server:

```
ridley.user.all
```

If you already have `knife.rb` with you, you can make use of `Ridley.from_chef_config` to set up the `ridley` client.

All the resources are accessed by the instance functions on a new instance of `Ridley::Client`:

- `ridley.client #=> Ridley::ClientResource`
- `ridley.cookbook #=> Ridley::CookbookResource`
- `ridley.data_bag #=> Ridley::DataBagResource`
- `ridley.environment #=> Ridley::EnvironmentResource`
- `ridley.node #=> Ridley::NodeResource`
- `ridley.role #=> Ridley::RoleResource`
- `ridley.sandbox #=> Ridley::SandboxResource`
- `ridley.search #=> Ridley::SearchResource`
- `ridley.user #=> Ridley::UserResource`

Most of the resources are able to perform **Create, Read, Update, and Delete (CRUD)** operations.

A new Chef object can be created with the `create` method or the `save` method. The `create` method can be invoked along with an attribute hash or an instance of a Chef object. The `save` method can be invoked on an instance of a Chef object or a Chef object built from serialized JSON.

For reading purposes, most of the resources support two read functions, namely `all` and `find`. The `all` function lists all of the Chef objects, while the `find` function can be used to retrieve a specific Chef object.

Any resource on the Chef server can also be modified using the `update` and `save` functions. The `update` function can be expressed in three different ways. It can be expressed with an ID of an object to update along with an attribute hash. It can also be expressed with an instance of a Chef object. Finally, you can use a `save` function on an instance of a Chef object.

A resource can be destroyed using a `delete` function. This function can be expressed either with an ID of an object to destroy, or with an instance of a Chef object. You can also destroy a resource using a `destroy` method.

For more details about using Ridley, refer to `https://github.com/reset/ridley`.

Summary

This brings us to the end of our journey into the world of the Chef server API and search. We have learned about the authentication mechanisms used by Chef API and we have also seen various endpoints provided by Chef to perform actions across multiple resources. We have also learned about Ridley, one of the very few popular Chef API clients. We have also seen how you can use the power of search to find details about resources present on the Chef server. You can build pretty nice tools to use by using the Chef server API. We'll see some of these tools in later chapters. Search is perhaps one of the most beneficial features of the Chef server and this can be used either in a command line or in your recipes to gain a quick insight into your infrastructure or the Chef server itself. With this knowledge in hand, you can build a really robust and scalable infrastructure with a very high degree of automation.

12
Extending Chef

So far, we have seen the different components of Chef and we have also seen what is possible by making use of the Chef server API. The Chef ecosystem is built for use by operations people and developers alike, and it comes with a bunch of tools such as Ohai, Knife, and so on, which can be used to manage your infrastructure easily using Chef.

However, every now and then you'll find that the available tools just aren't good enough to meet your requirements and this is the time when you can utilize the knowledge that you gathered about the API and internals of Ohai and Knife, and extend the Chef ecosystem by developing your very own resource providers, Ohai plugins, Knife plugins, or an all together different tool set using Chef API meshed up with other APIs.

We have already seen how to write our own custom resource provider and Ohai plugin in the previous chapters. In this chapter, we'll learn how to go about building custom Knife plugins and we'll also see how we can write custom handlers that can help us extend the functionality provided by a chef-client run to report any issues with a chef-client run.

Custom Knife plugins

As we saw in *Chapter 2*, *Knife and Its Associated Plugins*, Knife is one of the most widely used tools in the Chef ecosystem. Be it managing your clients, nodes, cookbooks, environments, roles, users, or handling stuff such as provisioning machines in Cloud environments such as Amazon AWS, Microsoft Azure, and so on, there is a way to go about doing all of these things through Knife. However, Knife, as provided during installation of Chef, isn't capable of performing all these tasks on its own. It comes with a basic set of functionalities, which helps provide an interface between the local Chef repository, workstation and the Chef server.

The following are the functionalities, which is provided, by default, by the Knife executable:

- Management of nodes
- Management of clients and users
- Management of cookbooks, roles, and environments
- Installation of chef-client on the nodes through bootstrapping
- Searching for data that is indexed on the Chef server.

However, apart from these functions, there are plenty more functions that can be performed using Knife; all this is possible through the use of plugins. Knife plugins are a set of one (or more) subcommands that can be added to Knife to support an additional functionality that is not built into the base set of Knife subcommands. Most of the Knife plugins are initially built by users such as you, and over a period of time, they are incorporated into the official Chef code base. A Knife plugin is usually installed into the ~/.chef/plugins/knife directory, from where it can be executed just like any other Knife subcommand. It can also be loaded from the .chef/plugins/knife directory in the Chef repository or if it's installed through RubyGems, it can be loaded from the path where the executable is installed.

Ideally, a plugin should be kept in the ~/.chef/plugins/knife directory so that it's reusable across projects, and also in the .chef/plugins/knife directory of the Chef repository so that its code can be shared with other team members. For distribution purpose, it should ideally be distributed as a Ruby gem.

The skeleton of a Knife plugin

A Knife plugin is structured somewhat like this:

```
require 'chef/knife'

module ModuleName
  class ClassName < Chef::Knife

    deps do
      require 'chef/dependencies'
    end

    banner "knife subcommand argument VALUE (options)"

    option :name_of_option
```

```
      :short => "-l value",
      :long => "--long-option-name value",
      :description => "The description of the option",
      :proc => Proc.new { code_to_be_executed },
      :boolean => true | false,
      :default => default_value

    def run
      #Code
    end
  end
end
```

Let's look at this skeleton, one line at a time:

- **require**: This is used to require other Knife plugins required by a new plugin.
- **module ModuleName**: This defines the namespace in which the plugin will live. Every Knife plugin lives in its own namespace.
- **class ClassName < Chef::Knife**: This declares that a plugin is a subclass of Knife.
- **deps do**: This defines a list of dependencies.
- **banner**: This is used to display a message when a user enters `Knife` `subcommand -help`.
- **option :name_of_option**: This defines all the different command line options available for this new subcommand.
- **def run**: This is the place in which we specify the Ruby code that needs to be executed.

Here are the command-line options:

- `:short` defines the short option name
- `:long` defines the long option name
- `:description` defines a description that is displayed when a user enters `knife subclassName -help`
- `:boolean` defines whether an option is true or false; if the `:short` and `:long` names define `value`, then this attribute should not be used
- `:proc` defines the code that determines the value for this option
- `:default` defines a default value

The following example shows a part of a Knife plugin named knife-windows:

```ruby
require 'chef/knife'
require 'chef/knife/winrm_base'base'

class Chef
  class Knife
    class Winrm < Knife

      include Chef::Knife::WinrmBase

      deps do
        require 'readline'
        require 'chef/search/query'
        require 'em-winrm'
      end

      attr_writer :password

      banner "knife winrm QUERY COMMAND (options)"

      option :attribute,
        :short => "-a ATTR",
        :long => "--attribute ATTR",
        :description => "The attribute to use for opening the
connection - default is fqdn",
        :default => "fqdn"

      ... # more options

      def session
        session_opts = {}
        session_opts[:logger] = Chef::Log.logger if Chef::Log.level ==
:debug
        @session ||= begin
          s = EventMachine::WinRM::Session.new(session_opts)
          s.on_output do |host, data|
            print_data(host, data)
          end
          s.on_error do |host, err|
            print_data(host, err, :red)
          end
```

```
        s.on_command_complete do |host|
          host = host == :all ? 'All Servers' : host
          Chef::Log.debug("command complete on #{host}")
        end
        s
      end

    end

    ... # more def blocks

  end
 end
end
```

Namespace

As we saw with skeleton, the Knife plugin should have its own namespace and the namespace is declared using the `module` method as follows:

```
require 'chef/knife'
#Any other require, if needed

module NameSpace
  class SubclassName < Chef::Knife
```

Here, the plugin is available under the namespace called `NameSpace`. One should keep in mind that Knife loads the subcommand irrespective of the namespace to which it belongs.

Class name

The class name declares a plugin as a subclass of both Knife and Chef. For example:

```
class SubclassName < Chef::Knife
```

The capitalization of the name is very important. The capitalization pattern can be used to define the word grouping that makes the best sense for the use of a plugin.

For example, if we want our plugin subcommand to work as follows:

`knife bootstrap hdfs`

We should have our class name as: **Bootstrap**H**dfs**.

If, say, we used a class name such as **BootStrapHdfs**, then our subcommand would be as follows:

`knife boot strap hdfs`

It's important to remember that a plugin can override an existing Knife subcommand. For example, we already know about commands such as `knife cookbook upload`. If you want to override the current functionality of this command, all you need to do is create a new plugin with the following name:

```
class CookbookUpload < Chef::Knife
```

Banner

Whenever a user enters the `knife -help` command, he/she is presented with a list of available subcommands. For example:

```
knife --help
Usage: knife sub-command (options)
    -s, --server-url URL              Chef Server URL
Available subcommands: (for details, knife SUB-COMMAND --help)


** BACKUP COMMANDS **
knife backup export [COMPONENT [COMPONENT ...]] [-D DIR] (options)
knife backup restore [COMPONENT [COMPONENT ...]] [-D DIR] (options)


** BOOTSTRAP COMMANDS **
knife bootstrap FQDN (options)
....
```

Let us say we are creating a new plugin and we would want Knife to be able to list it when a user enters the `knife -help` command. To accomplish this, we would need to make use of `banner`.

For example, let's say we've a plugin called `BootstrapHdfs` with the following code:

```
module NameSpace
  class BootstrapHdfs < Chef::Knife
    ...
```

```
    banner "knife bootstrap hdfs (options)"
    ...
  end
end
```

Now, when a user enters the `knife -help` command, he'll see the following output:

** BOOTSTRAPHDFS COMMANDS **

knife bootstrap hdfs (options)

Dependencies

Reusability is one of the key paradigms in development and the same is true for Knife plugins. If you want a functionality of one Knife plugin to be available in another, you can use the `deps` method to ensure that all the necessary files are available. The `deps` method acts like a lazy loader, and it ensures that dependencies are loaded only when a plugin that requires them is executed.

This is one of the reasons for using `deps` over `require`, as the overhead of the loading classes is reduced, thereby resulting in code with a lower memory footprint; hence, faster execution.

One can use the following syntax to specify dependencies:

```
deps do
  require 'chef/knife/name_of_command'
  require 'chef/search/query'
  #Other requires to fullfill dependencies
end
```

Requirements

One can acquire the functionality available in other Knife plugins using the `require` method. This method can also be used to require the functionality available in other external libraries. This method can be used right at the beginning of the plugin script, however, it's always wise to use it inside `deps`, or else the libraries will be loaded even when they are not being put to use.

The syntax to use `require` is fairly simple, as follows:

```
require 'path_from_where_to_load_library'
```

Let's say we want to use some functionalities provided by the bootstrap plugin. In order to accomplish this, we will first need to require the plugin:

```
require 'chef/knife/bootstrap'
```

Next, we'll need to create an object of that plugin:

```
obj = Chef::Knife::Bootstrap.new
```

Once we've the object with us, we can use it to pass arguments or options to that object. This is accomplished by changing the object's config and the name_arg variables. For example:

```
obj.config[:use_sudo] = true
```

Finally, we can run the plugin using the run method as follows:

```
obj.run
```

Options

Almost every other Knife plugin accepts some command line option or other. These options can be added to a Knife subcommand using the option method. An option can have a Boolean value, string value, or we can even write a piece of code to determine the value of an option.

Let's see each of them in action once:

An option with a Boolean value (true/false):

```
option :true_or_false,
  :short => "-t",
  :long => "—true-or-false",
  :description => "True/False?",
  :boolean => true | false,
  :default => true
```

Here is an option with a string value:

```
option :some_string_value,
  :short => "-s VALUE",
  :long => "—some-string-value VALUE",
  :description => "String value",
  :default => "xyz"
```

An option where a code is used to determine the option's value:

```
option :tag,
  :short => "-T T=V[,T=V,...]",
  :long => "—tags Tag=Value[,Tag=Value,...]",
  :description => "A list of tags",
  :proc => Proc.new { |tags| tag.split(',') }
```

Here the `proc` attribute will convert a list of comma-separated values into an array.

All the options that are sent to the Knife subcommand through a command line are available in form of a hash, which can be accessed using the `config` method.

For example, say we had an option:

```
option :option1
  :short => "-s VALUE",
  :long => "—some-string-value VALUE",
  :description => "Some string value for option1",
  :default => "option1"
```

Now, while issuing the Knife subcommand, say a user entered something like this:

```
$ knife subcommand -option1 "option1_value"
```

We can access this value for `option1` in our Knife plugin `run` method using `config[:option1]`

When a user enters the `knife -help` command, the description attributes are displayed as part of help. For example:

```
**EXAMPLE COMMANDS**

knife example
  -s, --some-type-of-string-value     This is not a random string value.

  -t, --true-or-false                 Is this value true? Or is this
value false?

  -T, --tags                          A list of tags associated with the
virtual machine.
```

Arguments

A Knife plugin can also accept the command-line arguments that aren't specified using the `option` flag, for example, `knife node show NODE`. These arguments are added using the `name_args` method:

```
require 'chef/knife'
module MyPlugin
  class ShowMsg << Chef::Knife
    banner 'knife show msg MESSAGE'
    def run
      unless name_args.size == 1
      puts "You need to supply a string as an argument."
        show_usage
        exit 1
      end
      msg = name_args.join(" ")
      puts msg
    end
  end
end
```

Let's see this in action:

knife show msg

You need to supply a string as an argument.

USAGE: knife show msg MESSAGE

```
    -s, --server-url URL          Chef Server URL
        --chef-zero-host HOST      Host to start chef-zero on
. . .
```

Here, we didn't pass any argument to the subcommand and, rightfully, Knife sent back a message saying `You need to supply a string as an argument.`

Now, let's pass a string as an argument to the subcommand and see how it behaves:

knife show msg "duh duh"

duh duh

Under the hood what's happening is that `name_args` is an array, which is getting populated by the arguments that we have passed in the command line. In the last example, the `name_args` array would've contained two entries (`"duh"`, `"duh"`). We use the `join` method of the `Array` class to create a string out of these two entities and, finally, print the string.

The run method

Every Knife plugin will have a `run` method, which will contain the code that will be executed when the user executes the subcommand. This code contains the Ruby statements that are executed upon invocation of the subcommand. This code can access the options values using the `config[:option_hash_symbol_name]` method.

Search inside a custom Knife plugin

Search is perhaps one of the most powerful and most used functionalities provided by Chef. By incorporating a search functionality in our custom Knife plugin, we can accomplish a lot of tasks, which would otherwise take a lot of efforts to accomplish. For example, say we have classified our infrastructure into multiple environments and we want a plugin that can allow us to upload a particular file or folder to all the instances in a particular environment on an ad hoc basis, without invoking a full chef-client run. This kind of stuff is very much doable by incorporating a search functionality into the plugin and using it to find the right set of nodes in which you want to perform a certain operation. We'll look at one such plugin in the next section.

To be able to use Chef's search functionality, all you need to do is to `require` the Chef's `query` class and use an object of the `Chef::Search::Query` class to execute a query against the Chef server. For example:

```
require 'chef/search/query'
query_object = Chef::Search::Query.new
query = 'chef_environment:production'
query_object.search('node',query) do |node|
  puts "Node name = #{node.name}"
end
```

Since the name of a node is generally FQDN, you can use the values returned in `node.name` to connect to remote machines and use any library such as `net-scp` to allow users to upload their files/folders to a remote machine. We'll try to accomplish this task when we write our custom plugin at the end of this chapter.

We can also use this information to edit nodes. For example, say we had a set of machines acting as web servers. Initially, all these machines were running Apache as a web server. However, as the requirements changed, we wanted to switch over to Nginx. We can run the following piece of code to accomplish this task:

```
require 'chef/search/query'

query_object = Chef::Search::Query.new
```

```
query = 'run_list:*recipe\\[apache2\\]*'
query_object.search('node',query) do |node|
  ui.msg "Changing run_list to recipe[nginx] for #{node.name}"
  node.run_list("recipe[nginx]")
  node.save
  ui.msg "New run_list: #{node.run_list}"
end
```

knife.rb settings

Some of the settings defined by a Knife plugin can be configured so that they can be set inside the `knife.rb` script. There are two ways to go about doing this:

- By using the `:proc` attribute of the option method and code that references `Chef::Config[:knife][:setting_name]`
- By specifying the configuration setting directly within the `def` Ruby blocks using either `Chef::Config[:knife][:setting_name]` or `config[:setting_name]`

An option that is defined in this way can be configured in `knife.rb` by using the following syntax:

```
knife [:setting_name]
```

This approach is especially useful when a particular setting is used a lot. The precedence order for the Knife option is:

1. The value passed via a command line.
2. The value saved in `knife.rb`
3. The default value.

The following example shows how the Knife `bootstrap` command uses a value in `knife.rb` using the `:proc` attribute:

```
option :ssh_port
  :short => '-p PORT',
  :long => '--ssh-port PORT',
  :description => 'The ssh port',
  :proc => Proc.new { |key| Chef::Config[:knife][:ssh_port] = key
}
```

Here `Chef::Config[:knife][:ssh_port]` tells Knife to check the `knife.rb` file for a `knife[:ssh_port]` setting.

The following example shows how the Knife `bootstrap` command calls the `knife ssh` subcommand for the actual SSH part of running a bootstrap operation:

```
def knife_ssh
  ssh = Chef::Knife::Ssh.new
  ssh.ui = ui
  ssh.name_args = [ server_name, ssh_command ]
  ssh.config[:ssh_user] = Chef::Config[:knife][:ssh_user] ||
config[:ssh_user]
  ssh.config[:ssh_password] = config[:ssh_password]
  ssh.config[:ssh_port] = Chef::Config[:knife][:ssh_port] ||
config[:ssh_port]
  ssh.config[:ssh_gateway] = Chef::Config[:knife][:ssh_gateway] ||
config[:ssh_gateway]
  ssh.config[:identity_file] =
Chef::Config[:knife][:identity_file] || config[:identity_file]
  ssh.config[:manual] = true
  ssh.config[:host_key_verify] =
Chef::Config[:knife][:host_key_verify] || config[:host_key_verify]
  ssh.config[:on_error] = :raise
  ssh
end
```

Let's take a look at the preceding code:

- `ssh = Chef::Knife::Ssh.new` creates a new instance of the `Ssh` subclass named `ssh`
- A series of settings in Knife `ssh` are associated with a Knife bootstrap using the `ssh.config[:setting_name]` syntax
- `Chef::Config[:knife][:setting_name]` tells Knife to check the `knife.rb` file for various settings
- It also raises an exception if any aspect of the SSH operation fails

User interactions

The `ui` object provides a set of methods that can be used to define user interactions and to help ensure a consistent user experience across all different Knife plugins. One should make use of these methods, rather than handling user interactions manually.

Method	Description
`ui.ask(*args, &block)`	The ask method calls the corresponding `ask` method of the HighLine library. More details about the HighLine library can be found at `http://www.rubydoc.info/gems/highline/1.7.2`.
`ui.ask_question(question, opts={})`	This is used to ask a user a question. If `:default => default_value` is passed as a second argument, `default_value` will be used if the user does not provide any answer.

`ui.color (string, *colors)`	This method is used to specify a color.
	
	For example:
	
	``ruby
	server = connections.server.
	create(server_def)
	  puts "#{ui.color("Instance ID",
	:cyan)}: #{server.id}"
	  puts "#{ui.color("Flavor", :cyan)}:
	#{server.flavor_id}"
	  puts "#{ui.color("Image", :cyan)}:
	#{server.image_id}"
	  . . .
	  puts "#{ui.color("SSH Key", :cyan)}:
	#{server.key_name}"
	print "\n#{ui.color("Waiting for
	server", :magenta)}"
	``

`ui.color?()`	This indicates that the colored output should be used. This is only possible if an output is sent across to a terminal.
`ui.confirm(question, append_instructions=true)`	This is used to ask (Y/N) questions. If a user responds back with N, the command immediately exits with the status code 3.
`ui.edit_data(data, parse_output=true)`	This is used to edit data. This will result in firing up of an editor.
`ui.edit_object(class, name)`	This method provides a convenient way to download an object, edit it, and save it back to the Chef server. It takes two arguments, namely, the class of object to edit and the name of object to edit.

Method	Description
`ui.error`	This is used to present an error to a user.
`ui.fatal`	This is used to present a fatal error to a user.
`ui.highline`	This is used to provide direct access to a highline object provided by many `ui` methods.
`ui.info`	This is used to present information to a user.
`ui.interchange`	This is used to determine whether the output is in a data interchange format such as JSON or YAML.
`ui.list(*args)`	This method is a way to quickly and easily lay out `lists`. This method is actually a wrapper to the list method provided by the HighLine library. More details about the HighLine library can be found at `http://www.rubydoc.info/gems/highline/1.7.2`.
`ui.msg(message)`	This is used to present a message to a user.
`ui.output(data)`	This is used to present a data structure to a user. This makes use of a generic default presenter.
`ui.pretty_print(data)`	This is used to enable the `pretty_print` output for JSON data.
`ui.use_presenter(presenter_class)`	This is used to specify a custom output presenter.
`ui.warn(message)`	This is used to present a warning to a user.

For example, to show a fatal error in a plugin in the same way that it would be shown in Knife, do something similar to the following:

```
unless name_args.size == 1
    ui.fatal "Fatal error !!!"
    show_usage
    exit 1
end
```

Exception handling

In most cases, the exception handling available within Knife is enough to ensure that the exception handling for a plugin is consistent across all the different plugins. However, if the required one can handle exceptions in the same way as any other Ruby program, one can make use of the `begin-end` block, along with rescue clauses, to tell Ruby which exceptions we want to handle.

For example:

```
def raise_and_rescue
  begin
    puts 'Before raise'
    raise 'An error has happened.'
    puts 'After raise'
  rescue
    puts 'Rescued'
  end
  puts 'After begin block'
end


raise_and_rescue
```

If we were to execute this code, we'd get the following output:

```
ruby test.rb
Before raise
Rescued
After begin block
```

A simple Knife plugin

With the knowledge about how Knife's plugin system works, let's go about writing our very own custom Knife plugin, which can be quite useful for some users. Before we jump into the code, let's understand the purpose that this plugin is supposed to serve. Let's say we've a setup where our infrastructure is distributed across different environments and we've also set up a bunch of roles, which are used while we try to bootstrap the machines using Chef.

So, there are two ways in which a user can identify machines:

- By environments
- By roles

 Actually, any valid Chef search query that returns a node list can be the criteria to identify machines. However, we are limiting ourselves to these two criteria for now.

Often, there are situations where a user might want to upload a file or folder to all the machines in a particular environment, or to all the machines belonging to a particular role. This plugin will help users accomplish this task with lots of ease. The plugin will accept three arguments. The first one will be a key-value pair with the key being chef_environment or a role, the second argument will be a path to the file or folder that is required to be uploaded, and the third argument will be the path on a remote machine where the files/folders will be uploaded to. The plugin will use Chef's search functionality to find the FQDN of machines, and eventually make use of the net-scp library to transfer the file/folder to the machines.

Our plugin will be called knife-scp and we would like to use it as follows:

```
knife scp chef_environment:production /path_of_file_or_folder_locally /
path_on_remote_machine
```

Here is the code that can help us accomplish this feat:

```ruby
require 'chef/knife'

module CustomPlugins
  class Scp < Chef::Knife
    banner "knife scp SEARCH_QUERY PATH_OF_LOCAL_FILE_OR_FOLDER PATH_
ON_REMOTE_MACHINE"

    option :knife_config_path,
      :short => "-c PATH_OF_knife.rb",
      :long  => "--config PATH_OF_knife.rb",
      :description => "Specify path of knife.rb",
      :default => "~/.chef/knife.rb"

    deps do
      require 'chef/search/query'
      require 'net/scp'
      require 'parallel'
    end

    def run
      if name_args.length != 3
        ui.msg "Missing arguments! Unable to execute the command
successfully."
```

```
        show_usage
        exit 1
      end
                Chef::Config.from_file(File.expand_
path("#{config[:knife_config_path]}"))
        query = name_args[0]
        local_path = name_args[1]
        remote_path = name_args[2]
        query_object = Chef::Search::Query.new
        fqdn_list = Array.new
        query_object.search('node',query) do |node|
          fqdn_list << node.name
        end
        if fqdn_list.length < 1
          ui.msg "No valid servers found to copy the files to"
        end
        unless File.exist?(local_path)
          ui.msg "#{local_path} doesn't exist on local machine"
          exit 1
        end

        Parallel.each((1..fqdn_list.length).to_a, :in_processes => fqdn_
list.length) do |i|
          puts "Copying #{local_path} to #{Chef::Config[:knife][:ssh_
user]}@#{fqdn_list[i-1]}:#{remote_path} "
          Net::SCP.upload!(fqdn_list[i-1],"#{Chef::Config[:knife]
[:ssh_user]}","#{local_path}","#{remote_path}",:ssh => { :keys =>
["#{Chef::Config[:knife][:identity_file]}"] }, :recursive => true)
        end
      end
    end
  end
end
```

This plugin uses the following additional gems:

- The parallel gem to execute statements in parallel. More information about this gem can be found at `https://github.com/grosser/parallel`.

- The net-scp gem to do the actual transfer. This gem is a pure Ruby implementation of the SCP protocol. More information about the gem can be found at `https://github.com/net-ssh/net-scp`.

Both these gems and the Chef search library are required in the `deps` block to define the dependencies.

This plugin accepts three command line arguments and uses `knife.rb` to get information about which user to connect over SSH and also uses `knife.rb` to fetch information about the SSH key file to use. All these command line arguments are stored in the `name_args` array.

A Chef search is then used to find a list of servers that match the query, and eventually a parallel gem is used to parallely SCP the file from a local machine to a list of servers returned by a Chef query.

As you can see, we've tried to handle a few error situations, however, there is still a possibility of this plugin throwing away errors as the `Net::SCP.upload` function can error out at times.

Let's see our plugin in action:

Case1: The file that is supposed to be uploaded doesn't exist locally. We expect the script to error out with an appropriate message:

```
knife scp 'chef_environment:ft' /Users/mayank/test.py /tmp

/Users/mayank/test.py doesn't exist on local machine
```

Case2: The `/Users/mayank/test` folder is:

```
knife scp 'chef_environment:ft' /Users/mayank/test /tmp

Copying /Users/mayank/test to ec2-user@host02.ft.sychonet.com:/tmp

Copying /Users/mayank/test to ec2-user@host01.ft.sychonet.com:/tmp
```

Case3: A config other than `/etc/chef/knife.rb` is specified:

```
knife scp -c /Users/mayank/.chef/knife.rb 'chef_environment:ft' /Users/
mayank/test /tmp

Copying /Users/mayank/test to ec2-user@host02.ft.sychonet.com:/tmp

Copying /Users/mayank/test to ec2-user@host01.ft.sychonet.com:/tmp
```

Distributing plugins using gems

As you must have noticed, until now we've been creating our plugins under `~/.chef/plugins/knife`. Though this is sufficient for plugins that are meant to be used locally, it's just not good enough to be distributed to a community. The most ideal way of distributing a Knife plugin is by packaging your plugin as a gem and distributing it via a gem repository such as `rubygems.org`. Even if publishing your gem to a remote gem repository sounds like a far-fetched idea, at least allowing people to install your plugin by building a gem locally and installing it via `gem install`. This is a far better way than people downloading your code from an SCM repository and copying it over to either `~/.chef/plugins/knife` or any other folder they've configured for the purpose of searching for custom Knife plugins. With distributing your plugin using gems, you ensure that the plugin is installed in a consistent way and you can also ensure that all the required libraries are preinstalled before a plugin is ready to be consumed by users.

All the details required to create a gem are contained in a file known as `Gemspec`, which resides at the root of your project's directory and is typically named the `<project_name>.gemspec`. `Gemspec` file that consists of the structure, dependencies, and metadata required to build your gem.

The following is an example of a `.gemspec` file:

```
Gem::Specification.new do |s|
  s.name    = 'knife-scp'
  s.version = '1.0.0'
  s.date    = '2014-10-23'
  s.summary = 'The knife-scp knife plugin'
  s.authors = ["maxcoder"]
  s.email   = 'maxcoder@sychonet.com"
  s.files   = ["lib/chef/knife/knife-scp.rb"]
  s.homepage = "https://github.com/maxc0d3r/knife-plugins"
  s.add_runtime_dependency "parallel","~> 1.2", ">= 1.2.0"
  s.add_runtime_dependency "net-scp","~> 1.2", ">= 1.2.0"
end
```

The `s.files` variable contains the list of files that will be deployed by a gem install command. Knife can load the files from `gem_path/lib/chef/knife/<file_name>.rb`, and hence we've kept the `knife-scp.rb` script in that location.

The `s.add_runtime_dependency` dependency is used to ensure that the required gems are installed whenever a user tries to install our gem.

Once the file is there, we can just run a gem build to build our gem file as follows:

```
→  knife-scp git:(master) × gem build knife-scp.gemspec
WARNING:  licenses is empty, but is recommended.  Use a license
abbreviation from:
http://opensource.org/licenses/alphabetical
WARNING:  See http://guides.rubygems.org/specification-reference/ for
help
  Successfully built RubyGem
  Name: knife-scp
  Version: 1.0.0
  File: knife-scp-1.0.0.gem
```

The gem file is created and now, we can just use `gem install knife-scp-1.0.0.gem` to install our gem. This will also take care of the installation of any dependencies such as parallel, net-scp gems, and so on.

You can find a source code for this plugin at the following location:

`https://github.com/maxc0d3r/knife-plugins`.

Once the gem has been installed, the user can run it as mentioned earlier.

For the purpose of distribution of this gem, it can either be pushed using a local gem repository, or it can be published to `https://rubygems.org/`. To publish it to `https://rubygems.org/`, create an account there.

Run the following command to log in using a gem:

```
gem push
```

This will ask for your email address and password.

Next, push your gem using the following command:

```
gem push your_gem_name.gem
```

That's it! Now you should be able to access your gem at the following location:

`http://www.rubygems.org/gems/your_gem_name`.

As you might have noticed, we've not written any tests so far to check the plugin. It's always a good idea to write test cases before submitting your plugin to the community. It's useful both to the developer and consumers of the code, as both know that the plugin is going to work as expected. Gems support adding test files into the package itself so that tests can be executed when a gem is downloaded. RSpec is a popular choice to test a framework, however, it really doesn't matter which tool you use to test your code. The point is that you need to test and ship.

Some popular Knife plugins, built by a community, and their uses, are as follows:

knife-elb:

This plugin allows the automation of the process of addition and deletion of nodes from Elastic Load Balancers on AWS.

knife-inspect:

This plugin allows you to see the difference between what's on a Chef server versus what's on a local Chef repository.

knife-community:

This plugin helps to deploy Chef cookbooks to Chef Supermarket.

knife-block:

This plugin allows you to configure and manage multiple Knife configuration files against multiple Chef servers.

knife-tagbulk:

This plugin allows bulk tag operations (creation or deletion) using standard Chef search queries. More information about the plugin can be found at: `https://github.com/priestjim/knife-tagbulk`.

You can find a lot of other useful community-written plugins at: `https://docs.chef.io/community_plugin_knife.html`.

Custom Chef handlers

A Chef handler is used to identify different situations that might occur during a chef-client run, and eventually it instructs the chef-client on what it should do to handle these situations. There are three types of handlers in Chef:

- The exception handler: This is used to identify situations that have caused a chef-client run to fail. This can be used to send out alerts over an email or dashboard.

- The report handler: This is used to report back when a chef-client run has successfully completed. This can report details about the run, such as the number of resources updated, time taken for a chef-client run to complete, and so on.

- The start handler: This is used to run events at the beginning of a chef-client run.

Writing custom Chef handlers is nothing more than just inheriting your class from `Chef::Handler` and overriding the report method.

Let's say we want to send out an email every time a chef-client run breaks. Chef provides a `failed?` method to check the status of a chef-client run. The following is a very simple piece of code that will help us accomplish this:

```
require 'net/smtp'
module CustomHandler
  class Emailer < Chef::Handler
    def send_email(to,opts={})
      opts[:server] ||= 'localhost'
      opts[:from] ||='maxcoder@sychonet.com'
      opts[:subject] ||='Error'
      opts[:body] ||= 'There was an error running chef-client'

      msg = <<EOF
From: <#{opts[:from]}>
To: #{to}
Subject: #{opts[:subject]}

#{opts[:body]}
EOF
```

```
    Net::SMTP.start(opts[:server]) do |smtp|
      smtp.send_message msg, opts[:from], to
    end
  end

  def report
    name = node.name
    subject = "Chef run failure on #{name}"
    body = [run_status.formatted_exception]
    body += ::Array(backtrace).join("\n")
    if failed?
      send_email(
        "ops@sychonet.com",
        :subject => subject,
        :body => body
      )
    end
  end
end
end
```

If you don't have the required libraries already installed on your machine, you'll need to make use of chef_gem to install them first before you actually make use of this code.

With your handler code ready, you can make use of the chef_handler cookbook to install this custom handler. To do so, create a new cookbook, email-handler, and copy the file emailer.rb created earlier to the file's source. Once done, add the following recipe code:

```
include_recipe 'chef_handler'

handler_path = node['chef_handler']['handler_path']
handler = ::File.join handler_path, 'emailer'

cookbook_file "#{handler}.rb" do
  source "emailer.rb"
end

chef_handler "CustomHandler::Emailer" do
  source handler
    action :enable
end
```

Now, just include this handler into your base role, or at the start of `run_list` and during the next chef-client run, if anything breaks, an email will be sent across to ops@sychonet.com.

You can configure many different kinds of handlers like the ones that push notifications over to IRC, Twitter, and so on, or you may even write them for scenarios where you don't want to leave a component of a system in a state that is undesirable. For example, say you were in a middle of a chef-client run that adds/deletes collections from Solr. Now, you might not want to leave the Solr setup in a messed-up state if something were to go wrong with the provisioning process. In order to ensure that a system is in the right state, you can write your own custom handlers, which can be used to handle such situations and revert the changes done until now by the chef-client run.

Summary

In this chapter, we learned about how custom Knife plugins can be used. We also learned how we can write our own custom Knife plugin and distribute it by packaging it as a gem. Finally, we learned about custom Chef handlers and how they can be used effectively to communicate information and statistics about a chef-client run to users/admins, or handle any issues with a chef-client run.

In the next chapter, we'll go about building a set of tools that can be used to manage your infrastructure with a lot of ease using Chef. These tools will combine the Chef API with some other APIs to accomplish goals that otherwise would be very difficult to accomplish.

13
(Ab)Using Chef

We've explored various aspects of the Chef ecosystem and we've tried to get our hands dirty with the exploration of Chef's wonderful API as well. However, as a common practice, nothing is good enough on its own, and the real benefits of a particular technology or tool can be only realized once we've used it along with other tool sets. This is true for Chef too. Chef on its own is a wonderful piece of software; however, once we start integrating it along with other tools, we realize the true benefits of Chef. In this chapter, we'll look at a few such integrations and also see how we can extend Chef by mashing together various different APIs with Chef's API. This chapter is going to be very code intensive and you'll be introduced to a few APIs outside Chef. These APIs can change at any point in time and if you plan on using the code given in this chapter directly, ensure that you have read through the API documentation. If the API provider has introduced any changes, make sure you've taken care of incorporating those changes into your code. Last but not the least, since we are trying to specify our infrastructure as code, it makes a lot more sense to ensure that the code we are writing works as expected in the production environment. We'll see how we can go about writing code that is tested thoroughly before it's pushed to the Chef server.

The dynamic server list in Capistrano using Chef

Capistrano is a remote server automation tool. It can be used to execute an arbitrary set of tasks on remote servers. It's primarily used for the purpose of remote deployments. As per their official documentation, Capistrano can be used to:

- Reliably deploy to any number of machines simultaneously, in the sequence of a rolling set

- Automate audits of any number of machines

- Script arbitrary workflows over SSH

Although Chef also provides a deploy resource, I personally prefer push-based deployment solutions such as Capistrano, as they provide more control and I can easily hook them up with a release management system to provide visibility.

Capistrano considers a list of servers as a role and it can either deploy to an individual host or an entire fleet. Usually, this list of servers is maintained in configuration files, or supplied as a command line option during execution. This works pretty well for environments where the total number of servers isn't too big and also where the infrastructure isn't very fragile. For example, say you are running a web app shop, consisting of a couple of web servers, a couple of application servers, and maybe three or four database servers in a data center. With such a setup, it's pretty easy to manage the list of servers in a configuration file, and to allow Capistrano to handle deployments by reading configuration files and figuring out the right set of servers to deploy the code to.

However, in today's world, where most shops are moving to cloud-based deployments, this approach isn't very well suited. In a cloud-based deployment, there are two concerns in terms of deployments:

- **Scaling**: One of the main reasons for hosting an infrastructure in a cloud-based environment, is the fact that they allow for the easy scaling of the infrastructure. You can set up Auto Scaling groups, which can increase/decrease capacity of your infrastructure depending on your requirements.

- **Fragile nature of the infrastructure**: The infrastructure in a cloud-based environment isn't as robust as a classic data center. The virtual machines in cloud-based environments can go down at any point in time, and when you bring up new instances in lieu of instances that were lost, you might get a different IP address for a new instance and all these issues will add to the complexity of deployments.

In all these cases, we see that the infrastructure isn't static and is very dynamic by nature. With such a setup, you need a mechanism to map machines with services dynamically. One way to go about doing this is to use some sort of service discovery mechanism such as Consul, Etcd, and so on. However, you can very easily rely on Chef and use it to discover services in your infrastructure, and map services with machines. We'll make use of Chef's search API along with the attributes to find the machines associated with the services running in your setup, and use this information to deploy code using Capistrano.

Before we go about integrating Chef with Capistrano, let's take a quick look at how Capistrano manages deployments. We'll be considering a use case for a PHP application.

We'll be only looking at Capistrano 3.x, and if you are using Capistrano 2.x, you might find a few subtle changes. However, the way we'll be integrating Chef will remain the same for both versions of Capistrano.

Installing Capistrano

Capistrano can be installed easily using a gem package as follows:

```
$ gem install capistrano
```

You can verify the installation by issuing the following command:

```
$ cap -version
Capistrano Version: 3.3.5 (Rake Version: 10.1.0)
```

Preparing your application:

Go to the project directory of your application and run the following command:

```
$ cd /path/to/app
$ cap install
```

This will create the following files/directories:

```
.
|-- Capfile
|-- config
|   |-- deploy
|   |   |-- production.rb
|   |   `-- staging.rb
|   `-- deploy.rb
|-- config.rb
`-- lib
    `-- capistrano
        `-- tasks
```

Let's look at the purpose of these files :

- `Capfile`: It's similar to a bootstrap. All the necessary configs generally go in here. It's the basic file of Capistrano and is mandatory.

- `config/deploy.rb`: Tasks that are common across environments go in here.

- `config/deploy/{production,staging}.rb`: Tasks that are concerned with a specific environment go in here.

- `lib/capistrano/tasks`: You can create any number of files with the `.rake` extension in this directory, and you'll be able to use the tasks that you've declared here automatically.

Roles:

Roles are how the division of responsibility between servers is taken care of. You can map a role such as `:web` to a bunch of machines running a web server, while `:db` can map to servers where our database is residing.

For example, the following code will map `webserver01.sychonet.com` and `webserver02.sychonet.com` to the `:web` role:

```
role :web, %w{ webserver01.sychonet.com webserver02.sychonet.com}
```

Tasks:

Tasks are a unit of execution in the world of Capistrano, and you can create as many tasks as you need. You can also create before and after hooks that allow you to decide which task is supposed to be called once a particular task is called upon, or once it's over.

The following is a sample task that runs the `'uptime'` command on remote server(s):

```
desc 'uptime'
task :get_uptime do
  on roles(:web) do
      execute 'uptime'
  end
end
```

You can execute this task using the following command:

```
$ cap get_uptime
```

This will in turn run the `'uptime'` command across `webserver{01,02}.sychonet.com`.

Use case:

We've a couple of web servers hosted on Amazon AWS. AWS provides hostnames such as `ec2-12-34-56-78.us-west-2.compute.amazonaws.com`, where the name consists of the AWS domain, the service (in this case, `compute`), the region, and a form of public IP address.

We have two such web servers with the following FQDNs:

- `ec2-12-34-56-78.us-west-2.compute.amazonaws.com`
- `ec2-12-37-59-104.us-west-2.compute.amazonaws.com`

We've set up our role called `:web` as follows in our Capistrano configuration:

```
role :web, %w{ ec2-12-34-56-78.us-west-2.compute.amazonaws.com
ec2-12-37-59-104.us-west-2.compute.amazonaws.com }
```

Since AWS doesn't guarantee the life cycle of an instance, one of the instances goes away (`ec2-12-37-59-104.us-west-2.compute.amazonaws.com`) and our provisioning system automatically takes care of bringing up a new instance in lieu of the instance that has been terminated, and finally Chef takes care of bootstrapping the instance correctly. Let's presume that this instance as FQDN, `ec2-12-34-59-114.us-west-2.compute.amazonaws.com`.

Now, however, our new instance is up and running, the Capistrano `config` is still considering `ec2-12-37-59-104.us-west-2.compute.amazonaws.com` to be a server where our web application needs to be deployed.

We can go about manually editing the Capistrano scripts and making the required change. However, this is where we can use the power of the Chef search API and generate a list of servers for Capistrano dynamically. Since the instance has been provisioned with Chef, we can always query the Chef server to get the list of nodes, which are of type `web server`. The type can be identified by `run_list` or by some attribute. Though we could have used roles for this purpose, often we find roles to be generic in nature and hence, I prefer the attribute way as it allows me to use an attribute as a tag and also allows me to modify my run lists at any point in time. Let's call our Chef attribute `server_type`, and this attribute can have a value `webserver`. The following code will help integrate Chef with Capistrano and get the list of servers dynamically:

```
require 'chef/rest'
require 'chef/search/query'

def set_role(rolename,value)
  roles.delete rolename.to_sym
  role(rolename){value}
end

Chef::Config.from_file(File.expand_path("/path/to/knife.rb"))
query = Chef::Search::Query.new
query_string = "server_type:webserver'
nodes = query.search('node', query_string).first rescue []
```

```
set_role('web',nodes.map(&:name))

    . . .

    desc 'uptime'
    task :get_uptime do
      on roles(:web) do
        execute 'uptime'
      end
    end


    . . .
```

Now, if we run the following command:

$ cap get_uptime

The script will first query the Chef server for the name of the node (generally FQDN) for machines, which have the `server_type` attribute with the `webserver` value. The query will return a list of nodes, which we'll assign to the role called `:web`. Since we are considering a Chef server to be a source of truth for our infrastructure, we'll get the updated list of servers every time we go about triggering deployment.

> If you have been watching this closely, we've not yet removed the instance that has been terminated from the list of nodes on the Chef server, and this can result in a search query yielding results that contain servers that aren't present anymore. You need to be aware of such a scenario, and either clean up the Chef server automatically, or ensure that deployment scripts don't error out if an instance is not reachable. I'll leave this as an exercise for you to figure out the right way to handle this issue.

Capistrano style deployments using Chef's "deploy" resource

Capistrano is a very popular push-based deployment tool used extensively in the world of Ruby on Rails applications. However, once you've moved your infrastructure to the cloud, in addition to the automatic provisioning of machines, you also need to be interested in ensuring that once the machines are up and running, they come up with the right version of your application code. Now, the provisioning of machines is the domain of Chef, while application deployment is classically a task belonging to the realm of Capistrano. However, now with the "deploy" resource of Chef, you can deploy your favorite Ruby on Rails application, just as you would do with Capistrano.

The `deploy` resource is meant to provide the facility of the `deploy` and `deploy:migration` tasks in Capistrano.

The syntax of the deploy resource is as follows:

```
deploy "name" do
  attribute "value"
  . . .
  callback do
     # callback, include release_path or new_resource
  end
  . . .
  purge_before_symlink
  create_dirs_before_symlink
  symlink
  action :action
end
```

The various attributes of the preceding code are as follows:

- `deploy`: This tells the chef-client to use either the `Chef::Provider::Deploy::Revision` or `Chef::Provider::Deploy::TimeStamped` providers.

- `name`: This is the name of the resource block. If the `deploy_to` attribute is not specified, `name` is also used to determine where the deployment will take place.

- `attribute`: It has zero or more attributes that are available for this resource.

- `callback`: This represents an additional Ruby code that can be used to provide additional information to the chef-client during the execution of the `deploy` resource.

- `purge_before_symlink`, `create_dirs_before_symlink`, and `symlink`: These are attributes used to link configuration files, delete/create directories, or map files during the process of deployment.

- `:action`: This identifies which steps the chef-client will take to bring a node to the desired state.

Phases of deployment

The deployment happens in four phases:

1. **Checkout**: During this phase, the chef-client will use the SCM resource to get a specific revision of the application. The code will be either checked out or cloned into a directory called `cached-copy`, which is a subdirectory of the `deploy` directory. A copy of the application is finally placed in a subdirectory called `releases`.

2. **Migrate**: During migration, the chef-client symlinks the database configuration into a checkout (`configs/database.yml`) and runs the `migration` command. For Ruby on Rails applications, the migration command is usually `rake db:migrate`.

3. **Symlink**: During this phase, the directories for shared and temporary files are removed (log, tmp/pids, and public/system by default). After this step, the directories (`tmp`, `public`, and `config` by default) are created. Finally, the `releases` directory is symlinked to `current`.

4. **Restart**: During this phase, the application is finally restarted as per the restart policy specified in the application.

Callbacks

In between the deployment process, callbacks are allowed to be executed. The callbacks can be an arbitrary Ruby code or even a recipe. Each callback expects a shell command when providing a string as an input.

The following callbacks are supported:

Callback	Description
`after_restart`	A block of code to be executed after the application is restarted. The default value is `deploy/after_restart.rb`.
`before_restart`	A block of code to be executed before the application is restarted. The default value is `deploy/before_restart.rb`.
`before_migrate`	A block of code to be executed before migration. The default value is `deploy/before_migrate.rb`.
`before_symlink`	A block of code to be executed before symlinks are handled. The default value is `deploy/before_symlink.rb`.

Each of these callbacks can be used in one of three ways:

*   To pass a block of code
*   To specify a file
*   To do neither

Within a callback, there are two ways to get access to information about the deployment:

*   `release_path`: This can be used to get the path to the current release.

- `new_resource`: This can be used to access `deploy_resource`, including environment variables that have been set there.

Actions

The resource can have the following actions:

Action	Description
`:deploy`	This is used to deploy an application
`:force_deploy`	This is used to remove the existing release of an application and redeploy the application.
`:rollback`	This is used to rollback the application to the previous release.

Attributes

The deploy resource has perhaps the largest set of attributes:

Attribute	Description
`after_restart`	This a block of code or path to a file that is executed after the application is restarted.
`before_migrate`	This a block of code or path to a file that is executed before migration is started.
`before_restart`	This is a block of code or path to a file that is executed before the application is restarted.
`before_symlink`	This is a block of code or path to a file that is executed before symlinks are created.
`create_dirs_before_symlink`	This is used to create directories before a symlink.
`deploy_to`	This is used to specify a path where the application is actually deployed.
`environment`	This is a hash of environment variables of the `{"ENV_VARIABLE" => "VALUE"}` form
`keep_releases`	This is the number of releases for which a backup is kept.
`migrate`	If a migration command is required to be executed, this should be set to `true`.
`migration_command`	This specifies which migration command to execute.

Attribute	Description
`purge_before_symlink`	This specifies a list of directories from a checkout before symbolic links are created. This runs before `create_dirs_before_symlink` and symlinks.
`repo`	This is an alias for the repository.
`revision`	This specifies which revision to check out.
`rollback_on_error`	This attribute is used to decide whether or not we should rollback to the previous release if an error occurs during the deployment of a new release. The default value for this attribute is `false`.
`scm_provider`	This is used to define the name of a source control management provider. The default value for this attribute is `Chef::Provider::Git`. If using subversion, this value should be set to `Chef::Provider::Subversion`.
`symlink_before_migrate`	This is used to map files in a shared directory to the current release directory. The symbolic links for these files will be created before any migration is run.
`timeout`	This attribute is used to specify the amount of time to wait before a command is considered to have timed out.
`user`	This attribute is used to specify the name of the user responsible for the checked-out code.

There are a few other attributes available as well, and readers should refer to the official documentation of Chef for the deploy resource.

The following is an example of a deploy resource in action. It's going to deploy the `myapp` application available at the `git@github.com/maxc0d3r/myapp` to `/apps/myapp` directory on the server where the chef-client run is executed:

```
deploy "/apps/myapp" do
  repo "git@github.com/maxc0d3r/myapp"
  revision "xxxxx"
  user "application"
  enable_submodules true
  migrate true
```

```
migration_command "rake db:migrate"
environment "RAILS_ENV" => "production"
keep_releases 7
action :deploy
restart_command "touch tmp/restart.txt"
scm_provider "Chef::Provider::Git"
end
```

If you are deploying a non-Rails application and you don't need any symbolic links, you should use the following code:

```
deploy "/apps/myapp" do
  symlinks({})
end
```

Alternatively, you can use the following code:

```
deploy "/apps/myapp" do
  symlinks Hash.new
end
```

Extending Chef to bootstrap distributed systems

Most configuration management systems such as Chef, Puppet, CFEngine, Ansible, and so on, operate at a node level, and any configuration change that is required to be made is applied only upon the convergence runs that happen at the scheduled intervals and aren't event-based. For example, say you've a setup comprising of a load balancer (say HAProxy) and web servers. Now, you are running a website and you want to ensure that as soon as the traffic spikes up, you should be able to provision a new web server.

You've written the HAProxy cookbook so that it searches for nodes of type *webserver*, populates its config, and reloads the HAProxy process. You've also written the Chef code to bring up the web server; however, even once the server is up and running, your load balancer has no knowledge of this and either you have to manually trigger the chef-client run, or if you are running a chef-client as a daemon or cron job, you have to wait for the next run to trigger. This can lead to unnecessary delays in the deployment of a new web server and may eventually lead to business losses. It would've been awesome if the load balancer could automatically know that a new web server has joined the fleet and is waiting to serve.

There are many different ways to accomplish this. One of the popular ways is to make use of a service discovery solution such as Consul, and write a wrapper over Chef, which is able to trigger the chef-client run on a load balancer machine as soon as a new web server has registered the web server service with it. Another way is to make use of a service such as **Serf**, which is a decentralized solution for cluster membership, failure detection, and orchestration. You are encouraged to look at these options for this purpose. However, we are looking at one other alternative provided by the Opscode folks. It's called Pushy or opscode-push-job-server/client.

There are two additional components, which are required to be installed, the Push Job server and the Push Job client. The server component used to be a premium feature, but with Chef 12, you can just go ahead and install it alongside the erchef project. To install the Push Job server, issue the following command on your Chef server:

```
$ chef-server-ctl install opscode-push-job-server
```

Once the installation is over, you can configure it through the following command:

```
$ opscode-push-jobs-server-ctl reconfigure
```

After the preceding command, run the following one:

```
$ chef-server-ctl reconfigure
```

The client component can be installed using the `push-jobs` cookbook.

Once the components are installed, there are two things that you need to be aware of:

5. How to allow commands to be executed via "Push jobs"
6. How to start jobs

The commands to be executed are controlled by a `whitelist` attribute. The push-jobs cookbook can be used to set this attribute, and the cookbook also writes a configuration file `/etc/chef/push-jobs-client.rb`. This script makes use of the `node['push_jobs']['whitelist']` attribute to identify the commands that can be executed.

For example:

```
"default_attributes": {
    "push_jobs": {
        "whitelist": {
            "chef-client": "chef-client -j /etc/chef/roles.json"
        }
    }
}
```

Now the jobs can be either triggered from your workstation manually, or you can set up your cookbooks to trigger jobs.

Running jobs from your workstation

Before you can run a job, you'll need to install the `knife-push` plugin. This can be accomplished by running the following command:

```
$ gem install knife-push
```

This will add the following subcommands to your Knife arsenal:

```
** JOB COMMANDS **
knife job list
knife job start <command> [<node> <node> ...]
knife job status <job id>
```

Let's say we have configured the node to be able to execute the `chef-client` command as mentioned in the `node['push_jobs']['whitelist']` attribute earlier. Now, we can trigger the job using the following command:

```
$ knife job start chef-client <node_name>
```

You can search for a list of available jobs using the following command:

```
$ knife search 'name: node_name' -a push_jobs.whitelist
```

One of the great things about using push-jobs is that you don't need to worry about setting up SSH keys and you can use the same credentials that are used to access Chef, in order to fire commands.

Running jobs from within recipes

This feature is extremely useful if you want to orchestrate actions between different nodes. For example, let's revisit the use case we discussed earlier.

"We are setting up a web server and we want it to be automatically attached to a load balancer, once the web server is configured."

One way to go about doing this is to configure the chef-client run scheduled to happen at regular interval on the load balancer so that it can search for the available nodes of the type `web server` and add them to its backend list. However, this is not the most efficient way to do this as it would lead to delays. A better way would've been if somehow the chef-client run on the web server could trigger a chef-client run on the load balancer automatically.

To our advantage, Push Jobs can also be used inside recipes. There is an LWRP called "pushy", which can be found at `https://github.com/mfdii/pushy`. This LWRP provides a resource called "pushy" that can be used to run commands added to the `node["push_jobs"]["whitelist"]` attribute on remote nodes.

Here is how you can use it in your web server recipe:

```
pushy "chef-client" do
    action :run
    nodes ["haproxy"]
end
```

This code will in turn execute the chef-client run on a node named `haproxy`, provided we've configured the `node["push_jobs"]["whitelist"]` attribute on the `haproxy` node, and configured the `"chef-client"` command.

Push Jobs is really useful in the context of applications where coordination between services running across multiple machines is of grave importance.

Apart from triggering a full chef-client run, you can also perform some other tasks such as restart/reload of services, and so on.

You can even create your very own template engine that can generate configs on the fly and trigger a run of that engine upon an event.

For example, rather than triggering a full complete run of a chef-client, we could've set up a basic templating engine on a load balancer, which would've queried chef-server for the list of machines with type `web server`, and recreated the load balancer's configuration file. We would then add the command responsible for running the templating engine to the `whitelist` attribute and invoke the command from within a web server recipe, followed by a command to reload the load balancer process.

The following is an example of a templating engine:

```
#!/usr/bin/env ruby
require 'erb'
require 'chef/rest'
require 'chef/search/query'

Chef::Config.from_file(File.expand_path('/path/to/knife.rb'))
query_string = "type:webserver'
servers = query.search('node',query_string).first.map(&:name)

renderer = ERB.new(File.read('/path/to/haproxy.erb'))
File.write('/path/to/haproxy.cfg',renderer.result())
```

Ensure that this script is present on the load balancer, along with the `haproxy.erb` template. For easy use, let's place it at `/usr/bin/regen_haproxy_config`.

The following is a sample `haproxy.erb`:

```
global
  daemon
  maxconn           10000
  ulimit-n          65536
  log     127.0.0.1  local2 info
  stats     socket /tmp/haproxy level admin

defaults
  log global
  mode http
  option httplog
  timeout connect 60000ms
  timeout client 60000ms
  timeout server 60000ms

frontend webapp
  bind *:80
  default_backend webservers
  option http_proxy

 backend webservers
  option http_proxy
  <% servers.each_with_index do |server,index| %>
  server server<%= index %> <%= server %>:80 check inter 2s rise 5
fall 2
  <% end %>
  balance leastconn

 listen admin
  bind *:9090
  stats enable
```

Just add the script to the `node["push_jobs"]["whitelist"]` attribute as follows:

```
"default_attributes": {
    "push_jobs": {
        "whitelist": {
```

```
        "regen_haproxy_config": "/usr/bin/regen_haproxy_config",
     "reload_haproxy": "/etc/init.d/haproxy reload"
       }
     }
  }
```

Now, in your web server recipe, you can just call this command using the pushy resource, followed by the reload of HAProxy as follows:

```
pushy "regen_haproxy_config" do
   action :run
   nodes ["haproxy"]
end
push "reload_haproxy" do
   action :run
   nodes ["haproxy"]
end
```

Push Jobs is just one way to ensure that you are able to set up distributed machines with a lot of ease. However, there are many other ways to accomplish the same thing. One of the really nice ways to accomplish this feat is by making use of a framework called Ironfan. This is a framework developed by Infochimps, which provides abstraction over Chef and allows us to provision, deploy, and manage a cluster. Though there are projects such as Ambari and so on that allow you to configure a distributed cluster such as Hadoop, Ironfan allows us to retain the benefits of Chef while extending it outside the realm of a configuration management system for a node to a cluster management system.

Let's see how we can go about using Ironfan to set up a distributed Hadoop cluster:

Installation:

Install Ironfan using the documentation available at https://github.com/ infochimps-labs/ironfan/wiki/INSTALL.

Finally, in your homebase directory, rename example-clusters to clusters. This directory contains cluster files, which are sample definitions of clusters provided by Infochimps.

Let's run the knife cluster list command once:

```
$ knife cluster list
Cluster Path: /.../homebase/clusters

  +---------------+-------------------------------------------------------+
  | cluster | path |
```

```
+----------------+-------------------------------------------------+
| dev | /.../homebase/clusters/dev.rb |
| stg | /.../homebase/clusters/stg.rb |
...
```

So now, we are pretty much set to specify our very own cluster configuration. You can specify the following configuration settings in the cluster configuration file:

Cloud provider settings:

Ironfan provides support for various Cloud providers such as AWS, Rackspace, OpenStack, and so on. We'll look at AWS as an example over the course of this chapter. We can provide information such as which AMI to make use of, what type of instance to use, which region and availability zone should the server be created in, what security group to use for use on the instance, and so on.

Base role definition:

You can define a base role for the cluster and store the definition inside the $CHEF_HOMEBASE/ roles directory. This role can be applied to all the instances in the cluster. You can, however, override the definition for a particular facet or server.

Environment definition:

You can manage multiple environments using a single Chef server and this holds true for Ironfan as well. One can define multiple environments in the $CHEF_ HOMEBASE/ environments directory.

Various facets definition:

Facets are a group of servers within a cluster. For example, in a Kafka cluster, you might have a few instances as part of the zookeeper quorum, while the rest of them are acting as Kafka brokers. We can define one group of servers under the zookeeper facet and others under the kafka_broker facet inside the Kafka cluster.

Facet-specific roles and recipes:

You can define roles and recipes that are very specific to a facet. The following is a sample cluster configuration file that can be used to set up a Hadoop HDFS cluster:

```
Ironfan.cluster test01' do
  # Environment under which chef nodes will be placed
  environment :dev
  # Global roles for all servers
  role :base

  cloud(:ec2) do
```

```
      permanent true
      region 'us-east-1'
      availability_zones ['us-east-1c', 'us-east-1d']
      flavor 't1.micro'
      backing 'ebs'
      image_name 'ironfan-natty'
      chef_client_script 'client.rb'
      security_group(:ssh).authorize_port_range(22..22)
      mount_ephemerals
   end

   facet :master do
     instances 1
     cloud(:ec2) do
     flavor 'm1.small'
     security_group(:hadoop) do
     authorize_port_range(5700..5900)
     role :hadoop_namenode
     role :hadoop_secondarynamenode
   end
   facet :worker do
     instances 2
     role :hadoop_datanode
   end
 end
```

The preceding code will spin up a cluster with one `m1.small` instance running `namenode` and `secondarynamenode`, along with two `t1.micro` instances running `datanode`.

Just add this configuration file to the `$CHEF_HOMEBASE/clusters` directory under a file such as `my_first_cluster.rb`.

Now, when we issue the `knife cluster list` command, we'll see the following clusters listed in the output:

- Cluster management commands: With configuration at our disposal, now let's go ahead and look at a set of commands that would make the task of cluster management a lot easier.

- List clusters: This command will list the clusters available with us in `$CHEF_HOMEBASE/clusters`:

```
$ knife cluster list

Cluster Path: /.../homebase/clusters

+-------------+-----------------------+
```

```
| cluster      | path                     |
+-------------+--------------------------+
test01          HOMEBASE/clusters/test01.rb
+-------------+--------------------------+
```

- Launch a cluster: This command will launch a cluster as per the configuration specified in the cluster's configuration file:

```
$knife cluster launch test01
Loaded information for 3 computers in cluster my_first_cluster
Name                        | Chef? | State    | Flavor    | AZ
 | Env | MachineID   | Public IP      | Private IP      | Created On
 |

+---------------------------------+-------+---------+----------+------
------+-----+-----------+----------------+------------------+------
------+
 | test01-master-0  | yes    | running | m1.small | us-east-1c |
dev | i-a5 | 101.23.157.51  | 10.106.57.77   | 2012-12-10 |
 | test01-client-0  | yes    | running | t1.micro | us-east-1c |
dev | i-cfe117b3 | 101.23.157.52  | 10.106.57.78   | 2012-12-10 |
 | test01-client-1  | yes    | running | t1.micro | us-east-1c |
dev | i-cbe117b7 | 101.23.157.52  | 10.106.57.79   | 2012-12-10 |
+---------------------------------+-------+---------+----------+------
------+-----+-----------+----------------+------------------+------
------+
```

Launch a single instance of a facet using the following command:

```
$ knife cluster launch test01 master 0
```

Launch all instances of a single facet using the following command:

```
$ knife cluster launch test01 worker
```

Stop the whole cluster using the following command:

```
$ knife cluster stop test01
```

Stop a single instance of a facet using the following command:

```
$ knife cluster stop test01 master 0
```

Stop all instances of a facet using the following command:

```
$ knife cluster stop test01 worker
```

Using Ironfan can make the life of someone such as a Hadoop admin a lot easier, as it allows you to get a complete cluster view of your infrastructure, rather than looking at instances one at a time.

Last but not least, you are encouraged to make use of service discovery mechanisms, such as Consul and Serf, and integrate them with Chef. These tools are pretty stable for production use now, and the possibilities of using them for the management of a distributed cluster is very enticing.

Test-driven development with Chef

As we are trying to specify our infrastructure as code, it would be prudent of us to take some good stuff from devs practices and incorporate them into our coding practices. The following figure illustrates a few such ideas:

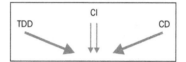

Ops:

- TDD: Test-Driven Development
- CI: Continuous Integration
- CD: Continuous Delivery/Deployment

Development without TDD

The usual practice followed by operations people can be understood from this flow chart:

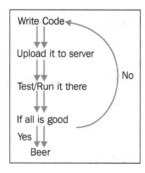

Development with TDD

With TDD practices in use, the following is how the development cycle looks:

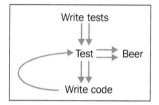

With TDD, the tests are an integral part of the development phase and either tests are written even before the code is written, or they are written alongside the code. So, whether you are building a new feature or fixing a bug, you'll always be writing test cases and running them continuously to ensure that things are behaving as intended. This is a habit that needs to be cultivated, and the following are the steps you need to take to follow the TDD practice for development:

1. Write tests to demonstrate a new feature or expose a bug.
2. Implement a feature or expose a bug.
3. Tests pass.

In this approach, you need to first think of test cases for new features or tests that will expose bugs. This will require a lot of practice, but you'll get the following immediate benefits by adopting this form of development practice:

1. Better test coverage
2. It allows you to think through the feature
3. It allows you to follow the practice of incremental development

Types of tests

The following are the two main categories of tests that are written by developers:

Unit tests:

These tests are meant to test an individual component and such testing is also known as "component testing". Ideally, each test case is independent of the other. It's written to ensure that the code meets its design and behaves as intended.

Unit tests are usually written before the code is written. When the tests pass, the code is considered to be complete. In case the test fails, it's an indicator of a bug in the code or test itself.

The following are the key points related to unit tests:

1. Tests only a single component.
2. Does not require other components.
3. Should be fast.

Integration tests:

Integration testing is a phase in software testing where individual software modules are combined and tested as a collective group. During the integration test, input modules that have already been unit tested are taken as input, grouped into larger aggregates, and the tests defined in the integration test plan are applied.

Integration testing is done to verify the functionality, performance, and reliability requirements of the overall system.

What to use where

Now that we know about different types of tests, we need to determine what kind of test should be used where. In the context of Chef, you can use the following approach:

Unit Tests	Integration Tests
Cookbooks	Chef server installation
Recipes	Chef client installation
Templates	Top-level role
Attributes	Application installation testing
Files	
Libraries	
Data bags	

How do we simulate a real-world scenario?

One of the major challenges of testing the Chef code lies in the fact that your development environment might be very different from your actual deployment environment. For example, you might be developing on a Mac while your servers are running Linux. Moreover, you might not be interested in actually running the Chef code locally on your machine as you don't want to install unnecessary components on your local box.

One of the workarounds to this problem is to make use of Cloud platforms. However, if, like most of us, you aren't interested in spending money over running test suites, one of the most used alternatives is Vagrant. Vagrant (https://www.vagrantup.com) is a wrapper over VirtualBox that allows you to spin up a cluster of virtual machines locally on your laptop/workstation. You can simulate an entire data center on your laptop, provided you've enough compute/memory capacity locally.

Tools

There are a large set of tools that allow for setting up the testing framework of your Chef code. For our purpose, we'll be looking at the following tools:

- ChefSpec (https://github.com/sethvargo/chefspec)
- minitest-chef-handler (https://github.com/calavera/minitest-chef-handler)
- Serverspec (https://github.com/serverspec/serverspec)

ChefSpec is a unit testing framework that runs on a local machine for the purpose of simulating the convergence of resources. One of the major advantages of ChefSpec is that it's blazingly fast as it doesn't provision a real node. It's also highly adaptable, in the sense that you might be running code on Mac, but want the recipe tested against a different platform. With ChefSpec, you don't really need to find the real node corresponding to the platform in order to run the test. However, with these strengths, comes a major disadvantage too. You cannot really verify the sanity of custom providers using ChefSpec. For example, say you've written a custom provider to install a package. Now, since ChefSpec will be doing a no-op, you won't really know if your custom provider will be actually doing installation of a software or not.

minitest-chef-handler is an integration testing framework that runs the minitest-chef-handler infrastructure as part of the chef-client run. It incorporates a report handler that tells at the end what really happened at the end of the run of minitest tests. The advantage of using this is that it actually runs on a real node, however, it's slow.

With the tools decided, we need to decide on the workflow. The following is one way to incorporate TDD practices into your coding workflow:

1. Create the ChefSpec test.
2. Modify the cookbook.
3. Ensure that chefspec tests passes.
4. Create a real test environment using virtual machines spawned through Vagrant.

5. Write minitest tests.

6. Ensure minitest tests pass.

7. Push code to Git.

Before we jump into details of writing unit tests using ChefSpec, and the integration test plan using minitest-chef-handler, let's look at how we can achieve continuous deployment by adhering to the following basic steps:

1. The master branch of your SCM should always be ready for deployment.

2. Each feature/bug fix should be committed to a master, while ensuring that no dependencies break the master.

This approach requires that you have tests for all the commits and no commit is made to master a branch until all the tests have passed.

ChefSpec is perhaps one of the most widely used "unit test frameworks" for Chef.

Install ChefSpec using the following command:

```
$ gem install chefspec
```

Also, since we'll be writing all our test cases inside the specs directory in the cookbook, install the knife-spec gem as well:

```
$ gem install knife-spec
```

This gem will ensure that the specs directory is automatically created whenever a cookbook is created using the knife cookbook create command.

The following code shows the basic structure of a unit test described with ChefSpec:

```
require '../spec_helper.rb'
describe 'cookbook_name::recipe_name' do
  let (:chef_run) {
    ChefSpec::ChefRunner.new.converge('cookbook_name::recipe_name')
  }
  it 'should_do_something' do
    expect(chef_run).to ACTION_RESOURCE(NAME)
  end
end
```

Let's look at each line of code and see what's happening out here:

- The ../spec_helper.rb path directs to the spec_helper.rb file, typically found in root of the /spec folder that contains ChefSpec unit tests.

- The `describe` method is a RSpec method used to define the unit test. There is another method called `context` that is used to group specific contexts.

- The `cookbook_name::recipe_name` variable is used to identify a recipe in a cookbook that is being tested.

- The `let` method is a RSpec method used to kick-start a chef-client run, using (`:chef_run`).

- The `it` method is a RSpec method that puts the context around each unit test. The actual test is defined within the `it` block. It generally looks like this:

```
                           expect(chef_run).to action('object)
expect().to is the assertion syntax in RSpec.
(chef_run) calls the Chef::Runner class to execute the mock chef-
client run.
ACTION_RESOURCE(name) is the action from a resource.
```

For example:

```
it 'starts service nginx' do
  expect(chef_run).to start_service('nginx')
end
```

minitest-Chef-Handler (`https://github.com/calavera/minitest-chef-handler`) is a wonderful integration testing framework. It works by gathering all the files that match the `files/default/tests/minitest/*_test.rb` path for cookbooks in your `run_list`. Once the regular chef-client run is over, minitest runs each of the tests and displays the results. It eventually makes use of a minitest framework (`https://github.com/seattlerb/minitest`) that provides support for writing unit, spec, mock, and benchmark test cases.

It can be installed using the following command:

```
$ gem install minitest-chef-handler
```

In order to make use of minitest-chef-handler, you need the actual machines on which the code will be executed. In most cases, using Vagrant is the best possible solution.

The following is a Vagrant file that can be used to set up VMs for testing your cookbooks:

```
Vagrant.configure(2) do |config|
  config.vm.box = "chef/centos-6.5"
  config.vm.box_check_update = false
  config.vm.provider "virtualbox" do |vb|
    vb.gui = false
```

```
      vb.memory = "256"
    end
    config.vm.provision :chef_solo do |chef|
      chef.cookbook_path = ["/code/chef-repo/cookbooks/"]
      chef.log_level = :debug
      chef.add_recipe "chef_handler"
      chef.add_recipe "minitest-handler"
      chef.add_recipe "docker::test"
    end
  end
```

Keep this Vagrant file at the root of your cookbook. We'll be using this file later on to start our VM.

Let's say we have a cookbook called `docker` with the following code in the default recipe:

```
package "docker-io"

cookbook_file "/etc/pki/tls/certs/ca-bundle.crt" do
  source "/certs/ca-bundle.crt"
  owner "root"
  group "root"
  mode "0644"
end

bash "enable_public_ol6_latest" do
  user "root"
  code <<-EOH
    yum-config-manager --enable public_ol6_latest
  EOH
end

package "device-mapper-event-libs" do
  version "1.02.90-2.el6_6.1"
  action :install
end

service "docker" do
  supports :status => true
  action :start
end

unless node["users"].empty? do
  group "docker" do
```

```
        action :modify
        members node["users"]
        append true
    end
end
```

This recipe will install the docker binary, manage certificates, install `device-mapper-event-libs`, start the docker service, and finally it will check for an attribute called `users`, and if we've the attribute present, it'll add those users to the docker group.

To set up test cases for the code, create a file `<recipe_name>_test.rb` inside the `files/default/tests/minitest` directory in the relevant cookbook. In our example case, our recipe is called `default.rb` and hence, we've a file called `default_test.rb`. In order to invoke the tests, either you can add the report handler to `client.rb`, or add the `minitest-handler` recipe to the run list:

- Option 1: Adding report handler to `client.rb`:

```
  require 'minitest-chef-handler'
report_handlers << MiniTest::Chef::Handler.new
```

- Option 2: Using minitest-handler:

```
chef.run_list = [
    "our recipes",
    "minitest-handler"
]
```

Let's now write our tests which will help ascertain the sanity of our Chef cookbook:

```
  require 'minitest/spec'
describe_recipe 'docker::default' do
include MiniTest::Chef::Assertions
include MiniTest::Chef::Context
include MiniTest::Chef::Resources
describe "packages" do
it "test_if_docker_is_installed" do
package("docker-io").must_be_installed
end
it  "test_if_device_mapper_events_lib_is_installed" do
package("device-mapper-event-libs").must_be_installed
end
end
describe "files" do
it "creates the certificate" do
file("/etc/pki/tls/certs/ca-bundle.crt").must_exist
end
```

```
end
describe "services" do
it "docker is running" do
service("docker").must_be_running
end
it "docker is configured to start on boot" do
service("docker").must_be_enabled
end
end

describe "users and groups" do
it "checks that group docker is created" do
group("docker").must_exit
end

it "checks that users are there having right membership" do
unless node["users"].empty? do
node["users"].each do |node_user|
user(node_user).must_exist
group("docker").must_include(node_user)
end
end
end
end
end
  end
```

Now, with code ready, let's start up our VM using the following command from the root of your cookbook:

```
$ vagrant up
```

This will use the Vagrant file we created earlier to spin up a VM.

Now, once the chef-run is complete, we'll see that at the end, we'll have our test cases executing and, in the event of any errors, report handler will report back with the errors.

Serverspec:

So, you have your servers configured via Chef, but how do you know if they have been configured correctly? This is where Serverspec comes into picture. Serverspec is a framework that allows you to write RSpec tests to verify the configuration of servers.

You can test the actual state of servers by running commands locally via SSH, the Docker API, and so on.

To install Serverspec, use the following command:

```
⊠  ~  gem install serverspec
```

Once Serverspec has been installed, you can use the `serverspec-init` binary to create the required directory structure and files.

This binary requires a few questions to be answered, such as which OS is the test suite meant for, what shall be the mode of execution of test suite: SSH/local, and so on.

Once you've the files in place, you can edit the spec file as per your requirements. Here is an example of spec to test the installation of `nginx` webserver:

```
require 'spec_helper'
describe package('nginx') do
  it { should_be_installed }
end
describe port(80) do
  it { should_be_listening }
end
```

With the test case in place, you can just execute this test case using the following command:

```
⊠  ~  rake spec
```

If you have opted for SSH as a mode of connection, Serverspec will try to connect to the remote machine as the user configured in `~/.ssh/config` or as the current user. If you want to modify this option, edit the `spec/spec_helper.rb` script and add the following:

```
options[:user] ||= Etc.getlogin
```

With the test setup ready, you can now hook up the entire setup with a CI server such as Jenkins and use it for the purpose of running the test suite, and once everything looks good, just do a `knife upload` of the cookbook to your remote Chef server from the CI server itself.

Using Chef in a dynamic environment such as the cloud

Today, with increase in the use of cloud-based environments, it's not too long before you might find yourself dealing with infrastructure in one of the Cloud environments. The benefits that Cloud-based environments give, which are agility and a dynamic nature, are also one of the major pain points. Managing an infrastructure spread across such a dynamic environment is a pretty challenging job on its own. Added to it are features such as Auto Scaling, wherein spot instances and the complexity can grow overwhelmingly and become a nightmare. Chef is a wonderful choice to provision instances in such an environment. However, you have to ensure that few things are taken care of, before we decide to make use of Chef for all the purposes such as service discovery, and integrate it in deployment workflows like we did earlier by tying Capistrano to Chef.

One of the major hurdles is with the fact that instances can come and go in a Cloud-based environment. This means that the state of infrastructure maintained on Chef might be different from what it actually is. There are multiple ways to get around this. One of the ways is to ensure that before the machine is terminated, a script is executed that takes care of the cleanup of the node/client information associated with that instance from Chef.

The following is a sample script that does this job:

```
#!/bin/bash
#
# chkconfig: 2345 74 26
### BEGIN INIT INFO
# Provides:          cleanup_instance
# Required-Start:    $network $named $remote_fs $syslog
# Required-Stop:     $network $named $remote_fs $syslog
# Default-Stop:      0
### END INIT INFO
source /etc/profile.d/rvm.sh
set -e

case "$1" in
  stop)
<% if node.attribute?("fqdn") %>
    knife node delete -y -c /etc/chef/knife.rb <%= node.fqdn %>  #
remove node from Chef
    knife client delete -y -c /etc/chef/knife.rb <%= node.fqdn %>  #
deletes the client certificate from Chef
    rm -f /etc/chef/client.pem
    <% end %>
```

```
    rm -f /var/lock/subsys/cleanup_instance
    ;;
  start)
    chef-client
    touch "/var/lock/subsys/cleanup_instance"
    ;;
  *)
    echo "Usage: cleanup_instance {start|stop}" >&2
    exit 1
    ;;
esac

exit 0
```

Save this script as a template in your `base` cookbook or any cookbook that is used across every machine in your infrastructure. Now, in your recipe, add the following code to set up this script:

```
template "/etc/init.d/cleanup_instance" do
  source "/cleanup_instance.erb"
  owner "root"
  group "root"
  mode "0755"
end

file "/var/lock/subsys/cleanup_instance" do
  action :create
  owner "root"
  group "root"
  mode "0644"
end

(0..6).each do |index|
  link "/etc/rc.d/rc#{index}.d/K74cleanup_instance" do
    to "/etc/init.d/cleanup_instance"
    owner "root"
    group "root"
    mode "0755"
  end

  link "/etc/rc.d/rc#{index}.d/S74cleanup_instance" do
    to "/etc/init.d/cleanup_instance"
    owner "root"
    group "root"
```

```
    mode "0755"
  end
end
```

 This code is meant for the RHEL/CentOS family. If you want to use this on any other Linux variant, modify the Chef code and script appropriately.

This code will set up the script. Now, whenever the instance terminates, the script will be invoked and the node/client entry associated with the instance will be removed from the Chef server. This approach will require you to push a chef-validator key to a machine, which can then be used for the purpose of reregistration. If you are using AWS, you can make use of the IAM role to pull the validator key from a secure S3 bucket. Remember to delete the validator key once the instance has been reregistered.

Another way is to monitor the instance and in case an instance goes down, the monitoring solution should trigger the cleanup code. Sensu (`https://sensuapp.org`) is a monitoring solution that is designed with this thought process in mind and can be used for the purpose of the deregistration of a node and client. The disadvantage of this approach lies in the fact that it might so happen that the monitoring instance itself is not able to connect to the remote host due to some issue and, in the event of such an issue, the clean up script might trigger on the monitoring host, leading to an unnecessary clean up of records.

Summary

In this chapter, we saw a few practical uses of Chef. We learnt how we can extend it to manage deployments using a dynamic server list via Capistrano. Next, we went about learning how to deploy applications using the `deploy` resource provided by Chef. This resource is extremely useful as it allows Chef to act as both a configuration management system and a deployment system. We also saw how we can use Chef to provision clusters and build distributed systems. Finally, we learnt about Test-driven development using Chefspec and minitest-chef-handler.

Index

Symbols

:nothing action 107
/search endpoint
  about 265
  GET method 265, 266
/search/INDEX endpoint
  about 266
  GET method 266, 267
  POST method 267-269

A

actions, Capistrano
  :deploy 311
  :force_deploy 311
  :rollback 311
API client
  existing client, deleting 50
  information, displaying 50
  listing 50
  managing 49
  new client, creating 49, 50
  reregistering 51
arguments 286
arithmetic operators 63
arrays
  about 76
  creating 76, 77
  destructive way, of selecting elements 81
  elements, accessing 77, 78
  elements, adding 79
  elements, removing 79
  elements, selecting 81

  iterating over 80, 81
  nondestructive way, of selecting
    elements 81
assignment operators 65
attribute file 189
attribute list
  building 186
attribute naming 186
attribute precedence 181, 193
attributes
  about 139, 185
  automatic 140
  default 140
  defining 189
  force_default 140
  force_override 140
  ignore_failure 108
  life cycle 189
  normal 140
  override 140
  provider 108
  recipe DSL methods 141
  retries 108
  retry_delay 108
  run_list, defining 141
  sources 189
  supports 108
attributes, Capistrano
  after_restart 311
  before_migrate 311
  before_restart 311
  before_symlink 311
  create_dirs_before_symlink 311
  deploy_to 311

G

gem repository
  URL 297
gems
  used, for distributing plugins 296-298
GET method
  parameters 266
global permissions, Enterprise Chef
  about 103
  create 103
  list 103
guard attributes
  about 109-113
  not_if 109
  only_if 109
guard attributes, arguments
  :cwd 110
  :environment 110
  :group 110
  :timeout 110
  :user 110

H

handlers, in Chef
  exception handler 299
  report handler 299
  start handler 299
hashes
  about 82
  creating 83
  iterating over 85
headers, request authentication
  accept 235
  Content-Type 235
  host 235
  X-Chef-Version 235
  X-Ops-Authorization-N 235
  X-Ops-Content-Hash 235
  X-Ops-Sign 235
  X-Ops-Timestamp 235
  X-Ops-UserId 235
helper modules
  about 137
  inline methods 137

  inline modules 137
  library modules 138
hints 208

I

if statement 67
infrastructure
  managing 163
instances, on AWS
  URL 200
integration tests 324
IRB 58, 59
Ironfan
  installing 318
  URL 318
  using 322

J

jobs
  running, from within recipes 315-322
  running, from workstation 315
JSON file
  key-value pairs 171
  using 168

K

key-value pairs 164
Knife
  about 17, 31
  API client, managing 49
  cookbooks, managing 34
  environments, managing 39
  knife command 32
  knife.rb 33
  node, bootstrapping 52
  nodes, managing 44
  options 223
  plugins 53
  roles, managing 42
  search command 51
  used, for encryption 223
  using 223
knife-azure plugin 54

N

syntax 270
wildcard matching 271
plugins
  knife-azure plugin 54
  knife-ec2 plugin 53
  knife-google plugin 54
  knife-push plugin 54
  knife-ssh plugin 53
  URL 55
polymorphism 86
proc attribute 285
process identification number (PID) 8
properties, Ruby files
  cookbook_versions 177
  default_attributes 177
  description 177
  name 177
  override_attributes 177
provider DSL
  action method 157
  converge_by method 157
  current_resource method 157
  load_current_resource method 157
  new_resource method 157
  updated_by_last_action method 158
  whyrun_supported? method 158
push jobs
  about 55
  components 55
  URL 55

R

recipe DSL methods
  about 141
  attribute method 142
  platform_family method 142
  platform method 141
  resources method 143
  value_for_platform_family method 142
  value_for_platform method 142
recipes
  about 105, 139, 190
  attributes 139
  data bag, using 217-222
  including 140

writing, best practices 143
request authentication
  defining 234-237
resources
  about 105-108
  attributes, evaluating 113, 114
  bash resource 130-133
  cookbook_file resource 117-120
  cron resource 126-128
  defining 106
  directory resource 120, 121
  execute resource 124-126
  file resource 122-124
  guard attributes 109-113
  package resource 114-117
  service resource 128-130
  template resource 133-136
  URL 114
resource template
  URL 139
Ridley
  about 274
  URL 275
role attribute
  defining 181
role/environment attribute 190
role file
  properties 167
roles
  about 42
  Chef API, using 169
  Chef server WebUI, using 170
  deleting 43
  editing 43
  information, displaying 44
  JSON file, using 168
  Knife, using 163
  listing 44
  managing 42, 163
  new role, creating 42, 43
  Ruby DSL, using 166, 167
Ruby DSL
  benefits 166
  using 166, 168
Ruby files
  properties 177

Thank you for buying
Mastering Chef

About Packt Publishing

Packt, pronounced 'packed', published its first book, *Mastering phpMyAdmin for Effective MySQL Management*, in April 2004, and subsequently continued to specialize in publishing highly focused books on specific technologies and solutions.

Our books and publications share the experiences of your fellow IT professionals in adapting and customizing today's systems, applications, and frameworks. Our solution-based books give you the knowledge and power to customize the software and technologies you're using to get the job done. Packt books are more specific and less general than the IT books you have seen in the past. Our unique business model allows us to bring you more focused information, giving you more of what you need to know, and less of what you don't.

Packt is a modern yet unique publishing company that focuses on producing quality, cutting-edge books for communities of developers, administrators, and newbies alike. For more information, please visit our website at www.packtpub.com.

About Packt Open Source

In 2010, Packt launched two new brands, Packt Open Source and Packt Enterprise, in order to continue its focus on specialization. This book is part of the Packt Open Source brand, home to books published on software built around open source licenses, and offering information to anybody from advanced developers to budding web designers. The Open Source brand also runs Packt's Open Source Royalty Scheme, by which Packt gives a royalty to each open source project about whose software a book is sold.

Writing for Packt

We welcome all inquiries from people who are interested in authoring. Book proposals should be sent to author@packtpub.com. If your book idea is still at an early stage and you would like to discuss it first before writing a formal book proposal, then please contact us; one of our commissioning editors will get in touch with you.

We're not just looking for published authors; if you have strong technical skills but no writing experience, our experienced editors can help you develop a writing career, or simply get some additional reward for your expertise.

Chef Essentials

ISBN: 978-1-78398-304-9   Paperback: 218 pages

Discover how to deploy software, manage hosts, and scale your infrastructure with Chef

1. Learn how to use Chef in a concise manner.

2. Learn ways to use Chef to integrate with cloud services such as EC2 and Rackspace Cloud.

3. See advanced ways to integrate Chef into your environment, develop tests, and even extend Chef's core functionality.

Configuration Management with Chef-Solo

ISBN: 978-1-78398-246-2   Paperback: 116 pages

A comprehensive guide to get you up and running with Chef-Solo

1. Explore various techniques that will help you save time in Infrastructure management.

2. Use the power of Chef-Solo to run your servers and configure and deploy applications in an automated manner.

3. This book will help you to understand the need for the configuration management tool and provides you with a step-by-step guide to maintain your existing infrastructure.

Please check **www.PacktPub.com** for information on our titles

Managing Windows Servers
with Chef

ISBN: 978-1-78398-242-4   Paperback: 110 pages

Harness the power of Chef to automate management of Windows-based systems using hands-on examples

1. Discover how Chef can be used to manage a heterogeneous network of Windows and Linux systems with ease.

2. Configure an entire .NET application stack, deploy it, and scale in the cloud.

3. Employ a step-by-step and practical approach to automate provisioning and configuration of Windows hosts with Chef.

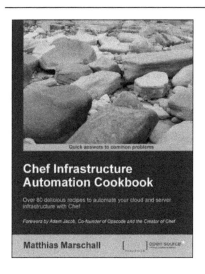

Chef Infrastructure Automation
Cookbook

ISBN: 978-1-84951-922-9   Paperback: 276 pages

Over 80 delicious recipes to automate your cloud and server infrastructure with Chef

1. Configure, deploy, and scale your applications.

2. Automate error prone and tedious manual tasks.

3. Manage your servers on-site or in the cloud.

4. Solve real world automation challenges with task-based recipes.

Please check **www.PacktPub.com** for information on our titles